BURGUNDY

New Directions in Anthropology

General Editor: **Jacqueline Waldren**, *Institute of Social and Cultural Anthropology, University of Oxford and Director, Deia Archaeological Museum and Research Centre, Mallorca*

Twentieth-century migration, modernization, technology, tourism, and global communication have had dynamic effects on group identities, social values and conceptions of space, place, and politics. This series features new and innovative ethnographic studies concerned with these processes of change.

For a full volume listing, please see back matter

BURGUNDY

A Global Anthropology of Place and Taste

Marion Demossier

berghahn
NEW YORK · OXFORD
www.berghahnbooks.com

First published in 2018 by
Berghahn Books
www.berghahnbooks.com

Library of Congress Cataloging-in-Publication Data
Names: Demossier, Marion, author.
Title: Burgundy : a global anthropology of place and taste / Marion Demossier.
Description: New York : Berghahn Books, 2018. | Series: New directions in
    anthropology ; Volume 43 | Includes bibliographical references and index.
Identifiers: LCCN 2017052483 (print) | LCCN 2018009554 (ebook) | ISBN
    9781785338526 (ebook) | ISBN 9781785338519 (hardback : alk. paper)
Subjects: LCSH: Wine and wine making--France--Burgundy. |
    Terroir--France--Burgundy. | Wine industry--France--Burgundy. |
    Vintners--France--Burgundy.
Classification: LCC TP553 (ebook) | LCC TP553 .D389 2018 (print) | DDC
    338.4/76632094441--dc23
LC record available at https://lccn.loc.gov/2017052483

British Library Cataloguing in Publication Data
A catalogue record for this book is available from the British Library

ISBN 978-1-78533-851-9 hardback
ISBN 978-1-78533-852-6 ebook

Contents

꧁꧂

ILLUSTRATIONS

ACKNOWLEDGEMENTS

In the course of more than twenty-five years of ethnographic encounter in Burgundy, I have come to realise that anthropologists, like other social researchers, are increasingly faced with competing duties, obligations and conflicts of interest, and with the need to make implicit or explicit choices between values and between the interests of different individuals and groups. Most of my informers are protected by anonymity. However, I have chosen to identify some of the main actors as they are well known, either in the world of wine, or at national or local level, and therefore any attempts to mask their identity is doomed to failure. I have tried as much as possible to involve them in my writing even when touching upon the most sensitive issues and I have also tried to explain my perspective, even when there was a strong disagreement between all parties concerned. Anthropology remains a science of critique and I hope that I have been able to preserve my professional ethical values while doing my job as an anthropologist.

This book has taken a very long time to write. Perhaps not surprisingly, a book that has been so long in preparation has allowed the author to accumulate a large number of debts to friends and colleagues. Over the years I have accumulated so many debts and I have met so many passionate and knowledgeable people in Burgundy and elsewhere that the list of thanks is almost endless. I have been extremely lucky to be able to build friendships and find wine growers keen to engage with my anthropological thinking. Particular thanks go to the Meunier-Confuron family, Claire Naudin and her husband Jean-Louis Bizot, Nathalie Tollot, Bernard Zito, Paul Meunier, Jasper Morris and Nick Mills, to cite only a few. The world of wine is one of sociability, sharing and community spirit and it is often paired with the world of gastronomy and food. Food and wine both play an important role in our society as they both convey social meanings and offer a platform to engage critically about the world we live in. My anthropological quest has been punctuated by these special experiences and the great generosity of the wine producers. I hope that the book will provide them with more food for thought.

I joined the Department of Modern Languages at the University of Southampton in January 2012 and became Head of Department in 2015 at a time of intense changes with regard to British higher education, Modern Languages as a sector, and British politics in terms of Brexit. I have been extremely privileged to be supported wonderfully across the Department, the Faculty and the University, which have all enabled me to pursue my investigations of an object which, at first glance, could be described as 'ordinary' and 'banal' and, in some cases, 'suspicious'. Yet wine offers an incredible platform to think critically about capitalist societies, nature and culture, science and empirical knowledge. I have not yet exhausted the richness of this fieldwork and the way in which it provides a bridge between different facets of what it means to be human. I wish to thank, in particular, all my colleagues at Southampton who have supported me throughout this new endeavour and have consistently expressed their intellectual support. To name just a few, Heidi Armbruster, Anthony Campbell, Jenny Jenkins, Mike Kelly, Clare Mar-Molinero, Ros Mitchell, Mary Orr, Roumyana Slabakova and Patrick Stevenson.

I thank the Faculty of Humanities for granting me a semester of study leave following my appointment, and for providing me with a set of regulations with which to conduct my ethnographic fieldwork in both France and New Zealand. My research complied with the Data Protection Act of the University of Southampton policy and the information generated by the interviews and participant observation has been stored and remained confidential. Anonymity was assured by coding our informers. The research ethics follows the Association of Social Anthropologists of UK and Ireland guidelines concerning the conduct of interviews and participant observation which can be found at https://www.theasa.org/ethics.shtml and conforms to the University of Southampton Ergo's ethical process.

I have some wonderful memories from my fieldwork in New Zealand, which was extremely generously supported by the New Zealand Wine Growers Association and COWA (Central Otago Wine Association). The trip helped me to distance myself from the Burgundian ethnographic site and to think more broadly about what it means to be a wine grower today. Again, several of these fantastic people graciously shared their time and thoughts with me and made my stay a very productive one. Nick Mills, James Dicey, Rudi Bauer, Marijana Brajkovich, Warren Morran, John Barker, Jeanine Bayliss and several others will recognise themselves.

Several friends and colleagues have read and commented on various versions of the book and their contribution has helped me to think more clearly and to refine my overall argument. Through my journey, I have also made several very good friends as wine has the power to establish relationships in a particular way. This is no doubt also true of my colleagues and I am grateful in particular to Ullrik Kockel, Peter Howland, Rachel Black, Mike Summerfield, Clelia Viecelli, Shawnee Harkness, Christopher Kaplonski, David Picard, Graham Harding, William Skinner, Julie McIntyre, John Germov and Kolleen Guy who have all been faithful friends, sources of inspiration or both. As I have worked through various drafts of the book, I have been extremely grateful for the comments of the three reviewers for Berghahn, although any remaining errors are my own. The Burgundy UNESCO team headed by Krystel Lepresle and led by Aubert de Villaine has been instrumental in the completion of this book as have my French colleagues, Jean-Baptiste Traversac, Gilles Laferté, Jean-Pierre Garcia and Julia Csergo. I have to thank, from the bottom of my heart, all those esteemed colleagues involved in the study of wine – whether from a historical or anthropological perspective: they will find themselves cited or acknowledged in this book. Finally, I have a special *pensée* for the late Professor Marinella Carrosso who tragically left us recently and who reminded me why the anthropology of wine growers remains a distinctive field of enquiry.

My husband Jules and our two daughters Margot and Louisa have been extremely supportive throughout my peregrinations and they have constantly reminded me that life has to be lived to the full. This book is dedicated to the three musketeers. The encouragement of Alain, Barbara, Emmanuelle, Gil, Ron, Jan, Paul and Pierre has helped to sustain me. Having been born after I embarked on this project, Louisa, ably seconded by her sister, has undeniably delayed its completion by diverting me in other more important directions.

INTRODUCTION

Never doubt that a small group of thoughtful, committed citizens can change the world; indeed, it is the only thing that ever has.

—Margaret Mead

On 4 July 2015, during a session of the 39th World Heritage committee[1] held in Bonn (Germany), the addition of the *climats de Bourgogne* to the UNESCO (United Nations Educational, Scientific and Cultural Organization) World Heritage list as cultural landscape was unanimously approved. That decision followed the adoption of amendments proposed by Portugal and Vietnam to heed the ICOMOS (International Council on Monuments and Sites) recommendations to list it as a cultural landscape rather than a site. Following the proposal, it was argued that the *climats de Bourgogne* offered the best possible example of a cultural landscape, not simply from the visual dimension, but also because of the progressive construction of the relationship between the people, the land and the soil. Burgundy, it was maintained, fitted this category better than that of cultural site and there were precedents to classify it as such.[2] Most of the discussions focused on the protection of the site, especially in relation to both the state party of France and the management plan set out by the Association pour les Climats de Bourgogne. The President of the Association and co-owner of the Domaine de la Romanée-Conti, known as DRC in the world of wine, concluded that 'the dossier reflects well French wine heritage which now becomes world heritage'.[3]

The subtle distinction between a cultural landscape and a cultural site was largely lost on the local population and most Burgundians understood the process as a UNESCO heritage stamp, irrespective of the category under which it was listed. 'This is going to be great for Burgundy!' exclaimed one of my compatriots, and she was not alone. The announcement became the pretext for a collective Paulée des climats,[4] a huge picnic

1

organised on 9 July 2016 in the Château de Meursault by the Association pour la Reconnaissance des Climats de Bourgogne. This celebration was something of a reprise of an older folkloric repertoire of festive sociability and wine tasting, given a modern and more democratic twist and involving the consumption of wine and food in an informal setting, while sitting on the grass. This was followed in the months to come by a series of events, promotional films and publications showcasing the 'culture' of the place and the Burgundy story built around the *climats de Bourgogne*, featuring conviviality, vineyards and artisanal production.

The concept of the *climats de Bourgogne* was invented locally in an attempt to renew the terroir ideology while positioning Burgundy wines in the context of an ever more globalised world of wine which has increasingly questioned the hierarchy attached to traditional regions of production. The *climats* are defined as Burgundy's own version of the terroir, with the term taking on a different sense to that usually associated with soil, exposition and meteorological conditions. According to the dossier, 'they are particular to Burgundy and designate a parcel of land dedicated to a precisely delimited vineyard, known by that name for hundreds of years, and therefore a precise plot, soil, subsoil, exposure, microclimate, and forming together within a vineyard characteristics that constitute a personality, unique to one terroir and one cru'.[5] According to this definition, the *climats* are another term for a historically created exceptional mosaic of vineyards with a hierarchy of crus and an international reputation. Superficially then, Burgundy might appear to be simply acquiring recognition for its unchanging landscape, tradition and culture. Yet, for all the power of its rich local identity, folklore and culture which is broadcast to the world, there hides underneath the comforting blanket of this seamless place, untouched by change or conflict, a far more complex reality. Burgundy's listing as a World Heritage landscape emphasises its international reputation as a traditional and historical site of wine production and opens a new chapter in the production and marketing of its quality, differentiation and authenticity. It is also about readjusting Burgundy and the *grands crus* in response to a changing global market and the shifting kaleidoscope of world wine values.

Burgundy, like other wine producing regions, has frequently experienced profound changes in economic and professional practices. It has also been buffeted by the effects of economic depression as in the 1930s, and by natural calamities, notably the phylloxera crisis of 1880 or more recently by the threat of the esca disease[6] (fungi). As we shall see, far from being an attempt to secure UNESCO approval for a unique, unchanging physical space and culture, the Burgundian bid is, in reality, the latest example of a response to professional and economic competition and forms part of a process of constant reinvention. For Burgundy, in the twenty-first century, claiming to be different means redefining some of its most prominent global references such as that of terroir which has been transformed into *climats*, once again linking place to taste by presenting the site of production as an authentic, stable, trustworthy and reliable place. My argument is that place – whether designated as terroir or *climats* – continues to be important, but it has to be regularly articulated or re-articulated to fit into the changing global wine story. I want to argue that 'Burgundy' offers a particularly relevant case-study for an in-depth exploration of the ways in which locality is produced not only at the local level where social groups like wine-growers, *négociants*, stakeholders and local wine experts might struggle and want to readjust themselves in their long-term self-narrative, but also at the transnational level by repositioning themselves as 'different' and the 'best' in the global world of wine. The power of the idea of terroir and its role in the elevation of Burgundy's winescape to World Heritage status lies in cultural differentiation based on human actions and reason rather than on superior natural endowment. This process is best described as one of self-reflexive imbrication by which individuals and groups imbricate themselves in the global economic world order, re-evaluating their place and their global story. This process is, however, far more differentiated than one assumes.

Yet Burgundy's application for UNESCO recognition also needs to be read in parallel with that of Champagne, which defined its own bid around the concept of landscape – 'Champagne Hillsides, Houses and Cellars' – rather than as a cultural site. The Champagne dossier proved to be less polemical than the Burgundian one and clearly demonstrated the powerful resonance of drinking Champagne for the members of the UNESCO delegations. By initially arguing for a different heritage category – that of site – and by seeking to establish a unique position in the global wine hierarchy,[7] Burgundy launched an ultimately unsuccessful bid to differentiate itself from Champagne. Heritage status is part of a process which aims to transform local places into objects of global interest, bringing local, national and international politics into the arena. Heritage valorisation is not only a fashionable trend, but also a source of social, economic and political power (Bessière 1998: 32). In the new global wine landscape, heritage recognition is therefore a potential trump card to help differentiate Old World wines from their rising New World competitors at a time of increased consumption and the transformation of tastes. As many commentators have pointed out, the worlds of wine have become increasingly complex, accommodating new regions and also different forms of production and marketing, from traditional and modern artisanal production, closely tied to place and vintage, to large-scale industrial production for a mass market (Banks and Overton 2010). As a result, claiming uniqueness and authenticity in terms of place of origin or provenance remains a matter of great importance.[8]

This powerful construction of place is often underlined by a series of hegemonic discourses about locality, which necessarily have an impact on the wide range of skills that actors deploy when making quality wine as well as the construction of sustainability in a rapidly changing economic context. Wine entrepreneurs in Burgundy do not necessarily seek to diversify and create multiple meanings of authenticity to accommodate, modify and, at times, resist, the effects of globalisation on local culture and economic life.[9] They seek to engage, take control and master global forces by consolidating, reinforcing and perpetuating the story of their origins and authenticity, thus creating a differentiated engagement from other producers at the local level. The heritagisation of a site is far from a collective and homogeneous process and we should not forget that it can often benefit some while alienating others. This is this story that we wish to tell. Interestingly enough, as a result of the broader heritage process, place becomes something else, thereby losing its character and its 'authentic' nature.

Visiting Beaune – widely recognised as the capital of Burgundian viticulture – in the summer of 2015, and staying in a local hotel rather than with my family, I was struck by how the town had changed. The majority of the local independent retailers devoted to clothes, food, jewellery and digital technology had disappeared, giving way to wine shops, luxurious gastronomic and artistic temples, restaurants and four-star boutique hotels. Even the Couvent des Cordeliers, which once belonged to the Patriarche wine merchants and was devoted to mass consumption and tourism, has now become the seat of a select, private wine club. Opposite the Couvent, another historic building, once a religious house, is now devoted to displays of contemporary art of an iconic and frequently tacky kind, while a wine tasting is orchestrated in a post-modern way.[10] The changes which have affected the sleepy town of Beaune over the last decade have accelerated the process of heritagisation and by the same token have contributed to the fossilisation of the site. There is a strong sense of pastiche and commercialism which contrasts with the traditional values through which Burgundy defined itself as a convivial and hospitable space.

These traditional collective values, which were at the core of the Burgundian experience, are rapidly being eroded by the intense economic transformation of the place. As one of the Dutch importers I met during my summer trip said: 'It is impossible to buy anything here, they have nothing to sell, I have to go South where good quality wines are still affordable'. Burgundy now faces the challenge of being, somewhat paradoxically, a public space, the heritage of humanity, and an economically inaccessible luxury product. By focusing on the place, the local elite can present Burgundy as if it were accessible to all, part of the world's patrimony, rather conveniently forgetting that only a tiny minority will ever purchase a bottle of Romanée-Conti. The Burgundy story therefore offers a fascinating insight into some of the fractures in our modern society and the constant battle between the different logics confronting human beings in a specific location. But it is also an example of a crafted and enduring construction of place, with every piece assembled in a seamless puzzle through historical junctures and elitist enterprise. This book is the story of that complex assemblage, viewed not only through a local prism, but also via its deployment on a global scale.

Burgundy as a Long-term Anthropology at Home

The Burgundy region has been famous for its high-quality wines for nearly '2000 years' and superficially it appears stable and unchanging, a region arrogantly proclaiming to be a 'terroir béni des Dieux' ('soil blessed by God') in a 1990s regional publicity campaign. When I started a doctoral thesis three decades ago on Burgundian viticulture under the direction of Isac Chiva, one of the founders of French rural anthropology, it was expected that a traditional ethnographic research project would focus on a single defined bounded site, clearly anthropologically conceptualised and with a strong emphasis on techniques and material culture. The model framework for the researcher was the administrative unit of the region, in my case the *département* of the Côte d'Or and the AOC (*Appellation d'Origine Contrôlée*) area as they together represented the ideal institutional, socio-economic and political contexts. In rural France, there is a persistence of regional forms of collective identification (Lem 1999) and wine regions are particularly noted for this. As a young ethnographer at the time, my topic – the wine growers of the Côte d'Or – was, however, a risky choice in the sense that the study of wine elites was largely underrepresented in the discipline of anthropology at home, but it seemed logical and unproblematic given the significance of wine growers in the traditional field of peasant studies.[11] Most of my training had been in African anthropology with Claude Rivière and Georges Balandier, and the study of rural Europe appeared to me less attractive than the African rituals analysed in class. Yet it was to become my prime subject of analysis over the next twenty-five years. As one of the local priests in Puligny-Montrachet informed me in the 1990s when I told him I was going to study their local festival, the Saint-Vincent Tournante:[12] 'We are all savages here as well'.

The difficulties associated with the study of a wealthy and secretive group of traditionalist wine growers meant that only those struggling to integrate or achieve recognition in the local professional sphere opened their doors to the long-term scrutiny of a female anthropologist. Progressing into the 'thick description' of the diverse deployments of what it meant to be a *grand cru* producer in this area, it quickly became obvious to me that a strict focus on wine production would only be one side of the story. Already the collective mentality of the viticultural profession was problematised ethnographically by the absence of a sense of collectiveness, and by a certain reticence when it came to talking about collective identity, unless it was the Burgundian regional one which is still a powerful trope in local, national and international discourses. The ethnography of the local wine festival of Saint-Vincent and of the main professional associations completed the investigation by providing a new dimension to the study of the global wine hierarchy and its deployment at the local level. Over the course of the last twenty-five years, the nature of the ethnographic encounter has changed and while my PhD was the result of more than ten years of fieldwork, my more recent ethnographic observations have been spread out across the late 1990s and 2000s, ending with my contribution to the scientific committee organised by the Association pour la Reconnaissance des Climats de Bourgogne. In the course of more than twenty-five years, I have published widely on the local wine industry, made a film on one of their emblematic wine festivals, the Saint-Vincent Tournante, organised several exhibitions in the local wine museum and, above all in the eyes of my interviewees, have the advantage of 'being local'.

My more recent work in the region goes back to the launching of Burgundy's bid for UNESCO status in 2008 when I was contacted by the Association pour la Reconnaissance des Climats de Bourgogne to act as the 'anthropological/sociological expert' on its scientific committee. As a result of this invitation, I witnessed part of the process of putting together a 'convincing and solid' application to UNESCO. In this context, the application provided me with a useful timeline to revisit some of my previous ideas and to conduct a different kind of anthropological investigation in the context of a more globally defined industry. Since 2008, I have returned to do fieldwork and I have taken every opportunity to revisit the sites of my original research with a different set of questions. I have expanded the number of informers, selecting them carefully for their more critical view of the UNESCO application.

I have to emphasise that working on this very traditional and often secretive social group of wine producers was not helped by the social configuration of the wine industry, especially the hegemonic position of wine merchants and elites who are highly powerful actors who want to remain in charge of the Burgundian global story. In this context, the political economy of the place has remained a challenge in methodological and ethical terms. More recently, I added a transnational dimension to my analysis by conducting two weeks of fieldwork in New Zealand in the context of an invitation by the Central Otago Wine Association to contribute to the 2013 Pinot Noir festival in Wellington. This contrasted terrain has revealed some powerful and differentiated examples of the construction of place and has helped me to situate my analysis in a more comparative perspective. A study of wine making in both Burgundy and New Zealand raises questions about the fate of the local environment and how individuals engage with it. The results of their labours depend on the level of engagement and commitment rather than on the arbitrary nature of the location. Yet location provides the framework through which the story and stories unfold. As the French historian Roger Dion[13] reminded us in the 1950s, never mind the location, the main issue is who is going to buy your wines.

In the case of the wines of Burgundy and the Côte d'Or, which have been the main focus of my ethnographic investigation, broader social and historical processes have constantly transformed the local and social configuration. One of the major changes affecting the community has been the rise of internet technology and the new opportunities for producers to tell their stories. It is only recently that digital communication has come to play an important role for the profession and that films, images, interviews and writings have started to showcase Burgundy and its *climats* in a more prominent fashion. This virtual development of the field of wine culture has played an important role in my research as it has enabled me to follow remotely through Facebook and other media some of the discourses, debates and recent shifts surrounding people, ideas and products. This digital *mise en scène* of wine growers by wine growers represents a major shift in the way in which individual stories are told, which has repercussions for the global world of wine with its paradoxical values, its constant process of imbrication cascading from the local to the national to the transnational and back and forth. The status of the wine grower today has become a feature of our modernity. Some of my long-term informers have also become more concerned about my own social status as a professor, and as the public image of Burgundy came to be more visibly articulated and was often in the national news, they found ways of not responding to my questions. Yet the majority of my longstanding informers have enjoyed the ethnographic experience, using it often in a self-reflexive way and have become close friends over long periods of time. The social trajectory of most of my informers[14] has been upwards and there are only a few cases where personal misfortunes have interfered with their livelihood. What is striking about the long-term encounters is their more self-reflexive engagement towards the world of wine and the increasing range of initiatives and positionings which have resulted. I have been able to follow closely the group of producers I first met in the 1990s and I have seen them become parents and take ownership of their domains (wine estates). Most of them now claim to be anxious to engage further with their own understanding of the wine they produce. For many, it is an ongoing process, defined by their constant reflections about their own positioning in the world. 'I make the wine I want to make' has become a major trope in the discourse of local producers.

One of the principal transformations of individual and social relationships has been in relation to the local village or community. At one time, *vignerons* defined themselves totally within the village context and as part of a professional group. Now they have a much more outwardly focused regard, not only across Burgundy and other French wine regions, but also internationally. Thus, the concept of culture, anthropologically speaking, has become a loose notion which requires a more ethnographically rooted approach in order to identify changes in core values, shifts in discourses and new positioning in the hegemonic national and global tapestry of politics. As part of the process of creating and empowering groups, the role of the individual has become the primary motor of change and our analysis requires a more holistic view of the forces at stake. Following the impact of globalisation necessitates the unpacking of the story in different locales and settings, while keeping the context in perspective and understanding how diverse and complex the responses are to global forces. The power of ethnographic location is that it provides a window onto the seamless and fluid nature of the social phenomenon, which enables the cutting out of the social reality that is magnified and reiterated through repetitive observation and emphasis on individuals and actors as part of the process. Mattei Candea (2007) speaks of the arbitrary nature of the location and the strengths of the multi-imaginary and multi-sited anthropological approach. For Candea, the bounded fieldsite rethought of as the arbitrary location becomes an explicitly 'partial' and incomplete window onto social complexity. The *climats de Bourgogne* offer just such a window.

The Winners of Globalisation or the Game of Global Imbrications

This book is about wine growers in Burgundy over more than two decades as they have adapted to the forces of globalisation and managed change while continuously weaving the terroir story and imbricating themselves in the seamless unfolding of modernity. This is a story which encapsulates both winners and losers, but which emerges as a powerful trope of an alternative way of thinking about modernity and engaging with it. Moreover, this is about the politics of identity in the present age of food and drinks globalisation. We cannot all become Burgundians, but we might want to learn a few lessons. In the study of what I define as the *grands crus* producers, the anthropological focus had to be multi-sited, multifocal, multi-layered and oscillating between individuals, permanent groups or those who are more ephemeral in nature, as well as the more pragmatic calendar of events in which the 'community' comes together. By 'community', I am referring to the fluctuating group of wine producers who attend specific events because they feel engaged or concerned by the agenda of the day. In 2017, it would be rather naïve to assume that the concept of wine growers refers uniquely to the definition of a bounded and clearly delineated social group and that locality, in this case Burgundy, confers collective meanings and values on their sense of belonging. They surely have in common specific views over 'being part of the Burgundy story', but they also effectively find individual ways of defining themselves and their families within this location. *Grands crus* producers characterise the arbitrary nature of the window I open, but it is by following both producers and products into their wider connections and circulations that I see them becoming ethnographically meaningful.

References to 'national', 'culture', 'artisanship', 'localities', 'place' are all linguistic examples of the arbitrary epistemological position that anthropologists often unconsciously favoured when working on specific professional groups such as farmers, wine growers or cheese producers. The methodological hurdle posed by the study of these highly regarded and protected crafts still challenges the observer. Even multi-sited ethnography leaves the anthropologist hungry for a better understanding of the complexities of scaling. It is, however, more useful to read places in a transnational and global perspective as agencies that mediate and shape, but are also being shaped and mediated in unintended ways by developments in local, national and transnational arenas. This assemblage (Ong and Collier 2005), friction (Tsing 2005), or what I prefer to describe as reflexive imbrication, is the key to understanding how models are transculturally mediated, translated or contested and reinterpreted by specific groups. Terrio (2000) noted in the case of the *chocolatiers* in France that they struggled with adaptation, while other industries such as viticulture flourished in the face of crisis. *Grands crus* producers have, in general, a positive and ambitious economic story to tell, but the social implications of this success might have adverse effects in the long term, and the terroir story has provided a point of anchorage and stability in a fast changing environment. Anthropology, with its intimate knowledge of alternative conceptual universes and local worlds, offers one of the few remaining critical vantage points from which to challenge the generalising claims of the global hierarchy of value (Herzfeld 2004: 4).

Drawing on more than twenty years of fieldwork carried out not only in Burgundy, but also in London, Paris and New Zealand, with some of the world's most famous wine producers, wine experts and wine lovers, this book seeks to demystify terroir and to describe for the first time the effects of the growing challenge from a generation eager to question the very essence of quality and to become more ecologically minded. The book tells the story of the often hidden debate over the issue of quality which is perceived as being hindered by the hegemony of the AOC legal system. It provides a unique long-term ethnographic analysis of what lies behind terroir in Burgundy and thus raises important questions about the future of quality wine in a global era and about terroir as a global ideology. AOC distinctions were based on complex factors that often had little to do with 'taste', quality or the market. The formalisation of these distinctions in the long process of creating AOC laws has been critical, however, in determining how communities of producers interacted and continue to interact with the commercial world (Guy 2003).

Key Anthropological Themes

The aim of this study is to provide an anthropological perspective on international debates about the discursive power of terroir, the relationship of this discourse to Burgundy as a community and landscape, the social and cultural constructions of global capitalism, and the leverage of mechanisms such as World Heritage status to enshrine commodity value for a region and a nation. Unlike other disciplines, anthropology focuses on people's representations and concerns the comparative study of human societies and cultures and their development. It also seeks to unpack social reality in all its complexity and in a long-term perspective. Anthropology is, after all, a science of critique and not a contributor to myth-making.

Anthropology, like other human and social sciences, has long demonstrated an interest in the study of drinking and alcohol, but wine was often studied alongside other beverages such as tea, coffee, rum and brandy and was never given top billing. The volume *Drinking Cultures, Alcohol and Identity*, published in 2005 by the anthropologist, Thomas Wilson, features only two chapters (out of twelve) devoted to wine, while the majority of the others deal with alcohol consumption across cultures. Until recently, anthropological research on wine was generally scant and wine as an object of enquiry was, first and foremost, located in a specific national and cultural context which was studied like other alcoholic drinks for its impact on identity and society. The specificity of the anthropological perspective was therefore to examine the consumption of alcohol as a way of life, one element of a given culture (Douglas 1987), rather than simply focusing on the site of its production. From Ireland to Hong Kong, Mexico to Germany, alcohol was seen as playing a key role in a wide range of functions: religious, familial, social and even political. Consumption within the context of these wider cultural practices revealed how class, ethnicity and nationalism were all expressed through this very popular commodity (Wilson 2005). It could be argued that wine serves as a pretext for a scrutiny of other traditional areas of anthropological investigation such as rituals, politics and kinship which were seen as going through major transformations and were therefore worth studying. The production and consumption of alcohol is an economic activity of consequence and its ceremonials and rituals reflect both real and imagined worlds (Douglas 1987).

It is only recently that wine has acquired an independent status in anthropological literature, and the publication in 2013 of *Wine and Culture: Vineyard to Glass* edited by Rachel Black and Robert C. Ulin was something of a milestone. For both anthropologists, the study of wine breaks new ground, but it is also linked to the critical issues at the forefront of the social sciences and humanities, especially in relation to modernity and complexity. In their introduction to *Wine and Culture*, Black and Ulin invoke the academic tradition of focusing on a single and bounded entity, with food and drink often being seen as part of the binding of social structures or other traditional forms rather than being the prime object of analysis. Yet wine also carried the shadow of the intoxicating and disordering nature of alcohol drinking cultures. In the USA, the ambiguous historical status of wine made it slow to be acknowledged as part of food studies, while, in France, the increasing mythologisation and politicisation of wine made it an object almost impossible to engage with unless to claim its unique quality. Such attitudes are still very present in contemporary analysis of wine in France and at times French historians, sociologists and geographers teeter on the edge of propaganda, arguing for the unique position of the French in relation to wine drinking culture. More recently, Chantal Crenn (2013) suggests that the anthropology of wine in France has generally been obscured by the emergence of rural France as a research field at the end of the 1980s as part of the national development of the discipline in the context of decolonisation. Anthropologists have been focusing on material culture, rituals and traditions (Chaudat 2012).

What is interesting in these transatlantic parallels is the fact that the majority of American anthropologists decided at the beginning of the twenty-first century to focus on European fieldsites, including France,

Italy and Bulgaria, rather than looking at their own vineyards, which are also the result of a long and complex historical and migratory transfer of resources, people and knowledge. French anthropologists, on the other hand, myself included, often focused on their own locality, practicing what was coined as 'anthropology at home' in the 1980s and 1990s without considering its transnational dimensions. These parallel conversations have been separated by the language barrier, but also by the impossibility of bridging two anthropological traditions rooted historically in different definitions of culture. What they have in common is the terroir perspective which has generated research on both sides of the Atlantic and has also, to some extent, provided a bridge between wine and food studies, legitimising the former. Several publications have been devoted to terroir and either to its translation from French into other contexts or its deployment in anthropological terms. The work of geographers, especially from New Zealand and Australia, has played a major role in allowing terroir to be analysed as a more transdisciplinary object.

Another major obstacle to the critical development of the anthropology of wine in Europe as an object of enquiry lies with the political, national and patriotic frameworks in which wine was defined, making it a difficult object to unpack and a very unpopular one to attack. In the French context, the new status given in 2014 to wine as a cultural heritage good has given a new protectionist impetus to its construction as a national emblem of identity. At the regional level, it is easy to find examples of the development of the propaganda embracing wine as a distinctive element of social life associated, paradoxically, with well-being in a global neo-capitalist society. This construction has implications for the ways in which wine is studied and how it is written about. Yet the growing importance of wine as a cultural product is beyond doubt and its study, as an object sensitive to the social structures in which it is made and consumed, can deepen our understanding of the contemporary world.

Finally, it is worth mentioning that wine does not necessarily appeal as an object of study to anthropologists because other than in exceptional cases such as the perpetual wines of Sicily, it does not have a kind of 'exotic' flavour or serious status. After informing my fellow anthropologists about what I am studying, I am often told cynically 'It must be hard to do fieldwork'. The anthropology of wine is traditionally associated with European fieldwork and would inscribe itself as part of what I would describe provocatively as 'soft anthropology', using the image of the ethnographer quenching his/her thirst after visiting one producer before lunching with other fellow wine drinkers. In the hierarchy of knowledge, it remains a marginalised area of research and it could be argued that interdisciplinarity has provided the anthropologist with a more than welcome home and an opportunity to gain more legitimacy. At least this has been my experience over the last two or three decades.

Amongst the key themes providing a framework for the development of my argument, globalisation, terroir and heritage deserve a brief introduction as they are at the core of this volume. Globalisation has often been described by anthropologists in terms of a clash of cultures or as the result of the external forces created by sovereign rule, market rationality and regimes of citizenship which have had a profound impact on communities, nation states and social life. Most of the anthropological literature refers to the intensification of global interconnectedness, suggesting 'a world full of movement and mixture, contacts and linkages, and persistent cultural interaction and exchange' (Inda and Rosaldo 2002: 2). Recent research has sought to capture globalisation in a more refined fashion using 'assemblages' (Ong and Collier 2005) or 'friction' (Tsing 2005) as metaphors to conceptualise the ways in which global forms have been articulated in specific contexts. Anthropological contributions have therefore helped to define more complex material, collective and discursive relationships to modernity. Yet they have largely focused on the negative impact of globalisation, presenting either a rather gloomy picture of the forces at stake and their devastating consequences for local cultures or a naïve and romantic analysis of resistance to it. I aim to place at the heart of my analysis the long-term effects that globalisation has on people, but more specifically, to understand how communities change and shape their worlds.

Terroir, a slippery concept as I will demonstrate, has long been a staple of French discourse and its more recent resonance on a global scale is testament to its power and capacity for myth making (Parker 2015). Yet very little is known of its transnational dimension (Black and Ulin 2013). The concept originated in the codification of the AOC in the Burgundy wine region in France as recently as the early twentieth century yet in the early twenty-first century has come to be considered as a natural law of the quality of wine and some other consumer products. Using my interviews and fieldwork observations since 2008, I have tried to map individual discourses on terroir, analysing it as a social construction of place in the face of global challenges. My argument is that terroir, and more recently *climats*, are the result of a single narrative that is shaped both within the region and around the globe. French wine makers are shown in dialogue with a global wine world that is being buffeted and shaped as much by markets as by climate change.

Finally, the concept of food and wine heritage has recently been recast: scholars have embraced an innovative and interdisciplinary approach to food and have engaged in a productive debate with the concept of food heritage, recasting food 'as a vehicle to express and shape interactions between humans' (Pottier 1996: 303). In their editorial introduction to the special issue of *Aofood*, Jacinthe Bessière and Laurence Tibère argue that the promotion of food heritage in contemporary France appears as a 'societal issue', a space for mobilising projects which contributes to the construction of cultural identities and to the dynamics of territorial development against the landscape of a global economic crisis (Bessière and Tibère 2011). This way of thinking and of using heritage seems unsurprising from a French perspective, the self-appointed land of food and wine, where the concept of culinary heritage was first coined and instrumentalised in the 1980s (Demossier 2000). Yet the concept of food heritage has now spread further in anthropological circles as part of the development of both food and heritage studies at a global level. This fascinating cross-fertilisation of two traditionally separate fields of research opens the doors to new areas of enquiry. By locating the anthropology of food heritage at the crossroads of the study of society, food production and consumption, as well as the politics of scale, new sets of questions have come to the fore which focus on contested anthropological concepts such as nostalgia, authenticity, territorial identities, tradition, political economy and innovation. I am interested in the contextual specificity of political processes and the mechanisms through which localities are differentially incorporated into larger scales of social, economic and political life. But this book is also about how specific localities incorporate broader processes and values into their global story in order to maintain the permanence of the fit between place, people and culture. All these constitute the bedrock of our modern, complex and fluid societies, against which individuals and groups seek to identify, negotiate and root themselves in the face of major economic upheavals. The study of wine heritage is thus linked to new theoretical perspectives which problematise heritage as 'essentially a political idea' (Schofield et al. 2008: 36).

Terroir From Local to Transnational

The organisation of the book follows the analysis of several ethnographic windows which have been carefully selected and are based upon a long-term investigation into the world of wine, allowing the development of a broader argument about place, quality, taste, terroir and the global world of wine. For centuries, Burgundy has been widely recognised as the home of the world's finest wines and as the birthplace of a model of terroir connecting taste to place. That concept was given legal form during the 1930s when the French state developed the system of AOC, emphasising the relationship between a given place, its micro-climatic characteristics and the local culture incarnated by wine growers and their traditional techniques.

The story of terroir seemed to guarantee the taste of place and to justify the high price of purchase for this closed gustatory experience. The terroir model has proved incredibly attractive and has rapidly expanded to the European and, more recently, global level and now provides a counter-story to that of globalisation, standardisation and industrialisation by challenging the vast array of anonymous, mass produced foods and beverages available to the consumer (Demossier 2010). Terroir has become a global phenomenon, encompassing everything from Portuguese wines to Fontina D'Aosta cheese. All manners of foodstuffs, artisanal products or techniques have sought to gild themselves with the blazon of terroir.

Yet as the Burgundian model of terroir has gone global, its very legitimacy has been challenged amongst the vineyards where it first took root. To understand the phenomenal success of terroir and why its whole ideology is now called into doubt, it is necessary to ask some fundamental questions: Why are the great vineyards of France located where they are? Why does one site produce a superior wine, while an adjacent plot that looks the same yields a lesser one? What is the taste of terroir? These are the questions being asked by the new generation of young wine growers who perceive terroir to be the fossilised and hegemonic system of the AOC which impedes any opportunity for innovation. Moreover, changes in consumer tastes are increasingly challenging traditional definitions of terroir and are questioning the work of producers (Teil 2012). The attempts of this new generation of wine growers to open a debate about what a good quality wine means has been blocked by the powerful and institutionalised model of terroir and its partisans, and the profound implications of the conflict are a major theme of this study.

Chapter 1 will examine the different meanings of place and terroir in Burgundy. The first part will engage with the geographical representation of Burgundy and the complexity of its patchwork of soils/vineyards through the four different denominations of origin it produces: *Grands crus, Premiers crus, villages* and regional denominations. It will discuss the historical and social construction of terroir and will analyse the ways in which specific groups have sought to empower themselves periodically by imposing new definitions of quality in a bid to combat fraud and cope with economic crisis and the deregulation of the worldwide wine market. The role of the connection between history and place will be critically assessed and contextualised in relation to the current debate on quality. Specific emphasis will be placed on the emergence and consolidation in social terms of various groups, from wine growers to wine merchants, who contribute to the emergence of a quality norm. Burgundian wine growers, with their internal struggles and their subordinate positioning within the commercial sphere, will be discussed in the light of their challenging relationship to the land. The chapter will then focus on the issue of ownership of 'place' and its continuity within the same family lineages. The social construction of place as an artefact of human imaginings and activities will be analysed through the transmission of a technical and cultural heritage within these families. It will discuss how each generation reinvents a special relationship to place, but also struggles to redefine its own contribution to the wine story. Finally, it will explore the complex social grammar of the landscape presented at the beginning and how this reading is transmitted from one generation to the next through a differentiated, but intimate, relationship to place and its diversity of products.

Chapter 2 focuses on the wine grower. Throughout the terroir debate, special emphasis has been placed either on soil and nature or on culture which have both been presented as uncontested and God given factors in the definition of quality wines at different historical periods. However, central to the definition of the product is the constant negotiation between the soil, climatic conditions and the work and knowledge of the wine grower. This chapter will focus on the discussion central to the issue of quality, namely the work of wine growers and their attempts to control nature and produce excellence in a context of climatic changes. It will engage with the growing social visibility of the group and its differentiated and hierarchical social composition. Issues of knowledge, cultural and social capital and engagement are thus central to the production of excellence, as are good marketing skills. This highly individualised and differentiated Burgundian wine landscape provides a range of economic niches which enable good and even bad producers to achieve distinction and excellence. However, only a small group of wine elites has achieved real economic success and has moved the goalposts of quality by redefining quality and terroir through more ecologically friendly practices and discourses. Interestingly, a few wine growers at the margins of Burgundian viticulture have joined them in promoting ecological methods in their production. This chapter will explore the ways in which each producer engages with the concept of quality through the work invested in his/her plots. Case-studies and the individual stories of wine growers will argue for a differentiated type of engagement in relation to terroir and the nature of the knowledge displayed in viticulture. Moreover, it is through the accumulation of experience and knowledge that producers are able to redefine their competence and *savoir-faire*. The chapter will also engage with the recent debate on quality and the attempt of some wine growers to produce more ecologically defined products and to defend quality wine in a more reflexive fashion. A discussion on biodynamic and biological wines will be included.

In Chapter 3, we explore the connection between taste and place which has been promoted as a characteristic of the Burgundian wine industry for at least eight centuries. Very early on, the history of Burgundy was associated with that of the *courtiers-gourmets* (wine brokers), a professional group founded in 1375 which played a key role in defining quality norms. They progressively established themselves as intermediaries, ensuring the quality, taste and authenticity of their products and facilitating the economic relationship between villages as places of production and towns such as Beaune and Dijon as centres of commercialisation. This chapter will explore the long historical association between a place and a taste and will analyse the role of intermediaries in constructing local reputations. It will also engage with the historical, social and political construction of taste by wine experts and their imposition of gustatory norms on the world of production and consumption.

The AOC system helped to consolidate the mythical image of an ahistorical terroir producing a wine with a taste unchanged since time immemorial. This view dominated the French wine industry until very recently, and has also been a major factor in the creation of an image of the wine grower as the embodiment of traditional agrarian values and as a guarantor of quality. Yet it is based upon a myth and despite its venerable history, the association between taste and place only became formalised very recently, in the 1990s, through the role of wine writers, experts and guides who helped to impose a gustatory reading and mapping of each AOC. The notion of the taste of place will be discussed in the light of this specialised wine literature and the role of experts by scrutinising its construction as a landmark in international and global tastes. For wine growers, the concept of a taste belonging to a specific plot is a new one as the emphasis was traditionally placed on the natural and geological characteristics of the vineyard rather than on the qualities of the final product. Taste was not articulated in a sophisticated way at the time because there was no normative discourse on taste in the wine market. Taste and its definition was first and foremost the prerogative of the market.

Chapter 4, entitled Winescape, will explore the role of regional wine culture in constructing Burgundy's reputation as the historical birthplace of quality wine. The first section will explore the historical dimension of this literature, which has always been transnational in scope and influenced by the role of specific groups that have argued for the exceptionality of place in viticultural terms. Several examples will be analysed in detail to demonstrate the role of the Burgundy story through its circulation among European and global elites. Wine in Burgundy is often discussed in the plural, defined as a wide and diverse range of precise geographic plots, some of them no larger than a small garden, but always clearly identified and named. The evocative power of Romanée Saint Vivant, Corton and Puligny-Montrachet, to name just a few, situates the drinker in an international language and culture shared by educated, wealthy, discerning and, until recently, predominantly westernised elites. Like Bordeaux wines, Burgundian *grands crus* reinforce ideas about lifestyle and class in a culturally differentiated world. In the Côte d'Or that experience takes on a new dimension. The international resonance of the *grands crus* story not only appeals to consumers seeking distinction in the Bourdieusian sense, but has also become emblematic in the world of wine production. The *grands crus* story acts as a form of cultural marker for the world wine industry, and is perpetuated, disseminated and transmitted through the various networks established between agents and brokers. The *grands crus* story is not only about the French classification system based on geographic origin rather than grape variety, as in the New World, but it is also about how the reading of these classifications operates in transnational contexts, through different drinking cultures. The chapter will discuss these categorisations and how they operate at a global level through culture. The second part of this chapter will discuss the contemporary literary construction of the product through a wide range of guides and publications focusing on specific *grands crus*, from the Guide Hachette to Robert Parker, which will serve as the basis for a discussion of quality and excellence and will enable us to understand the construction of imaginary worlds of taste.

Chapter 5, 'Beyond Terroir', will engage with the study of the wine growing elites who through diverse strategies have attempted to redefine their products by placing emphasis on the soil or more ecologically and environmentally friendly production methods in order to engage with their own consumers. What is emphasised is minimum human and technological intervention and an appreciation of nature/terroir as mediated through the wine which contrasts with the global and uniform technical approach promoted by oenologists and mass produced New World wines. Nature is constructed as the paragon of quality to contrast with the technical domestication which dominated wine production for much of the post-war period and was associated with the intensive use of pesticides and other chemicals. The example given by this group of wine elites, recognised as producers of excellence, provides a fascinating insight into the relationship between nature and man in the context of resilience – defined as the ways in which Burgundian communities have coped with the location of these vineyards and the difficulties encountered when growing wine at its climatic limits. This chapter will focus on the emergence of the discourse of 'Nature' since the end of the 1990s to discuss the power relationships at stake at the local and international level. It will place the debate on wine as a natural product closed to its place of production in the long historical traditions of the nature/science opposition and will discuss its modern form in contemporary wine discourse. Case-studies will be included to demonstrate how the discourse of nature or the natural resonates with new markets of wealthy consumers looking for authenticity and distinction through wine consumption. At the same time, the chapter will examine how the hegemony of terroir is debated at the local level, arguing that there is a tendency to use terroir as a local governance tool leading to homogeneity and rootedness, while supplying a means for individuals in localities to respond to globalisation. This new chapter in the construction of terroir could be read as a disjuncture relative to the traditional *grands crus* story, but it is also about different strategies coalescing to respond to greater differentiation in parallel with the consolidation of the terroir and the *grands crus* story worldwide. As one of my informants explained: 'If you are working very hard and you like your product and it sells, the AOC system becomes meaningless'.

Chapter 6 will examine how the terroir story has become a transnational marketing tool which is interpreted in a wide range of ways by a diversity of consumers and producers. Taking the example of the Japanese manga *The Drops of God*[15] and the Pinot Noirs producers in New Zealand as two different ethnographic vignettes, an investigation of terroir will enable us to investigate the multiple interpretations and imaginings associated with the taste of place and the deployment of terroir as a strategic European tool. The chapter will discuss these two examples as a means of understanding professional debates around the concept of quality and of opening new social avenues to wine consumption through its possible democratisation. The *grands crus* story offers a new insight into the social construction of quality at the local level and its circulation as an iconic discourse of the negotiated relationship between culture and nature. Through the concept of terroir and its globalisation, the *grands crus* model offers a classic example of a geographically and historically stable site and a fluctuating, but strongly culturally defined, group of producers working in a particular ecological milieu. Its success, so often praised internationally by wine lovers, experts and producers, could be defined as an archetypal transnational investment terrain and a successful worldwide cultural story. Its long-established reputation as a significant place producing the best wines in the world relies on the connections made between different imaginative discourses and experiences which promote place, producers and consumers in a quasi-religious encounter. The taste of place here takes on its full meaning, but is passed on in different ways from the knowledge about the place to the taste of a particular wine.

Chapter 7, translating terroir between Burgundy and New Zealand, between the old original model of European viticulture and the emerging Pinot Noir producing regions of New Zealand, offers a powerful example of the global process of culture and its flow. It is clear that the two regions are radically different. The New Zealand experience seems to have had little in common with that of Burgundy, which could be defined as almost hermetically sealed in its own materiality, temporality and self-experience. Central Otago, on the other hand, could be seen as open, soaking up external influences. Yet what both areas have in common is the global wine industry defined by capitalism as well as consumers cultivating 'differential distinction'. In this global context they started from different historical positions which explains where they are now in the pursuit for excellence. In this competition, the position they have respectively reached determines to some extent their attitude towards each other. For the majority of Burgundian wine producers, Burgundy has nothing to learn from Otago, while Otago has everything to gain from a cultural exchange. This is therefore an unequal relationship in the context of the global cultural economy. Globalisation therefore appears as both a homogeneous and heterogeneous process in which the notion of scale plays a major role. In Burgundy, the AOC system has put constraints on the local viticulture and in its capacity to innovate, borrow or change while in Otago the lack of a legal framework means that innovation is an intrinsic part of the global pursuit of excellence. The existence of specific networks of producers-buyers-wine critics-consumers attached to the production and the commercialisation of wines worldwide has created the conditions for encouraging differentiation and 'distinction'. Marketing, but more importantly, 'taste' as a social experience, is central to the process of identifying specific networks. The Burgundy model has through globalisation established itself as a benchmark for the discerning buyer who has a certain level of social, economic and cultural capital. This is considered as the model to aspire to in terms of wine production, but also in terms of taste and consumption. Otago's place in this hierarchy is still being defined and, as we shall see, its pathway is complex, multi-formed and partly inspired by the Burgundian model. It is still in the process of writing its own story.

Finally, using the case-study provided by Burgundy's campaign for UNESCO World Heritage status for the *climats de Bourgogne*, Chapter 8 investigates how Burgundian wine and its political and economic elites emphasise heritage, cultural traditions and ecological concerns by claiming the right to global recognition. Burgundy uses heritage as a new means to serve the definition of specific micro identities to counter-globalisation. Yet the application for World Heritage status and the debate surrounding it reveals the continuing strength of a traditional model of terroir amongst intellectual and cultural elites. The project was put together by the region of Burgundy, the department of Côte d'Or, the towns of Beaune and Dijon, the BIVB (Bureau Interprofessionel des Vins de Bourgogne)[16] and the Confrérie des Chevaliers du Tastevin. The owner of the Domaine de la

Romanée-Conti (widely known as DRC) was the president of the association established to campaign for UNESCO recognition and most of the meetings took place under his leadership. Having been invited as an expert to participate in the definition of the *climats de Bourgogne,* I was able to analyse the construction of a historical narrative around the notion of *climats,* an ill-defined term but one that is embodied in imagined notions of an enduring and thus authenticated social configuration. By exploring its deployment and internal contestation through the various debates and scientific committees that I attended, this chapter argues that the candidature was elitist driven and was far from achieving professional consensus. As the example of Burgundian *climats* demonstrates, beneath the seemingly harmonious discourse of terroir lies a far more heterogeneous and imaginative society. Special emphasis will be placed upon the tension between nature and culture through the debate surrounding the scientific commission as well as the fierce debate about terroir which raised questions about long-term ecological and environmental issues. Terroir thus provides a window onto the mechanisms by which societies are able to use globalisation and modernity to suit their own purposes. The paradox of this is that the global explosion of attention to terroir – or the national conditions of winescapes – conceals human intervention, local land politics and the homogenisation of many wine manufacturing practices in most parts of the world, including France. The chimeric qualities of the concept of terroir freight wine from Burgundy in particular with a sense of mythological excellence. What I hope I have achieved in this book is to uncover the layers of meaning, practice and myth that constitute the Burgundian wine community now and in the past, and to restore reasoned perspective to the discourse around Burgundy, terroir and heritage.

Notes

1. See http://en.unesco.org/events/39th-session-world-heritage-committee. Consulted on 2 February 2016.
2. See http://whc.unesco.org/archive/2015/whc15-39com-INF.19.pdf. Consulted on 15 February 2016.
3. My own translation. See http://whc.unesco.org/archive/2015/whc15-39com-INF.19.pdf, p.194. Consulted on 15 February 2016.
4. For more information on La Paulée de Meursault as a form of economic folklore, see Laferté (2006).

5. My own translation. See http://www.climats-bourgogne.com/fr/notre-dos-sier_17.html. Consulted on 2 February 2016. Crus is defined here as a specific AOC wine classification term which refers to several vineyards assembled to constitute a specific vintage.
6. Esca is a grape disease that affects mature grapevine trunks.
7. Only a few viticultural sites have benefitted from the cultural site classification and it is very often because of the cultural elements that they have been recognised as such. The site of Primošten in Croatia is one such example.
8. See the discussion on authenticity in Barrey and Teil (2011).
9. For a useful analysis of the social sources of authenticity, see Wherry (2006).
10. To this observer, it resembled the Californian wineries and their *mise en scène* of wine.
11. For an example, see the work of the anthropologist Claude Royer (1980), on French wine growers.
12. This work, funded by the Ministry of Culture, covered the year of preparation behind the Saint-Vincent Tournante and gave us the opportunity to make a film and to prepare an exhibition in the local wine museum. For more information, see Demossier (1999).
13. Dion (1959). For an analysis of the current debates in French geography around the legacy of Dion, see the work of Jacqueline Dutton (forthcoming).
14. I have followed over the years around ten families as well as twenty wine growers more closely. We have had discussions on a number of topics over the years. Long-term ethnographic participation in key events has also contributed to my thinking about the field.
15. *The Drops of God* best-seller in South Korea was also a smash hit in France (it has been translated by the publisher Glénat); it helped to introduce wine to the masses in parts of Asia, and had a massive impact on the wine industry in South Korea. The July 2009 *Decanter* publication of 'The Power List' ranking of the wine industry's most influential individuals placed the authors Shin and Yuko Kibayashi at number 50, citing their work as 'arguably the wine publication of the last 20 years'.
16. The BIVB or Burgundy Wine Board which is composed of wine growers, wine producers and wine merchants was created in 1989 as a regional non-profit organisation under the French law 1901. According to its website, it is built on the principle of each member having an equal voice, and it defends and promotes the unique skills of the profession of wine making, the *négoce* (wine merchant) trade and vine growing, and the heritage of a shared passion. For more information, see http://www.bourgogne-wines.com/. Consulted on 11 July 2014.

Chapter 1
WINE LANDSCAPES AND PLACE-MAKING

The Burgundian vineyard is a complex patchwork and each site of production has its own identity and unique history. The fragmentation of terroir as well as the predominance of small wine holdings is one of the major features of the region. Landscape and social organisation are mutually reflective and interdependent and they are both marked by distinct hierarchies. The French wine industry is highly specialised in those areas where AOC prevails; around 85,000 wine holdings cultivate 780,000 hectares of vines.[1] Burgundy holds a unique place because of its size and high concentration of small producers, with 4,100 family businesses cultivating 31,500 hectares. Most of these have been growing in size, increasing from 5.5 to 7.6 hectares on average between 2000 and 2010.[2] The wine landscape has therefore witnessed a very slow process of concentration of landownership into the hands of the bigger family estates. Although there are examples of individuals or companies acquiring vineyards over the last decade, they remain in a tiny minority. In 2012, for example, the Château of Gevrey-Chambertin and its vineyard were sold to a businessman from Macau for 8 million euros causing a storm in the region in large measure because it was so exceptional. Compared to other wine regions, the Burgundian landownership structure and the scale of the vineyard have deterred any major external investments from international companies, and even the wealthiest local wine growers have tended to look outside Burgundy in order to expand. As Antonin Rodet, a prominent Burgundian *négociant*, noted during an interview in the French magazine *Nouvel Observateur*: 'We are looking south because we are so crammed in our native Burgundy'.[3] Other well-known *négociants* have sought to increase their portfolios by developing new vineyards in Ardèche (Latour) or by investing in California (Drouhin). This phenomenon has expanded to include well-known families of wine growers seeking to create new joint ventures elsewhere. The son of one of my oldest informers, who had been trained in Chile and Lebanon, has recently bought a vineyard in the south of France.

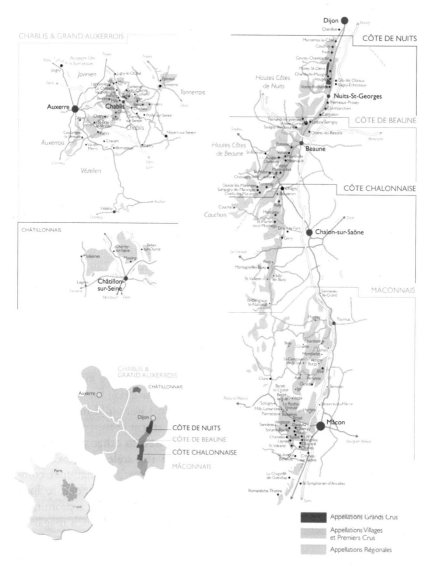

Figure 1.1 Burgundy and its vineyards © Bureau Interprofessionnel des Vins de Bourgogne (BIVB) (www.vins-bourgogne.fr)

The Côte d'Or has, since the consolidation of the AOC legal system in the 1930s, been represented in the local iconography as a stable hierarchy of crus defined on the basis of their geographical orientation and exposition with the National Road 6 and the railway dividing what have historically been defined as quality wines from the rest. The hills and slopes are central to the quality argument in global viticulture and along the sixty kilometres between Dijon and Saint-Aubin a myriad of crus are dispersed. The term *cru* has a complex etymology and it derives from French *cru,* 'vineyard', literally 'growth' (sixteenth century), from Old French *crois* (twelfth century; Modern French *croît*), from *croiss,* stem of *croistre,* 'growth, augment, increase', and ultimately from Latin *crescere,* 'come forth, spring up, grow, thrive' (see *crescent*). In the Côte d'Or, the *cru* is the equivalent of the AOC and of a particular taste historically associated with the *cru* which might include different plots blended together when the wine is made.

Despite its fragmented and heterogeneous nature,[4] what has always been compelling about the Burgundy story as a whole is its ability to resonate with consumers on several levels. At the macro-level the wine growing area encompasses the emblematic regional name 'Burgundy' and on a micro level it is presented as a list of villages from Côte de Nuits and the Côte de Beaune and the other major sites of production such as the Hautes-Côtes, Chablis, the Auxerrois, the Côte Chalonnaise, the Mâconnais, the Beaujolais and Pouilly-Fussé. In terms of volume, Burgundy produces 200 million bottles each year, covering over 100 different AOCs and representing only 0.5 per cent of the world's total wine production.[5] As a wine

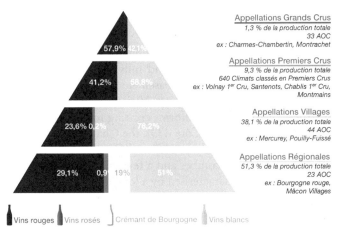

Figure 1.2 The geography of crus © Bureau Interprofessionnel des Vins de Bourgogne (BIVB) (www.vins-bourgogne.fr)

region, Burgundy is a complex puzzle which can be read from the websites dedicated to the region or the many ways in which local guides invite the visitor to explore its vineyards. Usually the encounter is accompanied by a range of sensations in which diversity, history, culture, tradition and tastes all contribute to the distinctiveness of the place. The historical investment is part of the story of place-making and no short cuts can be taken when trying to 'understand' Burgundy. The experience goes against the grain of contemporary society and culture with its diminishing attention span. Time is of the essence here. History and culture become embedded in the reading of the Burgundian vineyard, contributing to the resonance of authenticity in terms of the tourist's experience of the site. From the Cistercians to the Dukes of Burgundy, the reputation and notoriety of the place has been cultivated for centuries through the selling of distinctive village names to European courts, wealthy elites and, more recently, the global consumer.

Burgundy's geography and landscape have played a major role in establishing the reputation of the place and acting as long-term markers of quality, not on account of their aesthetic value, but because of the historical resonance of the site and its wines. After perusing the literature devoted to the region, it is clear that the wine landscape was rarely seen as an attractive feature of the place. Gilles Laferté (2011) even argues that the region was perceived as a site of historical interest but not as picturesque. In his book, *Terroir*, James Wilson (1998: 108) describes Burgundy as an area where wines are produced on hills and slopes along the western side of the Saône Valley. For the most part the relief is modest, the plateaux of the Côte d'Or being only 500 feet (115 metres) above the valley whose elevations average about 725 feet (220 metres).

According to Wilson (1998: 108), the landscape is characterised by a narrow band of scarps, fault blocks and hills with rocks dating back to the Jurassic and Triassic periods and basement granites exposing Paleozoic rocks, schists and old volcanic intrusion. Variations in the crust resulted in different structural styles and landforms creating four geologically defined viticultural compartments: the Côte d'Or, the Châlonnais, the Mâconnais and the Beaujolais. Structurally the Côte d'Or is one long north-south fault scarp, broken only by combes and a few small river valleys. Thus the Côte d'Or vineyards are characterised by a long and narrow hillside facing hilly valleys, which are fortuitously protected from the worst aspects of the continental climatic conditions. According to Jean-Pierre Garcia (2011: 11–12), the soil of the vineyards is predominantly clay and limestone, although in fact it is much more varied following faults and localised land movements. This combination of landforms, soils and micro-climates forms a multitude of diverse micro-territorialised natural sites. For most commentators, these conditions have shaped wine production and were exploited by the Burgundians who developed historically small-scale 'gardening viticulture'.

If the geological interpretation gives a sense of how the landscape is constituted, the anthropological perspective adds a very different dimension to our understanding of the wine landscape and local wine culture. My first encounter with the vineyards as a landscape and site of production dates back to the 1980s and to my years as a doctoral student conducting an ethnography of the *grands crus*. Having been born in Burgundy, I felt like many of my contemporaries that the vineyards were there and had always been there, but there was little aesthetic discourse or pleasure associated with their presence. The vineyard was mainly defined as a space for long walks or strolls on Sunday afternoons. Yet it was first and foremost a productive space for the local wine growing community. The landscape was largely fragmented, running in parallel with the nineteenth-century railway network and the more ancient National Road 6 which helped to form a barrier to further viticultural expansion. If today you were to drive south from Dijon to Santenay, along this road, most of the vineyard would be located on your right-hand side, visually presented as a tapestry or a patchwork of small vineyards assembled together and organised around a series of densely populated traditional Burgundian villages.

The local architecture has a chocolate box feel, with a series of quintessential French villages complete with church, châteaux and *mairies*. A sense of bustling activity defines these communities, there are still a few shops, and it is easy to meet the locals when walking around the streets. Wine production requires a workforce and these villages are characterised by the calendar of viticultural activities, from the hectic and noisy time of the autumn harvest to the more rhythmic winter and summer months which are punctuated by periods of intense labour. A sense of time dominates the wine landscape and the long-term occupation of the site is apparent from the monumental architectural presence of religious icons such as the Hospices de Beaune or the Clos de Vougeot as well as the smaller estates of generations of *vignerons* incarnated by stone walls and *cabottes* (small stone shelters) and the many walled *clos*.

It is only relatively recently that an awareness of the local landscape has taken centre stage in the context of the application for UNESCO World Heritage status (see Chapter 8). The prominence of landscape in heritage processes administered through the UNESCO has given a new meaning to viticultural landscapes and invested them with a political and cultural resonance. In 2006, for example, the United Nations deemed wine so integral to human history that it created and endowed an international chair for wine culture and tradition in Burgundy, which, revealingly, was given to a female climatologist specialising in the physical rather than the social or cultural aspects of the subject. Brock University in the USA and its CCOVI (Cool Climate Oenology and Viticulture Institute) was part of the driving force behind the creation of the chair. Proposed and spearheaded by the University of Burgundy and supported by CCOVI-Brock University, the Chair for Wine and Culture was established by UNESCO after much coordinated strategic lobbying.[6] This facilitated, as a result, deeper engagement with the concept of cultural landscape and how it could be more productively understood by local communities. Wine landscapes have therefore become inscribed in a broader set of frameworks, combining a wide range of characteristics from the historical formation of local viticulture to legal definitions of denomination of origin and the collective sense of ownership attached to them. It is now a fundamental part of the new heritage strategies put in place to refine the distinctiveness attached to specific sites in the global world of wine. This chapter seeks to engage with the complex process of making sense of wine landscapes and locating these understandings and engagements within a broader 'politics of scale' and 'politics of aesthetics', which mesh local and global together in a process of reflexive imbrications defined as a careful and selected process of elements which are then adopted and translated into the local context to be in turn projected onto the global wine market.

Place-Making and Wine

According to Glenn Banks (2013: 2) the new geography of wine is marked by diversity and distinction in terms of production arrangements and technologies, cultural meanings and understandings, and the resulting landscapes and communities. If Burgundy was a precocious example of place-making around wine, with its distinctive culture, folklore, architectural and historically emblematic heritage, as well as a model of hospitality which was already based on conviviality and sharing, it is only with the recent UNESCO application that a shift has taken place, recasting some of the global references linking place to taste by fossilising and historicising the site of production, which is presented as a stable, trustworthy and reliable place. Rather than competing with New World Chardonnay or Pinot Noir, Burgundy seeks to reinforce its image as a distinct elite product, with its Montrachet or Clos de Vougeot having a very different historic, geographic and cultural resonance associated with its newly adopted *climats*.[7] The successful UNESCO application will enhance and consolidate the identification between product and place of what is already defined as the 'lien au lieu' (link to a location). When drinking a Puligny-Montrachet

Premier cru Les Pucelles,[8] one should be able to visualise on the map the precise place of origin of the product, a small plot located on the hill. This strategy, which is similar to that developed in the luxury goods industry, emerges at a time when frauds in the wine industry are commonplace.[9]

The recent scandal of Rudy Kurniawan, who was arrested at his home in suburban Los Angeles and charged with what may ultimately go down as the wine crime of the century, is a case in point. Kurniawan was a thirty-five-year old Indonesian-born collector who, in the early 2000s, seemingly out of nowhere, became the biggest player on the fine-wine market, buying and selling millions of dollars worth of rarities. Kurniawan presented himself as a wine lover and the collector of rare bottles, who started to buy some of the most prestigious wines regularly at high prices. He then started to sell them, as well as other counterfeit bottles, through the same network of auction houses and some buyers trusted him sufficiently to pay up to one million dollars for the most precious vintages available. It was when the Burgundian wine grower, Alain Ponsot, was contacted by one of his friends, an American lawyer, who informed him that some of his wines from 1945, 1949 and 1962 were being sold at an auction, when the label did not exist before 1982, that the fraud was revealed. More than 4,700 bottles of counterfeit wines were discovered along with some authentic *grands crus*.

In the current global wine context, where all the traditional divisions in terms of viticultural practices and wine definitions seem to blur under the pressure of standardisation and homogeneisation, authenticity becomes a crucial area for differentiation (Barrey and Teil 2011). The significance of place in contemporary wine production is increasingly characterised by 'place-based' forms of marketing (Banks 2013: 3). In Burgundy the connection between history, quality and place-making has been a constant reference in the ways that place has been marketed and it is only recently with the UNESCO campaign that the region has reassessed its powerful terroir story. There is nothing new about sudden and often quite profound rethinking of what defines Burgundy and its wines. During the Great Depression of the 1930s, the AOC system emerged as a response to crisis. As for the recent invention of the *climats de Bourgogne*, that owes much to the consequences of what is described as fast capitalism and globalisation. Both periods are revealing of how Burgundy has negotiated difficult times and shown an ability to reposition itself in the global world of wine.

The 1930s were characterised by a period of intense economic restructuring of the wine industry in France. From the inter-war period, a regionalist movement of tourist development and gastronomy strongly influenced the construction of the image of the Burgundy region and its wines (Laferté 2006). During that period, tourism was no longer considered simply as the discovery of monuments and natural sites, and agricultural and viti-cultural folklore took on a new importance. Meanwhile, local cuisines became regionalised and were promoted as identity markers. Tourism and gastronomy acted as strategic levers, promoting the revitalisation of rural areas. This shift was made possible by the development of mass ownership of the automobile, as evidenced by the history of the Michelin guide. Viticulture was even more profoundly affected by the creation in the 1930s of the AOC system, emphasising the origin of wines which came to con-stitute a new standard of quality, and required the education of consumers through the promotion of these new appellations. As part of this process, Burgundian viticulture was advertised through a largely invented wine cul-ture based upon folklore and festivities featuring its wines and gastronomy, as part of a strategy of employing local heritage at a time of acute economic crisis (Jacquet 2009).

The creation of the Confrérie des Chevaliers du Tastevin in 1933 and its chapters is one of the best examples of this touristic and patrimonial enterprise; the touristic Route des grands crus was created at the same time (1934) as well as the wine auction at the Hospices de Beaune (1921) and the Paulée de Meursault (1923) which all became festive occasions for both the locals and their clients. What they have in common is an attempt to create a new reading of place constructed around a folkloric tradition and the convivial and exuberant celebration of wine (Laferté 2011). The desire to promote Burgundy as the natural home of the gourmet contributed to the development of regional agricultural products as well as viticulture. The creation of a museum dedicated to wine heritage and culture is par-ticularly evocative of the dynamics of heritage focused upon Burgundian viticulture which was led by actors external to the wine industry. Beaune was the first town in France to open a museum completely dedicated to viticulture, the Burgundy Wine Museum, established in 1938 and housed since 1946 in the former Hotel des Ducs de Bourgogne. Inspired by the retrospective exhibition of the Vine and Wine organised in 1920 by a committee of scholars of the history and archaeology of Beaune and teach-ers of the school of viticulture, the museum was conceptualised by Roger Duchet, Mayor of Beaune, Georges-Henri Rivière, the Parisian curator who designed the museum, and André Lagrange, the ethnologist who collected the majority of the exhibits. Both the museum and the folkloric tradition continue to prosper today and it forms part of the cultural encounter visitors experience when travelling to the region.

The new historical episode of the UNESCO application is yet another stage in recasting Burgundy's place in the world order. Yet the context is very different to the 1930s. As Jacques Maby has argued (2002: 198), it is only recently that a more organised approach to wine landscape has emerged in France and that oenotourism has developed on a significant scale. As part of the new global wine strategies, landscape has become a key part of the political economy, adding value to new categories of consumption. These strategies cannot be fully discussed without referring to the UNESCO heritage categories and how they have developed since their inception. The recent French initiatives to win UNESCO World Heritage status for a wide range of sites, landscapes and objects have to be read against the ways in which states can exploit UNESCO conventions in imaginative ways to suit their own purposes. The development and ratification of the UNESCO Intangible Heritage Convention (2003), which broadened the scope of an earlier convention act of 1972 by embodying 'a particular understanding and conceptualisation of the nature of both cultural and natural heritage' (Smith and Akagawa 2009: 1), has been highly significant. By exploiting, in different ways, the systems, language, definitions of culture and nature attached to the conventions of 1972 and 2003, national states and local actors have creatively combined different heritage registers to put together convincing cases of 'shared heritage'. Moreover, the scope of the UNESCO application goes further by integrating many different categories, including wine from historical landscapes (Tokaj wine region, historical cultural landscape), cultural sites (Piedmont) and cultural itineraries (Spain). In 2013, the ancient Georgian Qvevri wine-making method was inscribed onto the Representative List of the Intangible Cultural Heritage of Humanity. It is this broader context which provided the background to some of the discussions behind the UNESCO application in Burgundy as well as the debates on food heritage and authenticity (Barrey and Teil 2011).

Food heritage found its concrete expression at a time when UNESCO had begun to designate the food and cuisine of several European, Middle Eastern and Latin American countries as Intangible Cultural Heritage. That concept was first introduced in 2000 alongside the Masterpieces of the Oral and Intangible Heritage of Humanity as a way of addressing the criticism of its tendency to legitimise a particular Western – if not Western European – perception of heritage in terms of both policy and practice (Smith and Akagawa 2009: 1). This rise of heritage certification reflected a broader movement which has affected contemporary societies since the 1980s. Food heritage has become a political tool for the construction of identity in a context of globalisation. From Mexico to Kyoto, initiatives have recast national, regional and local identities through the recognition of gastronomic heritage which is defined in a new political context of rescaling and heritagisation. This food heritage fever forms part of an attempt to respond to societal concerns about the dangers of modern consumption, but also to feed a wealthy segment of our societies. It raises issues of economic development and causes us to think about new forms of post-productivist agricultural adaptation.

As part of this intense rescaling of the politics of heritage to suit local development purposes and to create new connections between the local and the global, wine landscapes have come to fill a central place in the new narrative about place-making. In a recent report published by ICOMOS (International Council on Monuments and Sites),[10] the broader international context which gave wine landscapes an institutionalised meaning is further explained. Vineyards are widely recognised to be amongst the most remarkable forms of landscapes created by human activity, both by the mark they make on the territory and by the cultural traditions associated with them. So it was hardly surprising that they found their way on to the World Heritage list almost as soon as the category of cultural landscape was created. Of all the many and varied agricultural landscapes, vineyards are the most commonly protected. UNESCO has accorded World Heritage status to six wine regions in which the landscape is essential and four regions in which it is not typical. There are only two other types of agricultural landscapes that have been recognised as World Heritage sites: those of tobacco crops and rice. Since 1992, when the introduction of the category of cultural landscapes in the World Heritage List took place, three major viticultural sites have been recognised, including those famous for some of the finest vines in the world: the old jurisdiction of Saint Emilion (Bordeaux Grand Cru); the valley of the Upper Douro (Porto) in Portugal; and the slopes of Tokaj (Tokaji aszú) in Hungary. In other cultural World Heritage landscapes, the vine plays a major role (Wachau, Cinque Terre, Val de Loire, the Rhine valley, etc.). Yet wine landscapes are not all remarkable aesthetically speaking and it has become difficult for UNESCO to differentiate and recognise their specific qualities.

To return to the example of Burgundy and its construction as an emblematic wine region, it is clear that tourism and hospitality played an important part in selling the region to both French and international consumers. In his book *The Story of Wine*, Hugh Johnson wrote a chapter entitled 'Journey to Gold Coast', focusing on the idea of pilgrimage tourism as a model of understanding the vineyard and the importance of history in the popular awareness of this part of the French landscape. Similarly, an anthropological approach to the Burgundian vineyard requires us to undertake a journey back and forth between production, marketing and consumption on a global scale. Burgundy as a touristic space was also built upon its relationship with wine and gastronomy (Laferté 2006). A unique consumer experience has been created on the model of a multiplicity of wines and the important role of history in the construction of regional identity. We can speak, in this case almost, of a true pilgrimage, or at least of a unique tourist experience, constructed around Pinot Noir and Chardonnay, and synthesising a remarkable diversity condensed in one place. The tourist experience is constructed continuously through the extreme differentiation attached to each varietal grape – Pinot Noir and Chardonnay – and the secular history of the place.[11]

Hospitality in Burgundy played an important part in the construction of a regional touristic identity and, unlike Bordeaux, it was until very recently relatively easy to meet the producer and taste wines in his/her cellar. Wine tasting was about an intimate social and cultural experience of encounter through the visit to the cellar, the knowledge of the producer, and the visual and gustative initiation to a particular location or plot. The story was about a real and authentic social experience embodied in the wine grower, usually the male head of the lineage with his close and enduring tie to the land that is recurrent in narratives about Burgundy. By meeting wine growers and their families, descending to the cellar, learning about the grammar of the *grands crus*, and memorising each of the wines through a unique social experience, the visitor had a unique visual, gustatory and sensorial experience as part of his or her encounter with this bounded culture. Yet the recent craze for its wines has meant that fewer and fewer good wines are available for purchase by the passing tourist.

In each of the successful reinventions of the meaning of Burgundy there was a need to protect the site from external pressures or to acknowledge its distinctive value in the world of wine. Interestingly, most of the wine regions that have been recognised by UNESCO are located on the European continent.[12] It is easy to draw the conclusion that for UNESCO only the emblematic, historic vineyards are considered to be worth listing (Mollevi Bortolo 2012). Similarly, debates have emerged relating to new dimensions of wine culture and heritage. The designation of a specific area as a World Heritage site implies the defence of its rural landscape, which is often threatened by other uses such as house building, commercial developments and roads. The debate on wine landscape and tourism is therefore inscribed in some of the current global concerns of sustainability, ecotourism and oenotourism and has still to find a common direction in the context of European vineyards. Local strategies continue to prevail in the management of wine heritage.

Wine tourism is, however, widely recognised for having a strong connection with the rural landscape and rurality (Mitchell et al. 2012: 312), which in Europe has a complex and wide-ranging resonance. Several authors have identified rurality as a core element of wine tourism and its promotion. In the context of New World wine regions, this romantic view of the rural wine setting has been described by Peter Howland (2008: 2) 'as a metro-rural idyll that essentially celebrates ... middle-class consumption of fine wine, gourmet food, upmarket accommodation, and intentional social connectedness'. In European vineyards, on the other hand, the discourse on wine tourism goes further as it seeks to develop in parallel a better awareness of the economic importance of landscape discourse and wine in terms of socio-cultural references (Maby 2002: 198). It has been suggested that wine tourism is both a contributor to, and a result of, winescapes and their components (Cambourne et al. 2000: 319). The Burgundy region is charged with meanings which are derived from the wine that is produced there, but also from carefully chosen elements of its history which have been evoked to construct the place. The very mention of Burgundy conjures up images of monks, monumental architecture, gastronomy and great wines. It is an imagined rural idyll that consumers are drawn to, which is accentuated by contact with wine growers and the simplicity of the encounter.

Despite some of the largest domains having developed wine tours and tasting facilities, wine tourism is still generally under-developed and it takes the form of individual trips organised by a wide range of actors, as demonstrated by the new website of the office for tourism in Burgundy[13] which proclaims, 'With a strong identity, Burgundy is a favourite destination for lovers of wine and food, art and history, but also recreational sports, nature, fishing and river walks'. The region recently organised a survey on the future of tourism led by the local authorities and the Tourist office as part of the UNESCO application. The result of the consultation presented Burgundy as the eighth most popular region to visit for foreigners and the fourteenth for French tourists. Overall it generated up to 6.2 per cent of regional GDP and employed more than 22,000 people and therefore it represents a vibrant and profitable economic sector.

The collective dimension of this new touristic enterprise is still under-developed and many different initiatives are being promoted. The BIVB (Bureau Interprofessionnel des Vins de Bourgogne, or Burgundy wine board) oversees the production and promotion of Burgundy wines, while the various tourist offices deal with other features of the region. A recent survey conducted by Atout France, 'Tourisme et Vin', in 2010 estimated that there were in the region of 2.5 million visits to Burgundy during the year for 650 cellars in total. Thirty-eight per cent of people interviewed responded that wine and the vineyards were the principal reason for their visit.[14] Interestingly, the same report underlines the fact that visitors have found the quality of its wines to be one of the principal attractions of the region, but many also describe it as inward looking, a bit distant and pretentious, as well as complicated and not very accessible. It is worth noting that while vineyards are not protected spaces, there are vineyards in Burgundy that are walled and inaccessible to the general public. Some are sites of pilgrimage for wine consumers from across the globe. The Romanée-Conti, for example, has even put up a sign forbidding public access to the plot.

As in Champagne (Mitchell et al. 2012: 330), the social significance of vines and wine is about sociability, while the nature of the wine industry remains highly individualistic. The rhetoric surrounding the communal, collective or cooperative nature of Burgundy is frequently undermined by the realities of the individualistic nature of wine production. Opening such sites to mass tourism might lead to challenging times ahead as viticulture and tourism do not necessarily cohabit successfully.

The Anthropology of Wine Landscape

Anthropologists were slow to appreciate the potential of landscape studies. It is only since the 1980s that they have begun to recognise the ways in which peoples' perception of their world and their material engagement with it are intimately bound together and are created, as well as shaped, by the landscape (Bender 1993: 323). In the anthropological tradition, landscape was interpreted only as land use, when something was done

Figure 1.3 Wall of the Romanée-Conti. Author's photograph

to the land, rather than as an object of study in its own right. Landscape was seen as the result of the impact of man on nature. Following Hirsch and O'Hanlon (1995), landscape should be conceptualised as a cultural process, one that is located between place and space, image and representation. Moreover, landscapes are perceived and understood in many different ways that are visible only in the eyes of the beholder, and through the historical and social experiences of that individual. Thus landscapes and culture are embedded in time, history, memory and meaning, producing multiple perceptions and understandings that act and interact together.

In the French context, Chaia Heller (2006: 331) has argued that actors tend to invoke romantic notions of space associated with traditional agricultural practice, encapsulating the socialisation of nature through human activity or labour. Seen from this perspective, terroir played an important role in redefining the relationship local communities had established with their land, giving new values to the landscape. For the anthropologist Amy Trubek (2008), the French conception of terroir relies on a way of seeing the world. Good food in France is not necessarily more natural or 'organic', but is more cultural, emerging from a particular agricultural soil and savoir-faire (Heller 2006: 332). This worldview means that the notion of wilderness, and by the same token nature, is intrinsically constructed as social and romanticised. Wine landscapes follow the same principle. Wine growers are, for the most part, acutely aware of their art, of their savoir-faire and of the implications of their productive activities. Hard work is deeply embedded in their engagement towards the landscape as a legacy of the post-war productivist ideology. Yet very few engage creatively with the landscape they live and work with (Maby 2002: 198).

In French anthropology, the study of wine landscapes has not therefore benefitted from close academic attention and it has often been analysed through the study of other social factors such as habitat, material culture or knowledge (Chaudat 2012: 94) which were all integral to a certain conception of history dominated by the French Marxist school of the 1960s and 1970s. For other French scholars working on the history and geography of wine, such as Roger Dion (1959), Gilbert Garrier (1995), Marcel Lachiver (1988) or Jean-Robert Pitte (2005), the quality of wine was, and still is, explained more by the history of humankind and culture than the geology of the vineyards (Chaudat 2012: 94). So it is true to say that the emphasis has been put on the role of culture, knowledge, traditional artefacts and folklore rather than on the landscape itself. The primacy of culture can be illustrated by the range of traditional themes and objects found in French museums devoted to wine, from tools for the cultivation of the vineyards to wine rituals surrounding the life cycle of communities. The Musée du

Vin in Beaune, which was created in 1937, illustrates this trend and its visual representation of wine culture promotes a wine heritage narrative that is typical of European wine museums. In this museographic tradition, landscape had no place and it is only recently that intellectual fashions have changed. To take the example of Beaune, the history of the vineyard is presented, from antiquity to the twentieth century, as a linear process and the lives of wine growers are portrayed throughout the exhibition via the labour of individuals or communities. This a-historical scenography cryst-allises an idealised, pre-modern view of French viticulture. The winery and cellar, dating back to the fourteenth century, house many presses spanning the period from the sixteenth to the nineteenth centuries, underlining the dominant narrative of a timeless society and means of production.

The wine museum in Beaune showcases the pre-agrarian ideal of nature domesticated by man and its labour. Similar patterns are detectable at the heart of the concept of terroir, and the Burgundian example exemplifies this conception (see also Chapter 6). By the dawn of the twentieth cen-tury, Burgundy had come to be seen as synonymous with its gastronomy and viticulture. The earlier aristocratic image of its wines was superseded by one of growers engaged in a labour of love (Laferté 2011: 37). The wine landscape gradually became an object worthy of investment as it guaranteed economic recognition for producers through its environmental quality and played an important role in rebranding the place. Yet it is only recently with the work of geographers and sociologists that a shift has occurred in terms of a better understanding of the way in which people operate in spatial constraints and engage with landscape (Bender 1993: 324). The specific category of wine landscape has been the focus of much recent attention amongst French geographers. The works of, among others, Yves Luginbühl (2014), or Jacques Maby (2002), seek to raise aware-ness both within wine growing communities and amongst the population at large of the uniqueness of wine landscapes and the complex web of meanings attached to them. Traditionally, wine producers thought of their landscape in a purely functional fashion. It was only through the terroir ideology that they gradually came to see it as a living object, albeit one whose properties cannot be evaluated using a strictly scientific methodol-ogy. Yet this engagement took different forms and the idea of a collective understanding of wine landscape is, in analytical and ethnographic terms, highly problematic. It could be argued that each wine producer has his/her own take on the landscape and that different ideologies contribute to a more complex understanding. Again, at any given time or place, individual attitudes will vary enormously, depending on the producer's character, economic position, culture and much else besides (Bender 1993: 323).

Landscape and History

Since the legal birth of terroir through the AOC legislation of the 1930s, the Burgundian landscape has always been part of a wider narrative attached to the production of excellence and craftsmanship. It is as if the most precious plots have always been there and have always been associated with wines of the highest quality. More than for any other agricultural product, the wine landscape incarnates a palimpsest which is marked by several centuries of occupation and land use (see Chapter 4). Located on the climatic edge of northern viticulture, the contemporary wine landscape of Burgundy offers a remarkable landform worked by man. As the result of long-term human activity, it condenses history, geography and culture shaped by the actions and skills that men and women have imposed upon it and the original social and cultural forms that have been associated with it. Over the length of the sixty kilometres from Dijon to Saint-Aubin, south of Beaune, sixty different appellations are visually displayed, defining a small territory, complex and remarkable thanks to its own unique hierarchy. Here you can see what you drink! This landscape, often admired for its subtle crafted appearance, is the result of the labour of generations of growers. On the eve of the French Revolution, the usually critical Arthur Young compared the vineyard of the Côte d'Or to the best gardens of England, such was the attention to detail and craftmanship displayed. In its physical appearance, it has changed little except that its exploitation has become more mechanised.

If the landscape is primarily the result of human intervention, wine landscapes have always been the focus of a particular and sustained attention due to wine's cultural status. Quality wines are valued for their long shelf life, and even more humble appellations are the product of the vine and therefore a long-term investment (Fournier and d'Onofrio 1991: 3). A preoccupation with the *longue durée* is a particular feature of wine landscape as both vines and producers are meshed together throughout the life cycle of production. The majority of producers know only too well when their vineyard was planted, and are familiar with the history of the grape (massale selection) or the provenance (clonal selection). For Yves Luginbühl (2004: 99), what is particularly striking about Burgundy is the presence of cramped plots, carefully manicured, mostly without vegetation cover between low vines, which are frequently separated by dry stone walls, the *clos* (walled plot). The paths are narrow, leaving very little space for manoeuvre with the tractor. This landscape has retained original features such as enclosed vineyards, stone walls, trees and slopes, but in some areas it has also been the object of intense use of the soil or relandscaping.

In the landscape narrative recounted by my informers, there is an acknowledgment that, for all the continuities, physical change has nevertheless occurred, and that history has left its mark. Echoing this, there is nostalgia for a pre-modern time before the rise of intense productivity when the landscape was more varied and less oriented towards viticulture as a specialisation. Polyculture dominated agricultural production here until the beginning of the twentieth century, and that was the case much later for some of the less prestigious vineyards of the Hautes-Côtes de Beaune or Nuits. History and culture have been embedded in the changing fortunes of the place, while, at the same time, they have been used to create a sense of permanence as a long-lasting site of human excellence. Specific mentions of episodes of viticultural expansion have always been tempered by a constant and reflexive discourse about wine production and the quest for quality. Interestingly, the aesthetic dimension of the landscape has rarely been mentioned by my informers as a feature or a subject of note. Amongst the educated and wine savants, Stendhal is often cited for his mocking description of the vineyards of the Côte d'Or, the golden hill, as 'the dry and small hill of Burgundy'. As we have seen, what has dominated the narrative about wine landscape is the human dimension, with the prestigious and historic influence of monks, kings and princes as well as a constant quest for excellence and quality in terms of production. Yet, the wine landscape was largely ignored by the local population and it is only with the recent Burgundy campaign for UNESCO World Heritage Status (see Chapter 8) that the vineyard has been discovered as a new category of perception, more environmentally friendly and imbued with post-modern flavours. For most wine producers, on the other hand, the story is very different; it is one of ambition and human success (Maby 2002: 206), largely defined by hardship and challenges as well as by community values and individual struggles.

To understand how *vignerons* perceive the landscape, it is necessary to appreciate the central preoccupation of their culture and society with physical labour. Following Black and Ulin 'wine is, in particular, very illustrative of this tendency towards both fetish and alienated labor' (2013: 180), which often obscures the social and historical conditions of wine production. For journalists and popular authors, wine landscape has tended to be portrayed as a crafted but naturalised object, which is often seen as reflecting the quality of local wine production. What is often hidden in this description of the landscape is the hard work involved even in maintaining it as a 'natural' site and the complex hierarchy of the workforce attached to a productive site. Several wine growers I interviewed in the course of my research summed it up by 'let nature speak'. Labour participates in the continuity of the landscape. It forms part of the commodification process discussed by Black and Ulin (2013: 180) when analysing wine under the conditions of contemporary capitalism. Interestingly, wine is on the one hand fetishised to the extent that very few studies actually focus on the workers (Crenn 2013), and on the other hand it is presented as the artistic triumph of an individual capable of mastering or domesticating nature. In Burgundy, the labour of generations of *vignerons* has ensured that often precarious hillside plots have survived the threat of erosion or have been brought back to life after long periods of neglect, as was the case in the villages of Pernand-Vergelesses or Saint-Aubin.

Viticulture is for many synonymous with intensive labour. Horse drawn ploughing has come back into fashion on the most successful domains and the mechanical maintenance of soil is discouraged. Yet very few producers mention the presence of workers and there is a strong emphasis on the wine grower as the only active worker of the land. Driving through the vineyards at different stages of the year, one quickly becomes aware of a very different story, that of a dense and skilled workforce of men and women fighting the elements. Indeed, quality viticulture has almost inexhaustible demand for intensive labour. In 2000, viticulture provided employment for 11,726 full-time workers, some 30 per cent of the overall regional agricultural labour force for a sector which represents only 18 per cent of employers and 1.7 per cent of the cultivated agricultural surface. In 2010, 3,770 domains employed 5,300 full-time workers.[15] Work is central to the local culture as it is associated with the process of emancipation for wine growing families. As *vignerons* have become economically independent of wealthy *négociants* and landowners, accessing ownership has been a prime objective for most of the local producers rooted in village life.

Landownership and Family Lineage

In the introduction to their collective volume on the ethnology of landscape, Françoise Dubost and Bernadette Lizet (1995: 226) argue that what matters is not so much understanding whether a space is perceived or not as a landscape, but understanding what the local society values in the landscape. Land tenure has a significant impact on landscape patterns and systems of production (including wine tourism), as it can influence landowners' economic decisions and behaviour.[16] Viewed from a long-term perspective, there have been many examples of transformation. Fragmentation took place following the implementation of a compulsory system of crop rotation in the 1740s, and the egalitarian inheritance laws of the revolution administered another shock that was closely followed by the effects on the land market resulting from the Civil Code introduced by Napoleon in 1803. It could be argued that after the French Revolution, land ownership became a key goal for the rural population as a means of ensuring economic autonomy and status.

In Burgundy, small-scale landownership remains the dominant key feature of the wine landscape and it is crucial to the familial and economic strategies of successive generations of wine growers. In 2000, 46 per cent of the vineyards were directly exploited and 43 per cent were rented from other local families. Sharecropping represented 11 per cent of the agricultural surface.[17] Land and families are intrinsically and deeply intertwined and kinship and business are inseparable. In 2010, official statistics confirmed that the biggest wine estates had seen their landholdings grow, while the number of producers owning vines had declined sharply, by some 26 per cent since 2000. One in five specialised holdings has disappeared and this trend has mostly affected the peripheral areas of Burgundy, especially in the south. This change follows the legal evolution of more complex forms of ownership created to facilitate the transmission of the vineyards from one generation to the next. Recent figures confirm the primacy of the family lineage in the social structure of local viticulture.[18] One of the most striking features accompanying this trend is the feminisation of the wine industry, with women representing no fewer than 26 per cent of the wine managers. Traditionally, families of wine growers encouraged the eldest son to take over, but following the rise in land prices, siblings – daughters included – have been integrated into the management of the wine estate, enabling the continuity of the domain. In contrast to the example of Languedoc, studied by Winnie Lem (2013), where the unit of family production has masculinised viticulture, in Burgundy, globalisation and capitalism have encouraged the feminisation of the industry. Yet the continuous rise in the price of vineyards, especially of the *grands crus*, has forced some families to sell emblematic plots, especially when one or more of the siblings left the domain and found themselves in need of an income. These difficult situations are rarely openly discussed, but they pose acute problems to the family and to the sustainability of its enterprise. This might be exacerbated by the acquisition of UNESCO world heritage status as it is likely to further inflate the already astronomical value of individual plots.

Over recent decades, wine landscapes have acquired greater economic value which has had an impact on the ways in which they are perceived. In the Côte d'Or, land prices have increased continuously since the 1990s and are still rising. Driven on by the *grands crus* which saw their average price reach 4 million euros per hectare in 2013, less prestigious plots have generally followed suit. Yet the notion of working the land means that landownership takes on a different meaning compared to elsewhere because for most producers the relationship to the vineyard is dictated by the personal affinity built up with it over many years and it is not simply dependent on its legal status. A special emotional bond binds the wine grower to some of his/her plots which are perceived as emblematic of the family history. That sense of history has remained central, despite the massive increase in the price of the vineyards and is embodied in the long-term durability of vines whose lifespans can be as long as a century. Each family has deep markers in the historical memory of each parcel, its climatic accidents, great vintages or dates of replanting. Historically, plant selection took place within families and within the same village. The history of the vineyard often coincided with that of the family lineage, its connections to other families and domains through replantation. A strong identification of the producer to the plant and the product characterises the wine environment. Whatever the mode of relationship to the land, a special emotional bond binds the wine grower to some of his/her plots which are perceived as emblematic of the history of the family and its past struggles and recent successes.

As a result of the enrichment of the families of wine growers and the rise in value of their land assets over the last three decades, the concept of working the land, which was central to their self-definition, has had a direct impact on the division of labour. As their financial means and personal wealth have increased, especially where *grands crus* and *premiers crus* owners are concerned, they have found themselves less attracted by hard labour and the attendant difficulties of working the vines. As I have argued elsewhere (Demossier 2011), wine growers traditionally defined themselves as the 'workers of the land', and even if this category has become fashionable in public discourse, wine growers differentiate amongst themselves, identifying those who really work the land from the rest. The emphasis is placed on direct contact with vines, the hard labour and the micro-knowledge that wine growers have acquired of their plots. The experience of many years of intensive fieldwork makes it clear that the majority of wine producers are in agreement with this definition. However, when it comes to landowners who own, but do not work the plots, employing a workforce instead, they tend to emphasise the symbolic and moral value of 'work' as a way of belonging to the local professional community. Yet in this traditional discourse of work and labour, it is noteworthy that neither gender nor ethnicity had a place, these workers being invisible.

Following Robert C. Ulin (1996), in Burgundy, as in Bordeaux, work and labour are both fundamental values underpinning the self-identification of wine growers in a world where both are becoming contested by 'flying wine makers' (Lagendijk 2004), capitalism and the standardisation of technologies. Despite the increasing wealth that some producers have enjoyed over recent decades, work remains the primary social marker of their distinctive and rooted profession, one associated with social emancipation and hard labour. Several informers, even though they are now reaching the age of retirement, still define their identity in terms of 'aller à la vigne' ('going to the vineyards'). From one generation to the next, the development of the domains has meant that when siblings remain involved there is a division of labour delineating who is in charge of what. The traditional authority of adults over children exercised by the family patriarch remains uncontested for some, but more and more that traditional culture is being challenged. One of my informers now has all of his three children – two boys and a girl – on board and each of them has a specific area to deal with, either the cellar or the vineyard, with his daughter specialising in the commercial development of the domain. The division of labour cuts across the two main sectors of activities, those of the vineyards and the production of wine. Specific training and skills are required for each and the management of the estate and its integrity are still in the hands of the father and mother who are both in their fifties.

If we focus on the issue of work and labour and to what extent a range of discourses have been deployed by local actors to define their community, it is clear that reading the landscape is one of the skills developed by each wine grower when working the land. It is also one of the first things they teach to their children, who almost from infancy are expected to know the boundaries of each of their plots. Working, eating, drinking and romancing were part of everyday life in the vineyard and the harvest period is a telling example of this social activity. Boundaries are thus seen as central to the self-identification of the lineage even if the plot is rented rather than owned. From the outset, wine landscape offers a means of visually reading the map of producers and the range of plots or AOC, and it is easy to see which skills have been mastered. The physical state of the vineyards is also a key for identifying the producer and where he/she stands in relation to ecological or more environmentally friendly practices. The visual impression conveys the image of a tapestry, a mosaic carefully ordered and woven, but each inflexion brings more complexity to the overall picture. It reinforces the image of a socialised environment, illustrating respect for the equilibrium between nature and culture. Yet any individual inflexion risks destroying the overall collective portrait and this remains part of the long battle between traditionalists and modernists.

These vineyards are presented as part of an unchanging, historically stable landscape which is crucial to their reputation. But this sense of order and equilibrium breaks down when one has to work in the vineyard as the contact is closer and more intense. It is through this physical engagement with the soil and the plant that knowledge is constructed and that 'quality' can emerge. Yet 'quality' means different things to different producers and consumers. Each wine producer acquires knowledge through the work conducted on his/her plots and it is this subtle process of differentiation that emerges as part of the narrative about wine landscape. Most of the producers I encountered know their plots intimately and can list the natural specificities attached to each of them as well as how each vintage has affected the quality of wine, especially if their families have worked the land for generations. Yet their engagement with the landscape is still largely defined by their social positioning, their level of education and their worldview.

The Domain and the Village

The classic image of Burgundy is of a vast patchwork of small plots with *vignerons* eking out a living. In the sea of plots juxtaposed one on top of each other, it is easy to identify ownership or individual sites of production. The vineyards are omnipresent in the landscape with villages or small towns spread along the National Road 6. In much of France, the village is the main focus for viticulture and the resulting wine tourism, which is a separate entity from the collective and individual vineyards, albeit intimately related to them (Mitchell et al. 2012: 324). Here the dense and busy character of the social organisation of viticultural communities characterises the local landscape. Each village is built around the institutional opposition between the church and the *mairie* which still has political resonance today, albeit more subtly than in the past. Over the last two decades it has become clear that some of these villages have gentrified and have become more opulent and more open to tourism. Meursault, for example, illustrates this economic *embourgeoisement* with several ostentatious wine cellars being established and new shops and restaurants opening their doors. Wine production is a rural-based industry but it has particular features which mark it out as a distinctive type of production.

Travelling through these villages offers a journey through the historical landscape of Burgundy and the recent success of some of the domains in attracting a new clientele. The overwhelming majority bottle and sell their own wines, and yet thirty years ago it was true of only the most commercially developed domains. Today the doors are open to the public and staff, often part of the kinship network, are there to welcome you and take you for a wine-tasting, especially in the most ostentatious wine cellars. The most successful domains have, however, opted for a more modest and discreet welcome as they have nothing to sell to visitors as their stock has already been reserved for existing clientele. The local professional union (*syndicat de l'appellation*) attached to the AOC ensures that a sense of community is maintained even if it is sometimes characterised by conflicts.

Each proprietor can be identified by a traditional banner with the name of the family lineage attached to it and an often monumental gate opening on to the domain. The names tell you the story of the lineage and the vicissitudes of its transmission. For example, Domaine Grin Frère et Soeur reflects the fact that Bernard Grin, one of Jean Grin's children, manages the domain, while Frère et Soeur refers to previous generations, the brother and sister of Jean Grin. Other examples include the reference to sisters joining the domain, or the eldest son taking over, or two families celebrating a joint venture through their children's marriage. These are all signs of the importance of the family lineage defined as the fruit of several generations and sometimes the inclusion of siblings from different generations. Village life is characterised by the presence of these family lineages and their presence is another example of their social weight. Each domain contributes to the financial management of the community with local taxes and through their involvement in community affairs. Sometimes, due to family frictions or dislikes, siblings go their different ways and establish their own domains independently. That is, however, difficult as it requires economic resources and enough land to allow the family estate to be split up without undermining its economic viability. Often the siblings end up being financially compensated or join the management of the family domain. Alliances between families have long been encouraged. Domains with a double name such as Choreau-Chaby are a perfect illustration of the necessity of preserving the land.

The emphasis put on the land is explained by its extreme fragmentation. Most domains own a range of plots covering a much wider geographical area than the village in which they are located. A grower in Chambolle might have several vineyards, some located in Chambolle, but others in villages such as Vosne-Romanée or Nuits-Saint-Georges. The vineyards might include *grands crus*, but also *premiers crus* or simple *village*. Families employ conscious strategies in order to keep a portfolio of good plots together, and the same principle applies where *métayage* (sharecropping) and *fermage* (a rent paid annually in money or bottles) are concerned. Producers will look first to family members – cousins, aunts and uncles – when they are seeking to establish new contracts. In this context, inheritance laws and transmission are often a source of conflict. In order to ensure the economic viability of their domains, producers often combine a portfolio of vineyards that they own, rent or have a contract of *fermage* (rent) for. Interestingly, it is the location of the prime plots, those with *grands crus* or *premiers crus* classification, that will determine to which of these syndicats the producers have a real sense of allegiance. Hierarchy characterises the productive space, and growers have an innate sense of this hierarchy of products. The *grands crus* and *premiers crus* are particularly cherished and are the object of intense care and deeper engagement on the part of the producer. In extreme cases, they are even occasionally ploughed using a horse and are meticulously cared for. But again, it would be naïve to conclude that all producers feel the same emotional engagement with their terroir.

In the complex relationship with the vineyard, the notion of 'lovely vines' has always been, and remains, a commonplace in the discourse of my informers, but the interpretation of it has changed, from one producer to another, from one generation to the next. It could also, in some cases, become an area of conflict between father and sons or father and daughters. If for the previous generation 'lovely vines' meant a healthy and growing plant, green in colour with lots of foliage and vigorously productive, cleaned and sanitised of any disease, it means something radically different today. The younger generation is now, in general, more critical of the use of pesticides, and likely to have a more holistic approach to viticulture especially if they are educated. This is partly driven by the most innovative and ecologically-minded producers, but also by the community at large which is keen to market a more 'natural' wine as part of the global shift. In some cases, a vineyard which has been left to its own devices can be seen as more environmentally friendly than one which has been purged of any uncontrolled vegetation.

Such distinctions are clearly visible at the village level to the community and on special occasions when producers meet each other, they often provide an opportunity to discuss viticulture in a more open fashion. Between producers, a certain degree of competition is almost inevitable, and if organic viticulture was likely to be met with mockery or scepticism a decade ago, this is no longer the case. Notwithstanding the shy, humble and discreet nature of the average wine grower, transparency and openness tend to prevail. However, this tendency sits alongside the approach of more traditional producers who, for different reasons, are rooted in the terroir ideology and therefore just reproduce what has been done before. This is especially true for the least educated and travelled wine growers, who are often described as the ones 'who have never left the cellar' or who are labelled *tractoristes* (always on their tractors) because they are keen to demonstrate their hard work through a form of productivist logic. An approach that became established after the Second World War, it was later associated with the development of clone selection, the increasing resort to oenology, and the use of pesticides and potassium hydroxide which radically transformed the landscape. That model has been challenged by a return to a more artisanal outlook, working on plant heritage, diminishing the use of chemicals and pesticides, engaging further with the vineyards and its life cycle and giving more space to nature (see Chapters 4 and 5).

The many villages that punctuate the landscape along the RN 6 are distinct communities and the locals have a sense of independence and attachment to the place where they live. Some villages are described as very wealthy, conflictual and competitive, while others are led by a handful of esteemed wine leaders and are seen as a place of constructive harmony, to be emulated. In the local discourse of place, each village is characterised by a number of features associated with the social definition of its *communitas* whether orientated towards a collective or an individualistic culture. The strong collective values attached to, for example, the old confraternities of Saint Vincent or to the mutual aid practiced at times of major crisis constantly resist the growing individualism which has accompanied the capitalist development of the wine region. These values are constantly advanced in debates at the local level, but they act more as cultural markers of an ideal world rather than a real belief that those values can be sustained in our modern age. French egalitarianism, born dialectically out of human conflict and the class divide, is institutionalised formally in the structure of a legally constituted production cooperative (Mitchell et al. 2012: 325). Some villages are described as composed of positive and engaged wine growers who are asking questions about their terroir while others find themselves categorised as unsuccessful in understanding theirs: 'In C, the ways in which they make wine does not work, it is not the same as the next village G and their style is not as good as G. In G they have very motivated wine growers, they have found the key, they are convincing', noted one *négociant*. One of my informers mentioned the dynamic social fabric associated with one of the wealthiest villages of the Côte, confirming that it leads by good practice and examples of excellence. Here the wine leaders shape the debate on wine quality.

Yet sometimes wine growers refuse to ask the right questions among themselves. As one my informers recalled: 'they did know why I was able to sell my wine at this price as we discussed it during one of our workshops on managing markets, but they did not want to go further or they did not ask questions about it. Some of them had no idea of their production costs, can you believe that?' This comment was also echoed by one of the wine buyers I interviewed when he mentioned that 'wine growers are not very chatty, they listen if they want, they take what they want and what they have understood'. It is often the engagement with concepts of terroir and quality which characterises the most successful producers and this is always picked up by wine buyers who are familiar with the changing landscape of what the market and individual consumers define as excellence.

If viticulture remains constantly at the heart of village life, the internet and modern technologies have opened up the community to the outside world. Wine producers have engaged with modernity and have established direct connections with their clients, restaurants, importers and with the global market economy. Again, the degree of individual engagement may vary as it depends on the ability to navigate through these new connections and on the level of personal training and education. Like other agricultural industries, wine production is linked to international markets by global value chains (Gwynne 2008), but these chains convey complex signals to producers (Overton and Murray 2012: 712). What is remarkable here is that some of the producers who have access to these global value chains and competence in managing them are able to understand what defines them or how they shift at the international level. These mediators or technicians of globalisation, who are often from a commercial or business background, play a major role in connecting local and global together, connecting local and global through a close imbrication with international wine culture and its hierarchy of values. Here the local transcends the global by asserting itself reflexively in the new competitive wine world order. Place-making relies on these technicians and on their ability to navigate different cultural zones and to pick up quickly the motifs or values in a particular industry or segment of society. Burgundy relies on constructions of its products which command higher market prices and build upon notions of high-quality fruit, tradition, hand-crafted wines and, critically, attachment to favoured places of origin (Overton and Murray 2012: 713). In turn, the very wealthy have the means to purchase and thus to define, at the very top end of the market by the wines' exclusiveness and apparent quality, the essence of what good wine should be (Overton and Murray 2012: 715) and they call the tune for the rest of the industry. Burgundy, through the wide range of products it offers and its social composition, sells the dream to the very wealthy, but also to the middle-class in quest of further distinction.

Conclusions

Throughout its history, Burgundy has sought to reinvent itself while maintaining its global reputation as a unique historical site, famous for artisanship and quality as key cultural markers in an increasingly fragmented and uncertain world. Superficially then, Burgundy might appear to be simply acquiring recognition for its unchanging landscape, tradition and culture. Yet, for all the power of its rich local identity, folklore and culture which is broadcast to the world, there lies underneath the comforting blanket a far messier reality. Burgundy, like other wine producing regions, has experienced profound change in terms of professional practice; it has also been buffeted by the effects of economic crisis as in the 1930s, or by natural calamities, notably the phylloxera crisis of 1880 or more recently by the threat of the esca disease (fungi). This chapter has examined the different meanings of place and terroir in Burgundy at different historical junctures, but it has also questioned the realities behind the seamless narrative of belonging. The Burgundy hierarchy of wines, from *villages* to *grands crus*, was established from the 1930s onwards as a way of repositioning the region within the local and global hierarchy of values. It was also a key moment in the growth of French tourism which was expanding both internally and internationally.

In this context, the uniqueness of the Burgundy story was associated with the historical and social construction of terroir and the claim that it was its birthplace. Earlier on, a quest for quality drove the region to establish its singularity and exceptionalism, yet its central geographic positioning in Western Europe made it a particularly attractive place for a political and diplomatic role in which wine served power. Yet this historical construction of Burgundy as a site of excellence forms part of its nostalgic and global deployment as the birthplace of terroir and as a lasting and enduring site of human endeavour which has been characterised by a constant struggle between productivity and quality throughout different historical junctures. While the nineteenth century saw the rise of mass production of poor quality wines destined for urban consumption, the most recent period of viticultural shift is associated with recasting Burgundy in the international arena. Wine landscapes have more or less evolved as a result of those seismic changes and it is only since the 1930s that Burgundy has become the object of growing interest while being reframed as a site of touristic aesthetic encounter.

In this context, the application to the UNESCO world heritage status provided a new impetus to put the house in order and to make sure that a collective synergy is redeployed as part of the global narrative of being the best vineyards in the world. Yet the background to this is of a different nature today, with an increasing number of international frauds and counterfeits, and the growing democratisation of wine consumption, accompanied by major shifts in drinking patterns and a strong attack by lobbies on alcohol as a dangerous drug. By playing different cards, such as the ecological revamping of the landscape or wine as commodity fetishism, while sustaining an image of authenticity, historicity, family roots and excellence, Burgundy is seeking to reposition itself in the new global order of wine where newcomers have become more aggressive, knowledgeable and capable of producing high-quality wines almost anywhere on the planet. Burgundy in the twenty-first century is first and foremost about wine landscapes and place-making, but it is also about the handful of producers who have led the changes and have cleverly adapted to the vicissitudes of world wine production by being self-reflexive and critical, while integrating social change within the wider global framework of modernity and fast capitalism.

Yet place-making is also the result of a long process of imbrication through the work conducted by generations of wine growers within the same family in the same plots. Dwelling could therefore be seen as central to this process of nesting the lineage in a specific relationship to the place and its economic productive cycle, which is largely dependent upon nature. Emotional bonds, hard work and more specifically the cycle of the seasons and the vicissitudes of the calendar year make the wine profession a world apart. Global pressures and calamities or crises have generally had an impact on the landscape. The vineyards that existed before the phylloxera crisis, or after the expansion of the popular Gamay in the nineteenth century, hardly resemble the *climats* of today. The wine landscape is result of a combination of often complementary factors, including periodic place-making projects, often centred on the *grands crus* and their place in the world wine hierarchy, and the influence of the market. History, quality and terroir play a major role in the reshaping of the Burgundy story and remind us, through generational continuity, that after all it is a story about being human, in all its contradictions and paradoxes.

Notes

1. http://agreste.agriculture.gouv.fr/IMG/pdf_primeur271-2.pdf. Consulted on 29 July 2014.
2. http://agreste.agriculture.gouv.fr/en-region/bourgogne/. Consulted on 29 July 2014.
3. *Guide Nouvel Observateur* 2000, 94.
4. Burgundy includes overall more than 100 AOCs.
5. For an overview see https://www.vins-bourgogne.fr/nos-vins-nos-terroirs/situer-la-bourgogne/la-bourgogne-une-localisation-privilegiee,2377,9170.html? Consulted on 8 November 2017.
6. See http://www.davidhulley.com/unesco-chair-created-wine-and-culture. Consulted on 22 July 2014.
7. For a definition of *climats*, see Chapter 7.
8. A *pucelle* is a maiden. For more information about the list of producers, see Morris (2010: 430).
9. http://www.decanter.com/features/counterfeit-wines-scandal-of-the-century-246011/. Consulted on 17 February 2016.
10. http://www.international.icomos.org/studies/paysages-viticoles.pdf. Consulted on 6 August 2014.
11. As the work of Peter Howland has illustrated in the context of Martinborough in New Zealand. Howland (2008).

12. See for example Roudié (2002) and Cleere (2004).
13. http://www.burgundy-tourism.com/. Consulted on 11 August 2014.
14. http://www.bourgogne-tourisme-pro.com/sites/default/files/commun/0010_porteur_de_projet/0010_je_veux_creer/FF%20Oenotourisme%20-%20nov%202011.pdf. Consulted on 11 August 2014.
15. http://agreste.agriculture.gouv.fr/IMG/pdf_R2611A14.pdf. Consulted on 23 July 2014.
16. Gobin, Campling and Feyen 2001, cited by Mitchell et al. (2012).
17. http://agreste.agriculture.gouv.fr/IMG/pdf/conjsynt239201406viti.pdf. Consulted on 23 July 2014.
18. http://agreste.agriculture.gouv.fr/IMG/pdf_R2611A14.pdf. Consulted on 23 July 2014.

Chapter 2
WINE GROWERS AND WORLDS OF WINE

Anthropological literature on globalisation has traditionally focused on the dominated, the losers of this world, and on the task of defending locality as a struggle. As a result, anthropologists have often underlined the differentiated negative impacts of cultural homogenisation and standardisation on groups, communities and individuals and how their responses have also been diverse and complex in terms of their cultural remit. The erosion of the perceived 'natural' connection between place and culture has tended to take centre stage in most of these analyses of a globalised world, which is increasingly represented as possessing a culture without space. The contemporary world is one of global embeddedness, ubiquitous rights movements and reflexive identity politics, universal capitalism and globally integrated financial markets, transnational families, biotechnology and urbanisation (Eriksen 2014). But it is also one of subtle resistance to these fast and disjointed processes of change, with places and groups engaging in a less conflictual and more harmonious manner. In such a context, the integration of culture, economics and politics takes a different form and is frequently dominated by powerful cultural elites.

All too often, we are presented with the 'black legend' of how communities are eroded, fragmented and trapped in a seemingly ineluctable vicious circle. Very few studies have explored the stories of those local communities that have engaged successfully with the forces of globalisation. Burgundian wine producers are one such example and they illustrate the innovative and creative work of local actors, led by a handful of leading producers or elites, who have been able to introduce new practices and representations to ensure the continuity of what they see as a coherent and stable social formation. On the one hand, globalisation provides an opportunity for these key actors to reinforce their position in changing international markets using the timeless imaginary of Burgundy's terroir, and its new guise *climats*. On the other hand, we have Burgundy as a powerful global wine story defined around quality, authenticity and history which seeks to reposition itself in a more competitive environment where quality and taste are subject to constant re-evaluation. For Burgundy, reaffirming its unique status involves re-enacting some of the global references linking place to taste by fossilising and historicising the site of production, which is presented as a stable, trustworthy and reliable place. Yet it is also about transforming that place by creating new images, norms and connections and adding a veneer to an old mythology.

In this chapter, I seek to engage with globalisation by developing a more positive and creative understanding of the complexities of the processes attached to the deployment of the terroir story. Burgundian wine producers offer a compelling window onto these broader and subtle processes, and, through a long-term ethnography, this chapter focuses on the concepts of 'place-making', 'being in location', 'authenticities' and 'politics of scale' to propose a differentiated reading of globalisation, that of 'reflexive imbrications'. Here the local transcends the global by asserting itself reflexively in the new competitive wine world order. A clear example of this process is provided by the recent campaign for UNESCO World Heritage status (see Chapter 8). But this chapter is also about how specific wine growers cultivate a new personal narrative through their professional activities to adapt to the local and global wine landscape.

In his analysis of place-making, the philosopher Edward S. Casey notes that 'To live is to live locally and to know is first of all to know the places one is in'.[1] Burgundian wine producers epitomise this tie to a place, 'being in location', which has been preserved, nurtured and narrated for many generations. The deeply rooted social construction of wine at the local level and its essentialisation has been until now a ubiquitous rhetorical device employed by producers when asked about past and present periods of economic growth or recessions. In this context, the concept of terroir presents a particular case of extreme localisation whereby three, four or five successive generations of the same family have established a working relationship with a particular milieu and a specific 'noble' plant, Chardonnay or Pinot Noir, in an ecological milieu which has been presented as immutable despite being the subject of constant social and economic change. These families have anchored themselves to a specific place and village and, consequently, they have accumulated a wealth of experience, even if that has not always been a synonym of 'quality'.

Despite their glowing reputation, Burgundy wines were for centuries characterised by unreliability and heterogeneity in terms of their quality. A slow process of imbrication has progressively redefined the quality of the product through its increasingly complex and diverse transnational commodification, accompanied by progress in the viticultural education of both producers and consumers. At its most extreme, Burgundy has enabled its commodification under various guises to encompass conceptions of wine as a work of art and aesthetics (with Domaine de la Romanée-Conti known as DRC, for example) and wine as a regional artisanal product (with wines from the Maranges, for example), even in some cases as a mass consumed drink (with Burgundy village wines). The strength of Burgundy wines lies in diversity, both in terms of quality and the *typicité* of the product, within a small and limited space while benefitting from the resonant and mythical global story of Burgundy wines.

Even if places are not, in reality, intrinsically bounded entities, but are constellations of connections within wider cultural circuits (Massey 1992: 3), it is nevertheless the case that in Burgundy these constellations have not only been maintained but also transformed over several decades by successive generations of producers, and that a sense of continuity is perpetuated by the tendency for wine growers, wine elites and wine experts to tell the same cultural story or to locate themselves within the Burgundy terroir mythology, while simultaneously entering into modernity in terms of their actions. It would, however, be erroneous to conclude that this long-lasting and close relationship to a place means that wine growers have perfected the art of growing grapes and making wines. Anthropologists and historians have in particular long demonstrated the capacity of human societies to tell a convincing tale even when the reality is far more complex and messy. Several crises, such as the recent USA wine frauds with fake *grands crus*, have had an impact on the ways in which the locality has reassessed itself as a collective entity. Being 'in location' in contemporary Burgundy requires not only the re-articulation of the terroir story, but also the adjustment of that story in the light of the political and moral economy attached to wine consumption. France as a nation has always endorsed wine ideologically as a unique cultural commodity, defending its supposed social and cultural values against the health lobby. This story has found many advocates over the years in political and economic circles and has proved no less resilient in the twenty-first century. The national context has therefore provided a receptive platform for the Burgundy terroir story. Fieldwork conducted over the years in this terroir 'blessed by God' has also revealed that the art of making good quality wine is far more complex than simply cultivating vines on a propitious estate. Trial and error define the wine landscape, and if in Burgundy one constantly hears the refrain 'we do not have bad wines', it is another myth.

In a world dominated by 'diverse mobilities of people, objects, images, information and tastes' (Urry 2001: 1), Burgundy seeks to offer a counter example: that of the isomorphism between place, culture, taste and people. Global changes have become progressively part of the local puzzle and they have imbricated within the social formation and within the 'place-making' project. By using the concept 'place-making project', I am drawing here on the ideas used by global ethnographers seeking to expand the links between three traditionally separated aspects of globalisation – namely global forces, connections and imaginations – by seeking out new definitions of social relations and boundaries (Gille and Ó Riain (2002). Burgundy remains a persuasive story because it is presented as the original and immutable site of the terroir ideology, while imbricating its global story to a constantly changing competitive international wine market. By imbrication, I mean '*a coating of imbricating scales*', an arrangement in which local and global overlap harmoniously and in a composite fashion, while re-adjusting under the pressure of change. The Burgundy terroir story has never been altered radically, it is about history, God – or the monks – and the goodness of the soil. These ingredients form part of the social construction of authenticity and the reinvention of tradition as illustrated by the *climats* story (Chapter 8).

Throughout history, the region has maintained its identification with a geographical space, despite the changing social structure and deep divisions between the workers and the owners of the land. In the century following the French Revolution, the local social structure experienced the shock of natural disasters, the phylloxera crisis, and the influence of economic change as the *vignerons* acquired vineyards in their own right. Yet until the 1960s most were concerned with the production of grapes, which were sold on to *négociants* or the larger landowners who actually made and bottled their wine. That traditional division broke down rapidly in the final decades of the twentieth century as the wine growers[3] increasingly became the masters of their own houses. Yet they had to share that privilege with the landowners who dominated the cultural story. As Laferté (2006) has shown, local elites have dominated the cultural landscape, establishing international networks for the sale and distribution of their wines. Globalisation and the expansion of the market for premium wines attached to monopoly rent[4] have thus enabled social actors to imbricate themselves in a reflexive fashion in a politics of scale where local and global respond to each other and where individual strategies have come to the fore. In this game, authenticity means wealth and money (Warnier 2013: 78), but for some it is also a way of being 'true to yourself'. However, the larger landowners had the advantage of accessing the market earlier on through their social and professional connections as most of them had another professional occupation, often linked to their education, social status and wider national and international networks.

The Rise of the Wine Grower or *Vigneron*

In the story of place-making, the *vigneron* producer has come to play a major role as one of the main actors of globalisation, offering an excellent illustration of the process of imbrication. The historical figure of the Burgundian wine grower has been mythically constructed over the centuries as integral to the place. Usually represented as a masculine figure, the patriarch at the head of the family domain is one of the ingredients of the region's success at global level. That said, it is only comparatively recently, within the last forty years, that the *vigneron* has come to occupy a significant place in the local power structure. The contemporary figure of the locally rooted wine grower in the global world of wine offers an alternative to more radical forms of modernisation; he incarnates the slowness of time, the return to a pre-modern era and the last bastion against modernity. Moreover in contemporary consumer societies, he symbolises a nostalgically and romantically rooted alterity through his construction as an authentic human being. Authenticity [here] is generated not from the bounded classification of an 'Other', but from the probing comparison between Self and Other, as well as between external and internal states of being (Bendix 1997: 17). Jasper Morris (2010: 13), a chronicler of Burgundy, has warned us against 'the temptation of placing *vignerons* on pedestals, investing them with hero status. They are human beings like the rest of us: some are better at the job than others'. Yet they have remained, despite the historical vicissitudes, part of the local landscape and their role in the global hierarchy of values has become as important as place. Yet despite their symbolic value they have remained, until relatively recently, silent in the social configuration. How do they see the world? How do they explicitly reconstruct boundaries around their products and how are they grounded in local socio-natural practices? How is this sense of grounding affected by external and internal changes? These are fundamental questions that need to be answered if we are to understand the cultural story of Burgundy, its wine producers and their wines.

Historically, wine growers have always been an active and politically turbulent part of the history of the Duchy of Burgundy, and in Dijon and Beaune they played a key role in the political and religious life of the towns. The historian, Mack Holt (1993), suggested that in the seventeenth century the political weight of the wine growers in Dijon increased along with the reputation of their wines. Everybody wanted to become a wine grower, including distinguished local notables such as the *maire* and échevins. Over three hundred years later, this fascination with the wine grower is alive and well and it has gained a new prominence at the global level with Hollywood stars keen to have their own vineyards as a mark of distinction. The film director, Francis Ford Coppola, has, for example, a vineyard which encompasses Sonoma and Mendocina Country to the north of California while, more recently, the actor Brad Pitt has invested in Provence to produce his own rosé.

Yet the glamour and romance attached to the ownership of a vineyard should not lead us to forget that the daily reality of being a wine grower in Burgundy is defined by hard labour and struggles. Moreover, throughout its history the profession of wine grower has remained dependent on the vagaries of the meteorological cycle, and hardship, taxes, poverty and economic precarity have been the norm. The term *vigneron* in Burgundy refers to a specific social context in which manual labour and a peasant mentality characterise the producer[5] in terms of their sense of belonging to a profession defined by specific collective values. The traditional image of the *vigneron*, defined as the person who cultivates vines to produce wine, is an enduring myth attached to the place. Yet the terminology surrounding the use of wine grower or *vigneron* has become even more blurred and confusing than before. According to my informers, true *vignerons* recognise themselves through the physical attributes of a worker which can be read easily on their hands. Yet the term *vigneron* has been borrowed by the elites who seek to emulate them (Laferté 2006) and work is often showcased as a virtue even by landowners 'who are not actually going to the vineyard' anymore.

Social change and economic prosperity have meant that an *embourgeoisement* of the wine growers has taken place, blurring the boundaries between both groups. More often today, a team of male and female workers, recruited within the kinship network, conduct the work in the vineyard under the management of the landowner or wine grower. What remains a factor of social differentiation in the community is the visible embodiment of the physical nature of the work attached to wine production. This definition remains central to processes of identification within the wine community, positioning each group in relation to the others, from *négociants* and courtiers to landowners and wine growers. The historicity of social relations upon which production and consumption are articulated is unwittingly concealed or marginalised in wine culture (Ulin and Black 2013: 67). Wine narratives all too often contribute to naturalising wine and its associated social relations (Ulin 1996). It is striking that when discussing quality wines, identification through place and the name of the producer is the first thing to spring to mind, obscuring the complex social field of production. Yet in most wine estates today siblings are given specific roles, and a strong division of labour characterises production. Spouses were, for example, for a long time invisible in the workforce while having many functions and being central to the overall organisation. Ethnicity is also remarkably well hidden as there has rarely been any mention of foreign workers – notably Algerians, travellers and East Europeans recruited for grape picking – and they only become visible when they occupy emblematic positions as oenologists, with the example of the Lebanese Guy Accad in the 1990s springing to mind, or as high-status individuals working as consultants.

The social tapestry which structures the Burgundy story is worth exploring as it enables us to better understand the originality of the local landscape. The key question is who tells the story today and to whom? How should we define the wine growers as a social group at the local level? Have they acquired more power through their increasing economic success? These key questions have to be discussed in the light of socio-historical conjectures and the ways in which, at different times, wine growers have explicitly defined themselves, at least in part, through contrasts or by saying what they are not. Ethnography therefore helps us to understand better how people parcel themselves into bounded groups. By *vignerons* or wine growers, we define a professional group that is heterogeneous in both social and economic terms. This is also a group which has diversified historically and sociologically. Yet it is also a group for whom terroir – and work – is embodied in their social positioning in the local milieu.

Like their terroirs, the local milieu is complex, diverse and hierarchised. The most successful *vignerons* have gentrified, while a separate group of wine elites dominate the social and political landscape. A few chose to distance themselves more radically by opting in the 1970s to follow a more ecological route, and their position was until recently marginalised in the local wine community. This social mapping has become more obvious in the light of the UNESCO application as a handful of wine owners have come to dominate the landscape. Yet what is interesting is the fluid nature of the category 'wine growers' as it is often invoked by our informers and the extent to which its use follows the social trajectory of other actors defined as being inside or outside of the group. What remains central to their judgement is 'physically working the land' which is at the core of their self-identification. In a conversation one well-known landowner made this apparent to me, while addressing the owner of another wealthy estate: 'You agree D, there is only one wine grower in Burgundy'. A strong discourse of social harmony dominates the local landscape, but the equilibrium remains fragile in the face of economic adversity and successive crises.

In his seminal article 'Une classe objet', Bourdieu discussed the symbolic production of the peasantry compelled 'to form their own subjectivity' through 'the gaze and judgement of others, they do not speak, they are spoken for' (1977: 4). The notion of the 'object-class' offers an interesting theoretical metaphor when discussing wine growers, who are regularly defined as artisans, and yet share some common features with the peasantry. The wine grower has a unique status as he/she is perceived as a peasant while economically being embedded in the world wine economy. Wine growers have, however, been largely silent in the symbolic field of wine culture and their voices are often narrated by the writers, intellectuals or elites. Laferté (2006) has argued that during the inter-war period the local republican elites sought to invent a marketing strategy for their wines based upon the traditional images of wine grower, terroir and authenticity and that they have imposed this model on viticultural communities. His argument calls to mind Bourdieu's symbolic representation model, but he fails to take into account the role of local wine growers themselves in the social process of economic folklorisation. Yet Laferté's analysis argues for their constitution as a new political force through the republicanisation of the countryside and the AOC establishment (2006: 40 and 59). It is striking that the model he describes was re-appropriated by the local wine growers during the 1970s and used as a reminder of the core ethical values of local culture, that is to say the folkloric features of economic regionalism. The Saint-Vincent Tournante, the principal wine fair, is a remarkable illustration of this re-appropriation (Chapter 4).

Another page is now being turned thanks to the success of the UNESCO initiative, but once again the elites seem to have imposed a new reading of the site. Looking at it from a more anthropological angle, the wine grower has appeared until recently as part of a new global symbolic field in which he still contributes unwittingly while at the same time maintaining his/her individual work ethic and identity based upon modesty, integrity and taciturnity. Such an interpretation could be seen as contrasting with the capitalist and entrepreneurial nature of their profession, but it contributes substantially to the true likeness of the place and the products, offering a form of authenticity. Most wine growers are aware of the tensions between the economic success of wine as a global commodity, which often borders on snobbery, and the necessity to remind themselves of their relatively humble origins. These characteristics are embedded in the linguistic materiality of their product. Like a work of art, a bottle of Burgundy tells a story through its label and shape: the family biography and the 'correct identification of the origins, authorship, or provenance' (Dutton 2003).

In the course of Burgundy's application for UNESCO heritage status, an increasing number of domains decided either to revamp their outdated websites or even to commission short professional documentaries about themselves. This growing *mise en scène de soi* forms part of a broader technological, cultural and environmental shift which is designed to recast the Burgundy story around the new concepts of *climats de Bourgogne*. It is a striking example of the phenomenal success of local elites in disseminating and promoting the *climats* story, rebranding authenticity around new notions such as ecology, nature and modesty. New technologies, especially the internet and Facebook, have facilitated the opening of these communities to the world. The deployment of these new media by individuals, domains or regional and professional bodies contributes to the reflexive imbrication of the locality into the changing wine political economy. The recent scandal of a biodynamic wine grower, who was prosecuted after refusing to spray his vineyard with pesticides to protect against an insect suspected of transmitting a devastating disease attacking vines, provides an excellent example of how information has amplified current local debates.

Thirty years ago, wine growers felt isolated, and, if they had no economic security or access to international markets, they were far more vulnerable. Most of the producers now promote their wines by visiting their importers and agents abroad, whereas two decades ago most were still opening their cellars to visitors. Their sense of identification was first and foremost defined at the local level through their family, the village community and social connections, as well as their commercial contacts who came to visit once a year. Wider economic engagement has been the key to their success, and their self-esteem and sense of purpose has been reinforced by the star status accorded to the most successful amongst them. The film director Jonathan Nossiter has certainly contributed to the visual shift with his films devoted to the worlds of wine: *Mondovino* (2004), in which Burgundy features prominently and *Natural Resistance* (2014). In *Mondovino*, Burgundy is presented through the figure of the now deceased Hubert de Montille, who incarnated the local traditional terroir-based viticulture of the Old World and the image of Burgundy as an unchanging place characterised by tradition. The far more dynamic reality of Burgundian viticulture was carefully hidden in this seminal documentary.

However, this construction of Burgundy as an unchanging society has progressively been eroded by economic competition and modernity. The figure of Hubert de Montille as the symbol of a *vigneron* resisting modernisation, as presented by his daughter, reveals how enduring the Burgundian myth of terroir is. De Montille, incarnating the local wine grower, is shown standing proudly in front of his house in Volnay, exclaiming that 'without wine there is no civilisation'. Such images are part and parcel of a traditional folklorisation of Burgundy which is showcased as fossilised in an immutable worldview. In *Mondovino* Nossiter chose to focus on de Montille, a former lawyer, landowner and notable, while ignoring the younger generation of talented wine growers who were keen to break away from the ideology of terroir while still producing quality wines. The concentration on a traditional rather than modern construction of Burgundy is very common, but is nevertheless being eroded. The internet revolution and the new technologies accompanying it are progressively transforming the global story.

Websites, documentaries and TV programmes are giving a voice to the traditionally silent wine producers. Their way of life has also altered; today most of them travel the world or sell their wines through new commercial networks, organise private tastings abroad or join other world producers on the global wine scene. These changes have engendered a certain degree of fragmentation. A study conducted in 2014 on independent wine producers and the internet[6] reveals that 30 per cent of French wine producers have a Facebook account, while 17 per cent have a Twitter account and 7 per cent actually use it. A minority even use Google to put videos of their activities on YouTube. The Burgundy campaign for UNESCO status has given an impetus to individual initiatives in this sector.

In 2012, the magazine *Le Point*, in collaboration with the Vin et Société association, set up a TV channel 'Vino Bravo', dedicated to programmes on wine. A young broadcasting and media production company, Bourgogne Live, was also launched at around the same time. Following one of its main advocates on Facebook, one can sense the cultural orchestration of the *climats de Bourgogne* propaganda campaign and the new culture of self-representation which has emerged. This also underlines the increasingly visible contribution of wine growers to the social and civic space provided by the internet, and comments are often posted in relation to issues facing viticulture or climatic accidents as well as in local debates. The first MOOC (massive open online course) dedicated to wine in Burgundy was set up in April 2015[7] by the University of Burgundy. What dominates most of the media is the focus on the landscape as a new visual and naturalised category, the aesthetic of terroir and the skills and work associated with the land as well as the *climats* narrative. Scientific experts continue to view nature as superior to culture, the impact of humanity as inferior to that of nature (Lowenthal 2005: 89).

Authenticity is constructed through the visual encounter with the place of production, as exemplified by the publication of new blogs.[8] 'Rather than drinking it, look at it' seems to be the new motto, which could be explained by the subversive attempts of the profession to circumvent the Evin Law.[9] Yet authenticity also needs to be understood in terms of the new ecological shift affecting most of the French wine regions and the need for Burgundy to position itself in the new moral economy. The vineyards have become inscribed in the Burgundian visual narrative in their own right. It is a trend that forms part of a global pattern, orchestrated through the UNESCO list, where landscapes are given a preeminent status and where the social has been hidden away. This heritagisation of wine culture is inscribed in a World Heritage construction of wine regions where landscapes obscure social realities and the true nature of labour. An exemplary illustration is the film *Les Vignes d'Or* (Golden Vines) by Valentin Dubach, which explores the Canton of Lavaux with its remarkable wine landscape,[10] deploying an extraordinary visual perspective of vineyards filmed by a drone against the musical background of Dragon Slayer and Ross Budgen with a focus on the vineyard and nature. What is striking is the total absence of wine growers and their labour.

The Wine Grower, between Peasant and Artisan?

Wines, especially the *grands* and *premiers crus* from the Côte d'Or, have long enjoyed a distinctive status as a global commodity which has been constructed and promoted as part of the Burgundy story. That story is not only told in relation to history, the ecclesiastical blessing and the diversity of terroirs, but it is also largely dominated by a small number of highly prestigious domains which are often presented as the quintessence of the place. The reputation of these domains has been the result of both a long process of constructing the reputations of the wines they produce, such as Romanée-Conti or the Clos de Vougeot, and of commercial and externally focused international marketing headed by innovative owners. One domain in Puligny-Montrachet is a good example of the genre; it first decided to launch its products onto the American market in the 1970s. Obviously quality and taste were some of the factors in the equation, but the importance of the historical reputation of these wines, acknowledged since the Middle Ages, cannot be underestimated, and this often preempts any actual discussion of quality.

Similarly, the ideal of the owner or wine grower as the quintessence of Burgundy plays an important role in the cultural story. Clearly, not all wines have been recognised for their quality or have benefitted from the same prestige and it is often the case that those sold at inflated prices today are produced by the most historically established domains or reputable plots, which are themselves the object of a particular historical narrative.[11] When conducting my fieldwork in the 1990s, I was struck by the internal wine hierarchy which was constantly reiterated to me by my informers. This local wine hierarchy, largely based upon the *grands* and *premiers crus*, has shifted to an extent to include the wines of new producers who are seen as talented and cutting-edge in their way of working. Throughout the Côte d'Or, a handful of names of producers are constantly cited for their reputation and that of their wines. When asked if my informers had tasted them, I was told: 'No I cannot afford them'. This internal social hierarchy was not always reflected in the media and it only emerged publicly during the 1990s with the development of wine culture and the oenological press in France (Fernandez 2004; Demossier 2010). In parallel, a wine hierarchy was established in the Anglo-Saxon world with the works of critics such as Robert Parker or Matt Kramer, but it relied on a different narrative around quality. The local landscape is, however, rapidly changing and new producers have come to the fore in the pursuit of taste and quality. Their wines often remain affordable.

The transformation of Burgundian viticulture and the image and economic position of the *vigneron* can be explained, in part, by globalisation and wider social and economic change. Firstly, an increasing number of wine producers have had access to higher education and consequently are eager to learn and to produce better quality wines by resisting standardisation in wine-making techniques. The price of the *grands crus* in particular was constantly rising throughout the 1990s, as were the land values and the prestige attached to specific plots at the top of the scale. It was only in 2016 that SAFER (the French rural land agency) decided to intervene and open the debate following the sale of vineyards in one of the prestigious villages of the Côte de Nuits. Over the course of my research, which now spans several decades, wealth accumulation has meant that the traditional lines of division between wine growers and landowners have become blurred. Access to international markets and the kudos of prestigious restaurants serving your wines is no longer a question of social class and status, but is increasingly dependent upon connections, friendships and negotiations. This global commodification has benefitted the wine producers, but it has also placed more pressure on landowners who wish to maintain their position in the market. Differentiation is often invoked by sociologists and anthropologists as a key vector of economic processes. In Burgundy, until recently, terroir was the key to explaining quality to both national and global wine consumers, but today the new narratives of *climats*, craft and artisanship have found their way into consumers' everyday understanding of global difference as well as into international, national, local and individual constructions of identity. This increasing quest for differentiation reflects the growing fragmentation of the wine market in terms of consumers' markets, and the rise of individualism attached to neo-liberal and post-colonial settings. In this new context, Burgundy incarnates tradition, unchanging time and authenticity while at the same time playing the diversity card.

It is significant that producers from the Côte d'Or have always claimed to be wine growers, rather than peasants or artisans. Despite the differentiated social structure ,with specific self-definitions attached to each group of producers (wine growers versus landowners versus *négociants*), the concept of artisan has never been a commonplace in their discourse. Interestingly, the south of Burgundy, the area of Maçônnais and Chalonnais, is more comfortable with the term, as is illustrated by the local websites.[12] The website presenting AVBS (Artisans Vignerons de Bourgogne du Sud / Artisans Wine Growers from the South of Burgundy) is a telling example amongst hundreds of this trend. Created in 2014, the association, which includes twenty-one domains, claims to promote and develop wines made using human and artisanal methods. Banks and Overton (2010) argue that the complexity of production and marketing of wines has rendered older categories attached to the world's wine industry obsolete. Instead, these categories, such as tradition/modernity, old/new world, can be seen as being characterised by complex processes of change in which the push towards integration, industrialisation and sameness are counterbalanced by those who are moving towards a continuation, even expansion, of a place-specific artisanal based production of premium wines (Banks and Overton 2010: 59). Throughout these transformations, the Côte d'Or has traditionally occupied a privileged place, at the top of the global hierarchy of wines. Yet these changes have brought uncertainties even for the most established producers, with greater competition, for example in the form of New World Chardonnays and Pinots Noirs. In addition, the local milieu has questioned and threatened the position achieved by some of the most established AOC producers as the overall quality of Burgundy wines is improving and new tastes are emerging. Quality and taste are ongoing evaluative and subjective notions and in the world in which we live even *vignerons* have little time to stand still. The pace of change has accelerated, and individualism, as well as a more critical engagement of the wine grower with the environment they live in, have had an effect. New strategies are being sought at the local level to ascertain the 'natural order' and to reaffirm the social hierarchy, and it is in this context that the UNESCO World Heritage application should be read.

To understand why some wine growers continuously distance themselves from the term 'artisan', it is necessary to reflect upon the fact that they wish to draw our attention to their social origin and trajectory and by the same token to emphasise their authenticity and the primordial role of nature in wine production. It is nevertheless the case that their products remain defined as artisanal in the context of an industrialised and modern food system. Wine growers, unlike the *grand cru* chocolatiers described by Susan Terrio (2000), control both the production of grapes and the making of wines; wine production and wine making form part of an annual cycle (Chapter 4) in which every part of the production process relates to the whole. Like the cheese producers studied by Heather Paxson (2010), wines are as diverse and distinctive in taste and quality as the lives and livelihoods of the people who make them. Wine is a constantly evolving, 'living', commodity, but unlike cheese, it acquires a form of stability through the maturation in the cellar until it is put in bottles. Most of the contemporary discourses surrounding the product are about controlling, checking, not intervening too much, 'leaving nature to do her job'. But again, this interpretation is not shared by all of the producers, some of whom might have a more interventionist and traditionally rooted way of working.

Differentiation is the key here. From the ethnographies I have conducted, it is clear that each individual has his or her own way of producing wine and, as Susan Terrio notes for *chocolatiers*, 'they are imbued with and are the bearers of the social identities of their makers and for this reason retain certain inalienable properties' (1996: 71). In the case of its wine producers, the Burgundy story has guaranteed a certain economic value for their production and the engagement with the notion of quality has taken various forms, making it difficult to draw firm conclusions. Going back to the informers I studied in the 1990s, some of whom I have continued to follow ever since, most claim that they have altered drastically the ways in which they are producing wines today, and they could not recognise themselves in the accounts I gave based on their ethnographies from the 1990s (Demossier 1999). 'I know that what you have written is true, you recorded everything, but still I cannot remember any of it. We just do things differently', said one of the wine growers. Going back to my informers, their stories have taken very different paths and if most of them have been highly successful financially – even being represented by the London wine company Berry Bros and Rudd – they remain focused on their wine production and their commitment to quality has increased. One of my informers also went into a financial venture, but decided to refocus on his wines a few years later. As was the case in the 1990s, Burgundy is represented by a wide range of producers and products, which reflects wider social and economic change (Miller 2008).

Another highly revealing aspect of contemporary agriculture is the public visibility of some of the domains. Over the last few years, I have observed an increasing number of YouTube videos created by wine producers for the promotion of their products. A number of successful domains have hired the local marketing and broadcast company Bourgogne Live Prod to make their films. One domain provides the perfect illustration of this trend with its recent YouTube clip in French and English, presenting the next generation of the family and their forty-seven hectares of *crus*. A domain in Chassagne-Montrachet offers another example as in 2014 it employed a photographer to follow the various stages of the vintage and take pictures. The Leuba domain in Pommard offers another variation on the theme with a clip of a horse ploughing the ground between the vines, emphasising traditional manual work. This showcasing of a return to a more artisanal way of looking after the vineyard plays an important role in terms of repositioning domains within the new narrative of *climats*. As illustrated by the leading domains, most of which employ *biodynamie*[13] or ecological modes of production, the terroir story needs to be accompanied by a less intensive mode of production and by an awareness of a conscious 'pampering' of the site by a rejection of mechanisation and pesticides. These practices contrast sharply with the new normative framework initiated and promoted by some of the key protagonists from the wine board. The Bailliage de Pommard,[14] a confraternity revived in 1981, is currently preparing a film following some of the initiatives developed by the Confrérie des Chevaliers du Tastevin (Jamais en Vain, Toujours en Vin / Never in Vain, Always in Wine) in the context of the reframing of Burgundy as a future heritage site. These new images and representations seek to document practices believed to be emblematic and illustrative of the new cultural story (such as ploughing) and to contribute to a new framing of Burgundy. In the context of global wine heritage, it seeks to reaffirm the particular and emblematic position of the region in the global story of terroir by creating new forms of authenticity through a more 'natural' mode of production. The ingredients used are the landscape in its immutable forms, monumental heritage sites, human labour incarnated by horse-drawn ploughs, and the perspective offered by a drone taking aerial pictures of the site.

Anthropology and Authenticities

In the global hierarchy of values, the concept of authenticity, which encapsulates place, product, producer and the consumer, plays a major role in wine markets. The analysis of the uses of authenticity should be positioned within the framework of transnational complex networks (Fillitz and Saris 2013: 21). It is not only about how authenticity is constructed at the global level between wine intermediaries and experts, but also about local understandings and deployments of authenticity and how they connect, or not, to global wine culture. Research has shown that the authenticity is a crucial ingredient in culinary tourism or, in this case, to the oenological experience and almost anything in today's market is associated with the notion of authenticity.[15] In the case of Burgundy wines, the production of cultural stories which characterise the authentic object and its provenance are often manipulated or simply constructed by traders, consumers, craftsmen and heritage officials. For Appadurai, these stories can be described as mythologies (Appadurai 1995: 48), and, as we have argued, they are, first and foremost, controlled by local elites and technicians of globalisation, taking a variety of forms and multiple expressions.

The anthropological literature exploring the concept of authenticity is growing rapidly.[16] In their introduction to *Debating Authenticity*, Fillitz and Saris acknowledge the existence of social practices that produce authenticity as well as the regional, national and global networks that make authenticity concrete for individuals, in particular the socio-historical circumstances. Emphasising the ambiguities attached to the ethnographic study of authenticity, they argue that studying authenticity remains a quest rather than constituting a beginning or an end. This search is often articulated as a rejection of ongoing modernity and the appropriation of traditions (Fillitz and Saris 2012: 9). Diversity is also represented as central to the contemporary culture of authenticity (Taylor 2001: 9). It is reflected in the anthropological scholarship which has moved in the direction of acknowledging the existence of plural, multidimensional authenticities (Field 2009) rather than a monolithic edifice.

Following Bruner's argument (Bruner 1993), we wish to examine authenticity within the cultural contexts of its production and to explore further some of the particular contradictions and dilemmas that authenticity can generate. Using the diverse deployment of the concept of authenticity through the encounter between producers, intermediaries, consumers and the product in a specific locale – Burgundy – or around a specific cultural idiom – Burgundy wines – allows for a perspective that acknowledges the reflexive imbrications at stake in the social construction of a global story. By doing so, we seek to follow Appadurai (1995: 41ff) by distinguishing two broad forms of knowledge, firstly connected to production and secondly connected to consumption. Yet in the case of wine, another form of knowledge is central to the construction of authenticity, that controlled by cultural brokers and technicians of globalisation. This framework will enable us to focus on the process of interconnections and cultural productions in the world of wine. Craft commodities such as wines do this cultural work for consumers, they make visible both a particular form of production (linking the conception of a product to its execution) and its attendant social relations (Terrio 1996: 71). The commodification process in the case of wine is a complex and fuzzy process of cultural encounters and trans-commodification which so far has been largely neglected. Moreover, wine production draws us to the values attached to French artisanship, which enjoys a positive resonance because small-scale, skills-based modes of family entrepreneurship dominated trade and industry well into the twentieth century (Terrio 1996: 1). That model continues to connect with the wider nostalgia for the past associated with the construction of authenticity.

For producers and consumers, the process of negotiating authenticities in wine consumption is constructed around specific cultural values, norms and experiences which might be very far apart. Place forms part of this process either as the site of experience or as an imaginary concept, but both producers and consumers play an active part in the construction of what is considered to be an authentic experience.[17] Different kinds of authenticities are staged in different contexts, and, in the world of wine, it is helpful to follow the multiple sites in which they are articulated or differentiated depending on context. Diversity is the key to this process. For example, the Burgundy story is translated in different ways in a wide range of cultural settings, while remaining unique and true to itself in its own right. Cultural brokers play a central role in translating the nature of the product in order to capture and shape consumer demand and the recent trends in wine consumption. In Japan, consumer culture might be defined as understanding the rich hierarchy of crus and deploying knowledge of it, while in Russia, for the new oligarchs, it could mean drinking the most expensive wines and deploying social status. Yet such processes underline the fact that authenticity is constructed and negotiated in a wide range of guises and fits into a global hierarchy of values which transcend the local and situate experiences of authenticity in a wide range of settings.

Individual Engagements: Authenticities and Worlds of Wine

Various ethnographic vignettes have been chosen for the purpose of our journey into the social construction of authenticities. My aim is to illustrate how a commodity such as Burgundy wines offers a wide range of deployments of authenticity which, in turn, become imbricated into the localities and the construction of the social experience of place. Subjectivities are an integral part of this process, and culture here is seen as 'contested, temporal and emergent' (Clifford and Marcus 1986). Diversity refers to the distribution and selection of what fits one's desire for the authentic, be it a behaviour, a state of mind or a particular type of object (Fillitz and Saris 2012: 15). But it is also about both the context in which authenticity is constructed through the various forms of its expression, and the process of cultural encounters or cultural translation which transforms the original and implicit meaning of the authenticity of the commodity into another object, which, in turn, is reinterpreted by the consumer. The Burgundy cultural story has always been one defined by hospitality, gastronomy and an authentic encounter with the wine growers. For a long time, wine merchants, who dominated the wine trade at the local level, used a specific cultural repertoire based upon these values, placing at the centre of the touristic experience the visit to the vaulted cellar. This encounter, which is generally organised around a wine tasting and a quasi-mystical meeting with the producer, contributes to this construction of an authentic wine drinking experience. Burgundian hospitality is also one of the historical ingredients of this touristic pilgrimage which has been perpetuated since medieval times.

How this local repertoire is changing and is articulated at the transnational level is another story. Burgundy has always developed a culture of hospitality based upon gastronomy, history and wine, but this culture was accessible only if the visitor came to the region. The case of the two American women who have opened a cooking class in Beaune is just the latest example of a long tradition of attracting visitors directly to the site.[18] According to the website, founded in 2008 by mother-daughter duo Marjorie Taylor and Kendall Smith Franchini, the *Cook's Atelier* offers cooking classes, seasonal suppers, and workshops throughout the year with the goal of educating local and international visitors about seasonal ingredients, classic French cooking techniques and Burgundy's wine capital. Their culinary approach has been well-received, inspiring guests to recreate the experience at home and prompting them to expand the brand with an on-site Wine Shop and culinary boutique, as well as an online retail site, coined The French Larder. The two women have also developed a gastronomic tour of the local market, taking American and Chinese visitors to the various producers and preparing a meal for them. The *Cook's Atelier* has been praised by local and international media outlets alike, and has been named one of the most 'Exciting New Culinary Trips' by Travel + Leisure and an 'Insider's Pick' by Fodor's Travel Guide. Marjorie and Kendall's curated products, recipes, wine selections and entertaining philosophy has also been featured in various magazines, including *Food & Wine*, *Kinfolk*, *Anthology*, *L'Express*, *Le Bien Public* and *Côté Est*.

During the 2013 Pinot Noir festival held in Wellington (New Zealand), the wine expert and raconteur Mike Bernie presented a YouTube clip, lasting approximately eight minutes, entitled 'Authenticity in wine, being true to oneself',[19] which explored one of the major contemporary values in the global hierarchy of wine. Interviewing a wide range of well-known wine growers, sommeliers and experts from Australia and New Zealand, Bernie tried to get a sense of how the world of wine gets to grip with, and defines, the concept of authenticity. While the first part of his talk was devoted to the broader definition of authenticity, the second part focused on the discussion of wines more specifically, illustrating to what extent they can be seen as a broader medium in the construction of identities. What came out strongly from the clip was the interaction between the place or terroir, the actors, wine grower or producer and honesty, truthfulness or even integrity. As one of the interviewees concluded, 'this is about the contrast between humans who can be true to themselves, but who are malleable whereas nature, the earth and terroir being authentic, it offers up only what it can, it does not think about it and the seasons come and they are what they are, it is what it is, and that is true'. The figure of the wine grower encapsulates both the fight against nature and respect for it, and he or she is presented as the quintessence of wine production. That image contrasts sharply with the reality of modern liberal economies, which tend to be marked by anonymity and standardisation in food production. Authenticity in Burgundy could be summed up by the phrase 'If you achieve something consistently, it builds authenticity'. In relation to this quest for authenticity, specific values are negotiated, from friendship to the integrity of the producer as well as the simplicity of the experience which contrasts with the economic value of the product.

Authenticity is also performed through direct personal contact with producers. During the festival mentioned above, a number of the New Zealand producers who participated in the organisation cited their networks of Burgundian producers, buyers and experts in order to recount their own version of the Burgundy story of terroir A few emblematic names of Burgundian producers were repeatedly invoked and acted as points of reference. For example, domain X was tweeted several times after its owner was cited by a celebrated Melbourne restaurant manager as 'My friend'. It was striking how often *vignerons*, especially the owners of elite estates, were described as 'my friend X'. When I asked about the nature of the relationship, it was clear that the friendship had developed over the years and that both had visited each other. Wine and its sharing clearly provided a springboard for the development of a more personal relationship. One of my informers even claimed that 'We share the same vision about wine and about where we want to be with our wines'. Following these networks of established friendships between producers and customers from different parts of the world, it rapidly became clear that bottles had been passed around in a circle of exchanges with gifts being made at various sites of production and commercialisation. In a practice that recalls what I witnessed at the Paulée de Meursault, with wine tasting taking place after the banquet,[20] some of the producers I sat with during the Pinot Noir festival in 2013 presented some expensive Burgundy wines at the end of the dinner to taste and share between 'friends'. Friendship and gifts of wine are part of the Burgundy cultural story and they say a lot about the various networks established between producers and experts or buyers all over the world. They also form part of the moral economy of the product, contrasting exuberant prices with the free nature of the gift and obliging reciprocity in a manner consistent with the famous model designed by Marcel Mauss.

Burgundian Hospitality: 'Being True to Yourself'

In the construction of authenticity Burgundian hospitality has always been one of the principal tropes associated with the historical reputation of the place. The majority of my encounters with Burgundy since the 1990s have been punctuated by remarkable wine tastings, especially when I was a student, and by a generosity difficult to describe or to reciprocate. As an academic anthropologist, I have never been able to purchase any of the fantastic bottles tasted and my long-term memory of people is undoubtedly associated with those quasi-religious moments of opening a prized vintage and sharing it for hours with knowledgeable and passionate producers, or enjoying a simple *casse-croûte* at 10 AM in the vineyard after a morning's labour. These encounters shaped my life as a young PhD student and have made it more difficult to turn towards new ethnographic horizons. The trope of hospitality is deeply embedded in the Burgundian way of life and distinguishes the region from others.

Interestingly, it is in the most expensive area of wine production that generosity has been the most deployed. Whether at the Saint-Vincent Tournante, Paulée de Meursault or in one of many visits to the cellars, hospitality has been constructed as a means of establishing loyal and trustworthy ties to a clientele. It has taken time for oenological tourism in this part of the world to be recognised as such because it always existed as a distinctive social practice. Jacquet and Laferté (2013) have shown that at the end of the nineteenth century, tour guides totally excluded vineyard visits and gastronomic activities from their Burgundy sightseeing tours. Only natural sites and medieval monuments were of interest to visiting travellers. They argue that gourmet products and wines were perceived at the time as being internationally recognised high-end upper-class luxury products, so not associated with any particular region. The commercial value of certain wines and the freedom enjoyed by vintners (to produce blended wines from grapes of different geographical origins) were major factors contributing to this situation. By the late 1930s, major changes had occurred in production and marketing standards in France, with the introduction of AOCs, together with a cultural renaissance based on regional traditions and a strong drive on the part of the Republic's political establishment to promote local 'homeland' areas. The rise of tourism in the 1930s helped to transform the ways in which the region was presented to the public. With the development of the direct sale of bottles at the domain, hospitality developed as a useful tool to establish relationships with a clientele as part of the regional and commercial marketing of folklore (Laferté 2006).

To understand how Burgundian hospitality is articulated, it is helpful to follow an example of an encounter with a local producer. In 2014 as part of my fieldwork I decided to visit one of the first young female wine growers I had worked with in the 1990s. Her name had been mentioned on several occasions over the subsequent years and she was also involved in the First Vinexpo held in Burgundy in 2011. I was aware that she had also been included in a book entitled *Les Nouveaux Vignerons* (The New Wine Growers), published in 2002 by Jacky Rigaux, a fervent believer in terroir. More recently, she had been granted the title of best female wine grower of the year in Japan during the Foodex exhibition. Annie took over the management of the domain in 1994, following in the footsteps of several generations of her family, implanted in the Hautes-Côtes; she faced challenging times before gradually putting her own stamp on the domain. As stated on the website: 'Committed to integrated viticulture, she refuses standardisation and prefers a traditional approach to sustainable viticulture, with minimal intervention. The wines of Burgundy are emotional wines, but also wines of the future, taking into account the carbon footprint. Female wine maker, passionate mother, she wants to pass on this heritage for our delight' (author's translation).

What defines her as a female wine grower in a world still dominated by a masculine culture is her high level of education – a degree in agricultural engineering and a national diploma in oenology, which is not common in this part of the world. Yet her constant questioning of her own practices and the whys and wherefores of viticulture make her far more approachable than some of her counterparts. Her family narrative is constructed around a deeply entrenched sense of place: 'our ancestors lived in one of the small villages in the Hautes-Côtes and have been farmers and labourers since 1500'. What struck me during my various encounters with Annie is the simplicity and honesty of her approach to life, illustrating the adage of being 'true to yourself'.

My encounter with Annie in 2014 took the form of a lunch invitation to her husband's family home with their three sons. The love for simple and down to earth food is one of the ways in which sociability is constructed. Her website always gives a few new recipes which showcase terroir and family traditions. The interview took the form of an informal family gathering, with a relaxed conversation around the table punctuated by the children's stories of school and discussions about travelling the world. I was immediately put at ease and made to feel part of something familiar and intimate as well as emotional in terms of memory building. It was difficult to keep to the thread of my questions as the familiar domestic setting made me relax. We tasted a wine from another natural wine producer from the Loire, and had a broader discussion about Burgundian viticulture and its past and future. Part of our discussion focused on terroir and the extent to which it crystallised viticultural techniques rather than encouraging the constant questioning of traditional practices. Throughout my encounters with wine growers, the tension between the economic and moral dimension of wine production has been implicit, serving as a line of separation between them. Burgundy, as a site of encounter, is typical of this *mise en scène* of a rural idyll with a return to wholesome values and authenticity, it is also part of the emotional construction of the site for the individual consumer, as memories will always be revived through the reactivation of specific moments. Shared in a fusional fashion with a producer, the Burgundy terroir story is about this social experience of authenticity which lies deep in one's emotional core.

In his blog, entitled 'Mes riches heures en Bourgogne' (My Special Time in Burgundy), Jacques Berthomeau, a wine consultant commissioned by the French Ministry of Agriculture to prepare a report in 2001, now known as the Berthomeau Report, describes his meeting with Annie in the same vein: 'The simplicity of her welcome, warm but without ostentation, as my mum would have said, characterises the sharing of our meal around a well-presented table facilitating the flow of conversation. The visceral connection between Annie and her family rooted in the Hautes Côtes is immediately felt'. This authenticity is not played out for the purpose of the visitor or client, it is intrinsically embedded in Annie's philosophy. Moreover, it forms part of her way of approaching her wines which she defines as 'natural' wines. Berthomeau notes: 'With our lamb's lettuce salad, guinea fowl, cheese and pie, we drink – I use the term drink and not tasting, we are at the table, not in representation – we drink just a Hautes-Côtes de Beaune'. This episode, commented upon on Berthomeau's blog, exemplifies the mediated construction of authenticity. This complex process of cultural transmission of social experiences through the sharing of a meal and wine contributes to the construction of authenticity at a global level via the websites lauding Annie's status as a natural wine producer. It also has commercial implications, in her meetings with importers and consumers, and illustrates the complex process of fabrication of authenticity throughout the commodity chain, which in some cases resonates or imbricates into a global and hierarchised world of values. The values deployed here resonate because they contrast radically with our daily experience, offering a counter-narrative, one of space, imagination, connections, trustfulness and strong emotional ties, simplicity and common sense.

Climate Change and Producing Values: 'Let Nature Speak'

Another form of authenticity deployed by local actors is related to the marketing of a specific form of viticulture in which nature is idealised and romanticised. The terroir discourse has often been characterised by a tendency to treat everything attached to wine culture as natural (Ulin and Black 2013). In order to articulate the terroir discourse and to demonstrate its authenticity, a wide range of strategies have traditionally been used by producers. Amongst them, the production of performative texts, films and other visual media have come to join the repertoire of wine culture. They are often deployed to give more legitimacy to the products, but they also have other symbolic functions as writing, reading and seeing are ways of making sense of the world in which we live.

In agricultural communities, the practice of keeping a diary is widespread (Joly 2004). While conducting research in the 1990s into the literary culture of wine growers in Champagne, Jura and Burgundy,[21] I argued that writing about wine production is a way of controlling the environment and, especially, space and time. In these texts, the weather is frequently the principal preoccupation of the author and the principal preoccupation of the author and it benefits from a thorough description as it is presented as one of the elements which is most difficult to forecast and control, and for many wine growers it is in God's hands. Little is known about the use of these texts, but they may well have rewritten or at least have been consulted and read by later generations. Time and weather form part of the same juxtaposition in terms of climatic sequences that the producer seeks to control or rationalise through his writings. In some cases, climatic accidents provide the opportunity for deeper reflections. Climatic descriptions might appear as short sentences or a brief description, prompting a reminiscence of the literacy style of the almanac when time was perceived as moving more slowly. When writing about weather, the author classifies natural phenomena and puts them into a rational framework, in an attempt to establish order in the reality he describes. One might wonder if writing fulfils a protective function like other symbolic practices: 'Verba volent, scriba manent…'. Another characteristic of these wine growers' diaries is the methodical, repetitive even incantational nature of the prose which reminds us of the cyclical and perilous nature of wine production. This sort of writing is still present in many families, but it is kept apart, hidden away from the observer, forming part of the family heritage. More recently, it has also been transferred to the computer, which has transformed the nature of the task. Despite these shifts, writing still represents a clear and protective function. Most of the domains take notes during the year, especially related to the harvest, but these papers are seen as private and are rarely shown. When I conducted my study in 1993, I was reminded constantly of the status and significance of these records, especially in the emblematic wine region. When I asked to see their archives, one of the Meursault producers responded: 'No I do not want you to see it, we have one, but you see my daughter will publish it one day'.

If such writings once formed part of the traditional private literary genre, they have been transformed with the use of computers, but they remain attached to the private and professional sphere. They were also sometimes found in wine guides, such as the *Guide Hachette*, but their use remained for a long time confined to the domain or the local archives.

Yet more recently they have re-emerged as part of the debate on quality. On 14 October 2014, the newspaper *Le Point*[22] published an extract of the annual report on the state of the harvest of DRC, written by the well-known co-manager. This re-use of wine growers' writings by producers themselves illustrates a need to introduce a new strategy of differentiation when describing annual weather patterns in the context of the terroir story at a time of increasing climatic pressure. A few other producers have also resorted to this method on their websites, but often their descriptions are very brief and not so informative about the perceived quality of their vintage. It is used here as a stylistic device rather than a value tool. This initiative could be read as an attempt to go back to nature and to position the philosophy of the producer in the global hierarchy of value. It also illustrates the rising visibility of Burgundy as a global story in the international world of wine, and its emblematic position that needs to be maintained in a competitive environment. It also establishes a new marketing strategy designed to link the *climats de Bourgogne* story to the ecological and environmental shifts that the author wishes to provoke at the local level. The text, reported by a journalist, is presented as a form of diary along the lines of the traditional descriptive and intimate writing that was once commonly used by the more educated members of peasant society. It is first and foremost written as a struggle against nature and its natural process of adaptation. Very little is said about the role of man, except during the organisation of grape picking. The narrative focuses on how the vineyard has an extraordinary capacity to adapt to the most extreme climatic conditions. The analogy goes as far as to present the happy end as a purely natural process, illustrated by the picture chosen to accompany the narrative: a contemplative image of the wine grower and his vineyards.

A performative dimension is from the start attached to the narration: 'We can divide into three acts the scenario written for us this year'. Meteorological changes are presented as the incarnation of 'nature and its whims' from the first episode of hail storms, followed by a short and welcome heat wave which ensured a bountiful harvest. The third act was a cold, rainy and humid July which at the end helped the grapes to mature, and the author concluded: 'From the beginning of September, the wine-grower will see coming together everything that he could wish for in his vineyards: North wind, dry and sunny weather, moderate heat'.[23] Yet the episode was to be disrupted by a violent storm on 19 September which happily did not damage the harvest. This series of unfortunate events finds its happy conclusion in the vintage and, especially, the quality of the harvest as the signs of success begin to appear as the wine becomes ready for consumption. The process of wine making is also described and annotated with positive comments which presage the happy outcome of the 2014 vintage.

Through this narration and writing about the power of nature, a sense of blessing emerges as part of the reiteration of the Burgundy global story. Nature is here domesticated through the act of writing, made sense of through the repeated meteorological accidents which were ultimately resolved, thereby producing a happy ending. These forms of writings, published in a newspaper known for its economic coverage, contribute to the construction and differentiation of what Karpik has named economies of singularities. Karpik (2010) has argued that because of the uncertainty and the highly subjective valuation of singularities such as wine or art, these markets are necessarily equipped with what he calls 'judgement devices' such as labels, brands, guides, critics and rankings, which provide consumers with the credible knowledge needed to make reasonable choices. In this case, the use of a wine report describing the climatic accidents and their impact on the vintage brings a new, unique and innovative judgement tool based upon the reputation of the owner and the authenticity of the *témoignage*. It is a case of what is written must be true, reaffirming the authenticity of the product and contributing to the debate on the quality of the vintage.

Nature here is presented in a specific way and the environmental shift seeks to reposition the wine region in the global hierarchy of value where ecological concerns have acquired ever greater weight. The UNESCO application and construction around the *climats* as the authentic site of a singular historicised value are part of that process – they are amongst the most expensive wines in the world – and they are not only part of the domain strategy, but they also tell a story about the place and its continuous struggle against the elements. The weather and the climatic uncertainties are now mentioned as part of the 'unfinished' commodity predicament (Paxson 2012). Consumers are warned of the capricious influence of nature and of the difficulties to be faced when trying to produce a reliable vintage. If most of the producers never mention the issue of vintage in terms of quality, they frequently rely on wine experts and wine tasters to comment for them. By taking up his pen, the co-owner of DRC tells his story directly to his consumers, and, by the same token, he not only takes control of the expertise of his wines, but also locates the product 'from an economy of uncertainty to a workmanship of certainty' (Paxson 2012 citing Pye 1968). DRC is well known for deciding that specific vintages which are not seen as being of the expected quality will not be sold. Rarity is a significant factor in this economic process, helping to increase the value of a given vintage.

Conclusions

Burgundy has traditionally conjured up images of gastronomic pleasure, great wines and stunning architecture while offering a long-lasting and monumental image of a terroir which has remained the same for centuries, promoting an international image of artisanal excellence and prestige. As discussed here this image has in fact been more dynamic and is anchored in a more complex history of discontinuities and battles for quality than is usually acknowledged, especially by the local elites. In the ongoing endeavour to manipulate and control this seamless story of excellence, local actors have at different points in its history played an important role in shaping the content of its international contours. Yet they have also progressively shifted some of the main elements in an attempt to adapt to modernity and to the new values driven by consumers. What is consistently reiterated is a story of permanence and excellence through place and terroir, but this process of adaptation has not just been an evolutive one, and it is also marked by crisis, ruptures and disjunction. Yet what characterised the Burgundy story is the role at different historical points of specific elites who continue to shape its image at the local and transnational level and to adjust the story and then communicate it through the commercialisation and marketing of their wines.

Wine growers have increasingly asserted their position in the global world of wine and they have sought to adjust to the new wine values circulating within the winescape and their positioning at the local level, ensuring that the Burgundy story remains constructed around terroir, history, authenticity and quality. Yet in the circulation of these ideas and experiences, attached to wine consumption and wine commercialisation, local actors engage in highly differentiated ways with global wine culture and what they perceive as their self-reflexive identification in relation to those values. Indeed, most of them project their own self-identity onto their products and the Burgundy story to some extent condenses particular conceptions of the world: that of greed, success and acute competition, but also friendship, authenticity and truth. It is through these diverse encounters that we are able to experience the richness and depth of local life, while being constantly faced with the pressure of modernity. The experience of consuming a Burgundy in the cellar of a wine grower far from the pace of modern life is about transcending daily preoccupations and proposing an alternative reading of our societal experience. What has been extremely successful in the Burgundy terroir story is this capacity to reinvent Burgundy while remaining the same. The recent UNESCO listing might radically transform the experience by fossilising it and by preventing a more democratic encounter with the place. As for Burgundy wines, their price is liable to continue to soar, making it impossible for all but the wealthiest to taste the fruits of their vines.

New strategies have to be sought to both inscribe Burgundy and its *climats* in the global story while weaving the production of authenticity through a wide range of new initiatives, positioning each producer in a different fashion into the changing global wine landscape. The role of individuals, be they wine growers or landowners, remains central to that process which needs to be carefully crafted into an alternative and critical collective endeavour into modernity.

Notes

1. Cited by the anthropologist Arturo Escobar (2001: 13).
2. *Typicité* is a French term in wine tasting used to describe the degree to which a wine reflects its varietal origins. The term is also used by the French wine profession when granting the AOC certificate to a specific wine. For more discussion about the concept, see Teil (2012).
3. I define wine growers as the workers of the land, while landowners do not directly cultivate their plots. Both own the vineyard, but there is a strong social division between these two worlds in terms of social networks and connections, lifestyles and social status as well as their positioning in local politics.
4. As Fourcade argues (2012: 536), in these multiple ways 'the "rent" that [appellations generate is] capitalised into the value of the vineyard', so that 'the rent process is circular and self-sustaining over extended periods'. The areas with the highest rents per unit area are able to maintain the most demanding viticultural and wine-making practices over time.
5. For a survey of the terminology, see http://www.cnrtl.fr/definition/vigneron. Consulted on 12 January 2015.
6. www.soluka.fr/.../etude-les-vignerons-independants. Consulted on 7 January 2015.
7. http://platform.europeanmoocs.eu/course_mooc_owu_open_wine_university_. Consulted on 24 April 2015.
8. For example, https://www.troisfoisvin.com/blog/les-climats-de-bourgogne/. Consulted on 11 November 2017.
9. The loi Évin (formally: 'loi n° 91-32 du 10 janvier 1991 relative à la lutte contre le tabagisme et l'alcoolisme', Law 91-32 of 10 January 1991 relative to the struggle against tobacco consumption and alcoholism) is the French alcohol and tobacco policy law passed in 1991. See, for example, some of the recent debates concerning possible changes to the Evin Law, 'Loi Evin François Patriat défend la presse': http://france3-regions.blog.francetvinfo.fr/politique-bour-

gogne/2015/03/31/loi-evin-francois-patriat-defend-la-presse.html. Consulted on 11 November 2017.

10. www.youtube.com/watch?v=RFtr6EgM5J4. Consulted on 12 January 2015.
11. See, for example, http://www.romanee-conti.com/#/ProfessionDeFoi. Consulted on 24 April 2015.
12. See, for example, http://www.artisans-vignerons-bourgogne-sud.com/. Consulted on 14 January 2016.
13. Biodynamic agriculture is a form of alternative agriculture which is very similar to organic farming, but which includes various esoteric concepts drawn from the ideas of Rudolf Steiner.
14. www.bailliagedepommard.com. Consulted on 12 January 2015.
15. See, for example, the work of Taylor (2001) and Wang (1999).
16. See, for example, Handler (1986), Bendix (1997) and Fillitz and Saris (2012).
17. See, for example, Kirschenblatt-Gimblett (2004), Molz (2004) and Bendix (1997).
18. https://thecooksatelier.com/our-story. Consulted on 13 August 2014.
19. https://www.youtube.com/watch?v=IIQHqE7s9XQ. Consulted on 13 August 2014.
20. The tradition is that a large number of bottles are brought every year by the Meursault producers and they are kept under the table to be consumed afterwards between close friends in order to reaffirm social relations.
21. See Mission du Patrimoine Ethnologique, Ministère de la Culture et de la Communication, report 'Moi je suis vigneron, carnets, calepins, agendas et livres de raison en pays de vignoble' (1994). http://www.culturecommunication.gouv.fr/content/download/43290/344874/version/1/file/Ethno_Demossier_1995_056.pdf. Consulted on 12 January 2015.
22. Le Point Magazine, 14 October 2014, available at http://www.lepoint.fr/vin/vendanges-2014-domaine-de-la-romanee-conti-22-10-2014-1874581_581.php#xtmc=14-octobre-2014-vendanges&xtnp=1&xtcr=1. Consulted on 20 November 2017.
23. Ibid.

Chapter 3
THE TASTE OF PLACE

❦

My first direct encounter with the sensorial world of wine goes back to my training as an anthropologist during the 1990s when I was invited to join one of the wine tasting sessions organised by the BIVB (Burgundy Wine Board). It was the first step on my ethnographic journey towards a PhD. At the time, the concept of oenotourism or wine discovery was still not fully developed and it was clear that when compared to its main competitors, Bordeaux or Champagne, Burgundy was lagging behind. The tasting sessions I attended were, first and foremost, about the complexity of the variations encountered with Pinots Noirs and Chardonnay at the regional level and the familiarisation with the tasting protocol promoted by the BIVB. One of their local technicians was managing the session in a light-touch fashion, without being too prescriptive. Two noble grapes were defined in a multitude of ways across a small geographic area, covering around 30,000 hectares, 100 different AOCs, 3,800 domains, 250 *négoces* and 23 cooperatives mainly located in the south of Burgundy. According to the BIVB website, 'this exceptional diversity of tastes, "a wonderful aromatic panorama", has its roots in the natural conditions of the vineyards. As such, there can be slight differences between two neighbouring plots in terms of their aspect and/or soil type. The winegrower of the Burgundy region is known to preserve these differences in character brought about by these tiny variations'. What dominated this initial experience and has continued to reverberate throughout the following three decades of field-work was the encounter with this complex and puzzling sensorial universe of tastes, which is difficult for the novice, or even *aficionada*, to grasp.

Burgundy, as a viticultural model, is characterised by the extreme diversity of the sensory qualities of place, but also by the emphasis placed upon the permanence and stability of the site in gustative terms. Several commentators have pointed out that Burgundy, unlike other French vine-yards, has resisted change. This evocative and powerful construction of the place as a natural site protected from any external pressures has progressively been consolidated in response to the increasing internationalisation of wine production and the growing competition in the market. It offers a counter-story to that of globalisation, standardisation and industrialisation as, increasingly, the taste of place is seen as a challenge to the vast array of anonymous, mass-produced foods and beverages now available to the consumer.[1] The main story is therefore one of a stable terroir, defined as an imaginary discourse about the historical relationship between a specific place – one acquired with difficulty and through hard labour – and a specific wine grower and his family. Yet the complexity on which it relies is part of the story attached to the consumption of fine wines. In his book *Inside Burgundy*, Jasper Morris underlines the complexity of the Burgundian model: 'Burgundy does not respond well to being put in a straightjacket. There are no set rules to making Burgundy; there are no set rules to appreciating Burgundy. It intrigues, fascinates, delights, infuriates, disappoints, charms, enraptures and puzzles. Very like the life of man, as long as it refrains from Hobbes definition – solitary, poor, nasty, brutish and short' (Morris 2010: 15).

During the New Zealand Pinot Noir festival held in Wellington in 2013 and throughout my ethnographic travels around New Zealand producing areas, I found that Burgundy, as a global model of reference, proved to be the leitmotif for Pinots Noirs producers (see Chapter 7).[2] Taste, colour and nose were emphasised as central to Burgundian wines and Pinot Noir was presented as a fine plant, with a liking for difficult and extreme climatic conditions but particularly well adapted to the Burgundian geography. Producing wine in this part of the world is defined as a constant battle against nature, as demonstrated by the hailstorms in June and July 2014 which destroyed localised areas of the vineyards of Volnay, Meursault and Pommard. During the festival in Wellington, a wine tasting was organised around a range of Burgundian Pinots Noirs bottles which had been brought over by the British wine buyer, Jasper Morris, to illustrate what Burgundy was about in sensorial terms. Again, during the tasting the interpretation each wine critic and producer gave to it was central to the discussions around the table. As Jasper Morris explained: 'The taste for pinot noirs is between a general framework for Pinot Noir, based on the general structure on the palate, and specific details which comes from the sense of place: flavour profile, balance of fruit, acidity, tannin etc.'.

When I interviewed a number of New World wine growers about Burgundy, it was clear that its model of viticulture dominated their discourse of excellence and was presented as a marker of quality in the world of wine that other producers wished to emulate. Yet when I asked more precise questions about it, most of them admitted that they were not sure about the realities of wine production nor about the subtleties of each wine. Their discourse was mainly about the artisanal, small-scale and unchanging nature of wine production and the ways in which terroir was given a voice through the careful light-touch intervention of the wine producer eager to preserve and let nature speak for itself. The global discourse on Burgundy as a reference in the world of wine resonated strongly with the local and regional construction of the place. Specific names came back as points of reference, often associated with emblematic domains or with very expensive bottles. For New World producers, Burgundy equals quality, terroir, artisanship and a unique and complex style of wines in terms of wine-making practices. Yet these references form part of a mythical construction of the region at the global level, which ignores the differences in the quality of wines under the same AOC roof. The increasing standardisation of wine making has also had an impact on wine styles and tastes, and the contested issue of the use of pesticides to combat the threat of disease is another factor that should not be ignored. The story is about Burgundy as a hegemonic worldwide wine discourse and its international deployment through a wide range of settings from restaurants, wine events, wine tastings or other drinking occasions. But it is also about the values deployed at the core of the viticultural model.

The definition of Burgundian terroirs and tastes deployed through different historical, social and geographical settings is a very modern preoccupation. The articulation of a sensorial field attached to 'noble' grapes such as Pinots Noirs and Chardonnay has been part of a major enterprise headed by specific groups and individuals in a differentiated historical politics of scale. Kolleen Guy (2003) has engaged with the romanticisation of the French peasantry and its terroir as a successful commercial strategy developed by Champagne producers from the nineteenth century onwards. The work of Gilles Laferté (2006) is also illustrative of a similar project at the local and national level during the inter-war period, but its international and contemporary dimension is yet to be fully explored. How has this cultural model been translated into different geographical settings, from New York to Shanghai? Who has conducted the translation? Does the Burgundian story still draw upon an agrarian and folkloric narrative of popular festivals such as the Gastronomic Fair of Dijon, the Paulée of Meursault, the Saint-Vincent Tournante and the annual wine auction at the Hospice in Beaune? These sites, each in their own way, drew attention to the unique qualities of the wines and suggested how they might best be consumed. The emphasis at the time was not so much on taste, but more on the act and context of consuming, sharing and socialising, the Burgundian peasant model of hospitality.

More recently, in the context of a growing competition, there has been an attempt to convince new consumers that they too can join the ranks of wine *aficionados*. The Paulée of New York and San Francisco, instigated in 2000 by the wine buyer, Daniel Johnnes,[3] was inspired by the same cultural strategy as the original Paulée de Meursault.[4] As noted by the website, 'a special feature of La Paulée de Meursault is that everyone brings wine which, no doubt, makes it the world's classiest "Bring Your Own Bottle" party. A friendly but intense competition reigns as bottles are uncorked, shared and imbibed'. According to its promoters, 'Anyone who appreciates fine wine and cuisine should try to attend this event, which captures the essence of Burgundy's joie de vivre'. La Paulée de New York is according to Daniel Johnnes, an acknowledged homage to La Paulée de Meursault and the traditions of Burgundy, characterised by a convivial and simple atmosphere around the sharing of a bottle. 'It is his humble attempt to transport the Burgundian spirit of generosity and camaraderie to an enthusiastic and passionate Burgundy loving American clientele', indicates the website. Another important aspect of this deployment of taste concerns the more professional dimension of wine culture through the role played by the Burgundy story in international professional settings such as the New Zealand Pinot Noir festival, but also the internal contestation of terroir and taste which calls into question the notion of change in tastes. Our main questions for this chapter are therefore how are tastes and terroirs deployed in this politics of scale? To what extent have they both changed? Finally, what are the relationships between the social and the sensorial in Burgundy?

Anthropology of Place and Taste

In anthropology, the study of place and taste has traditionally been confined to the literature on terroir. As Sutton (2010: 116) has pointed out, another approach to gustemology[5] might be found in writings that focus on the sensory aspects of food as part of constructions of senses of place or place-making projects. In her seminal book *The Taste of Place: a Cultural Journey into Terroir* (2008), Amy Trubek defines terroir as a 'foodview', that is to say a food-centred worldview, a folk category through which people understand their relationship to the land. She argues convincingly that terroir – a taste that is typically rationalised and associated with a specific local place, mode of production and consumption – is in fact produced by a particular history of social practices in France attached to the work of journalists, writers, folklorists, chefs and artisans. Trubek underlines the role that institutions and social practices play in shaping the ways taste comes to define place and vice versa. The world of wine was, first and foremost, the original site of experimentation for the terroir model which progressively became the reference not only for other European wine productions, but also other food and foodstuffs. Wine in France has long been the object of an ideological and cultural construction managed by the state and wine producers as well as, more recently, the world of wine critics.

Focusing on how terroir is locally constructed and crafted by producers, Heather Paxson (2010) goes further by arguing that it offers a theory of how people and place, cultural tradition and landscape ecology are mutually constituted over time. It echoes the view shared today by some wine professionals that 'An individual man puts his imprint on the wine, interprets the terroir, and mankind has shaped the vineyard across the centuries, making decisions which have resulted in the various terroirs being as they are today' (Morris 2010: 13). Through an ethnographical study of US artisan cheesemakers, Paxson (2010) convincingly demonstrates how the taste of place is adapted to reveal the range of values – agrarian, environmental, social and gastronomic – that producers and consumers believe constitute their cheese and distinguish artisanal from mass production in the New World landscapes. This process, which she describes as 'Reverse Engineering terroir', offers a useful theoretical platform to think about the relationship between place and taste in the case of the Old World and especially Burgundy wines and to analyse their production as a more dynamic process. The boundaries between Old and New World are, at least in the wine industry, more porous than is sometimes assumed and, indeed, need to be called into question (Banks 2013). Yet what is useful in Paxson's analysis is the multi-scalar dimension of US artisanal production. Rather than seeing it as a closed and detached agricultural process of innovation, Paxson engages with the socio-economic, political and ideological contexts of cheese production. As we shall see, the process she describes is now also taking place in one of the most traditional bastions of terroir ideology, Burgundy. Taste and terroir have become contested both from within the profession and also from outside by enlightened consumers (Barrey and Teil 2011).

Brad Weiss has shed further light onto the construction of locality through taste and his analysis offers some useful ideas for our case-study, even if most wine producers would not like to see their wines compared to and analysed in relation to pig farming. His work underlines the ways in which sites of production are a 'field in which "place" is constituted in action and experience and imbued with concrete meanings and orientations in the field of participation' (2011: 440). Through the process of raising pigs locally, producers engage with a complex construction of the place as a sensory field which is carefully crafted through a range of venues in a process attuned to the materiality of ecosystems, landscapes, grapes and wine; it is also built through social relationships amongst farmers, craftsmen and their activities (2011: 440). Moreover, for Weiss, inhabiting place in a local fashion is a matter of innovation, never just continuity and 'the pig permits places to be reinhabited through imagined connections to an alternative past' (2011: 440). The discussion on place and space, past and present and the notion of sensory fields are undoubtedly central to any discussions on terroir. What strikes me as a useful anthropological platform in Weiss's work is the discussion on agency and what could be defined as a place-making project. Individual agency sometimes leads to conflict with local perceptions of place-making and this clash between the individual and the collective seems, in the context of wine culture, to be the best way of understanding the finesse of the locality and its political economy. The concept of sensorial field, as defined by Weiss, also offers some parallels with the results of my Burgundian fieldwork, in this case the grape varieties Pinot Noir and Chardonnay. Moreover, the analysis could be pushed further in the case of Burgundy because the transnational sensorial field is part of the story and by opening the field to the global arena, it is possible to better understand how it is adapting to the global hierarchy of values around wine culture.

The issue of taste shaped by and shaping international standards has often tended to be neglected in the terroir literature. It is only recently that the notion of international tastes has started to be discussed. Yuson Jung (2014), in an innovative article on Bulgarian wines, questions the adjustments of lesser known locales to the global taste standards established through wine competitions. In addition, Jung argues that the taste of place is not an attribute available to any single wine producer, but is indeed the product of a global hierarchy of value that gives preference to certain forms of sensory experiences and knowledge over others. It is through the sensorial encounter that each producer decides to engage, or not to, with the global world of wine. In this encounter the wine expert plays a major role in dictating the standards and norms, choosing whether or not to give legitimacy to certain tastes or to fix a certain conception of gustatory expectations when consuming Pinots Noirs from a specific place. His or her expertise encompasses both the sensorial and the social as he/she is also a being-in-location. Unlike in Burgundy, where long historical taste narratives of Pinots Noirs and Chardonnay have shaped the global world of wine in hegemonic ways and still serve as markers of tastes, Bulgarian wines have to create their own sensory field in order to establish themselves. Yet what is interesting is how these recently established international standards are subject to change and reinterpretation by producers given the debates at the local level. The global story associated with place and recounted by local actors keeps everything together in an attempt to silence local debates or prevent internal contestation.

As we have seen, the anthropological literature on taste sheds some light onto important aspects of the cultural edifice of taste and place. But what could be learned from an anthropological approach to place and taste as discussed above? In the study of place and taste, there has been a scholarly tendency to construct locality in bounded, essentialised and representational terms as if it was a quest for a perfect fit and as if every producer was pursuing that aim in a collective fashion. Burgundy epitomises this relationship between place and taste and it provides us with a striking illustration of how the link between place and taste has been historically, politically, economically and socially reconfigured. Terroir is also characterised by a complex historical landscape of experimentations, failures, crisis, frictions and pressures to conform to the norm, a kind of Lévi-Straussien *bricolage*. Rather than looking at the perfect fit between place and taste, it is more useful, as Yuson Jung and Nicolas Sternsdorff Cisterna (2014: 2) have argued, to examine the co-constitutive relationship at the intersection of sensory experiences and the social, taste being understood as combining civic, ethical, political and economic processes. Yet this intersection is far from being a straightforward process as different values, understandings, representations and ideologies come together in a disjointed and conflicting way. Moreover, the historical depth of this intersection adds more layers and complexity to the Burgundian project under scrutiny. What I am trying to argue is that regardless of the success of the terroir story at the global level, the relationship between place and taste has never been a homogeneous and continuous site of encounter and it could be read more as a site of friction, power struggles, mobilisation and human agency.

In the case of Burgundy, and drawing upon the anthropological literature, several questions can be asked. What has changed in relation to taste and place? Who is driving the change? How has it become an evocative and powerful model in global commodity discourse? What are the values at the core of their relationship? These and other questions are at the heart of this book. The historical cultural construction of 'tastes' as a permanent feature of the site of production and as a complex sensory field embedded in a politics of scale is undoubtedly part of Burgundy's success. But this could not have been sustained without the role of cultural mediators and elites in maintaining the mythical link between place and taste.

I want to argue that 'Burgundy' offers a particularly relevant case-study to explore, in depth, the ways in which locality is produced not only at the local level where social groups might struggle and want to readjust themselves in their long-term self-narrative, but also at the transnational level by repositioning themselves as 'different' and the 'best' in the global world of wine. Burgundy as a wine region is constructed as a stable cultural formation, rich and historically powerful, resonating in regional, national and international terms with consumers and the wider public alike. The Côte d'Or *grands crus* offer a classic example of a geographically and historically stable site and a fluctuating, but strongly culturally defined group of producers working in a particular ecological milieu and in a specific niche market. It is because this story has hardly changed that it has acquired a powerful resonance for other producers worldwide. However, in Burgundy perhaps more than anywhere else, terroir is recognisable as the productive outcome of market capitalism and trade regulation, while simultaneously speaking to the intimate, sensory apprehension of, and semiotic significance given to, being-in-location (Escobar 2001: 152–53 cited by Paxson 2012). Moreover, it is about experiencing being-in-location through a displaced and mediated consumption of singularities. The discussion of terroir, which has often been artificially separated from the political economy of commodities, needs to engage more critically with the process of commodification.

The fine wines market in France has a venerable history in which *grands crus*, haute cuisine and social elites have long been intertwined (Karpik 2010: 136). The issue of authenticity in terms of reliable identification helps us to better understand how terroir resonates so strongly today in the market place. Authenticity is defined in Burgundy in various guises, from the unique bottle of wine bought expensively as a prestigious commodity to the wide array of possible encounters with the product, which include contact with the producer and participation in touristic activities. As Karpik has argued (2010: 136), 'inalienability and true bearers are the producers of a unique work' although, in some cases, they may have merely participated in a co-production that combines human skills and natural sources. The Romanée-Conti and other emblematic wine domains exemplify this process of extreme singularisation. This is less about the authenticity of the wine, its taste or its vintage, than the authenticity of the object produced and how it is both tracked and traceable throughout its life cycle as an object of consumption. These wines are authentic and cannot be replicated elsewhere, even if fraud has been a recurring problem in the wine sector.[6] Some of the emblematic wine villages of Burgundy combine these characteristics, but the majority of producers benefit from the imaginary story weaved around these wines and their consumption. The agency between the place, as an immutable and historically located site of tastes, and its ability to redefine itself without changing contributes to its long-lasting construction as a unique and economically priceless site. This growing singularisation of wines derives from a strategic alliance between critics, producers and *haute cuisine* (Karpik 2010: 143). This is this complex edifice of terroir that the following will investigate from its historical construction to its institutional development and through its social and transnational deployment.

The Historical Construction of Place and Taste in Burgundy

For the most reputable vineyards, the history of wine has traditionally been associated with the concept of place. Even in its most primitive form of production, wine was subject to enormous variations in quality. What caught the attention of our ancestors was therefore mostly the effects of the beverage and it is only very recently that taste has emerged as a central feature in wine culture. As Martine Chatelain-Courtois (1984: 5) puts it, 'No other food, but wine has such an intimate relationship to language ... It is the only product that requires comment' (author's translation). Consequently, very early on, the place of production provided a way of identifying the origin of a wine more accurately. As Steven Shapin (2012: 54) commented: 'The Romans took as a matter of course that there were very good, good, mediocre, and bad wines; they knew quite well which regions produced the best wines (Falernian wine was evidently the gold standard); and they ascribed degrees of goodness partly to taste and partly to medical consequences'. Over the centuries, tastes in wine have come to play a more substantial part in the product's definition, but what has remained central to its appreciation is its relationship to place and the desire to locate the area and the year of production when consuming the beverage.

The transition from the sparse to the elaborate, from medicinal implications to aesthetic analysis, from a leading concern with goodness (authenticity and soundness) to an interest in the analytical description of components, flavours and odours in wine, characterised the main historical shifts attached to the discourse of taste (Shapin 2012: 54). From Aristotle to Henri d'Andeli's satirical poem *La Bataille des Vins*, wines have been the object of contestation and discernment and a wide range of appreciations which have often been geographically rooted. In this *bataille* Burgundy has often been held in high esteem because of its historical reputation as an ancient site of production and it has long been associated with a plurality of tastes as well as a wide range of places such as Beaune or Volnay. For example, Cyrus Redding, a British journalist and wine writer, was already commenting in 1833 about the plurality of distinctive tastes attached to Burgundy and its villages: 'Among Côte d'Or burgundies, Nuits-St. George possesses exquisite flavour, delicious bouquet and great delicacy. *Le Montrachet* is notable for its finesse, lightness, bouquet and exquisite delicacy, having spirit without too great dryness and a luscious taste without cloying; and Volnay is a fine, delicate, light wine' (Redding 1833: 67). Yet this is still far from contemporary descriptions of tastes.

In a recent book devoted to the history of the idea of terroir, Thomas Parker (2015: 9–12) argues convincingly about the broader context in which terroir, from the Renaissance to today, has developed, providing an insight into how gastronomic mores were linked to aesthetics in language, horticulture and painting and how the French used the power of place to define the natural world. Citing a wide range of historical sources and encompassing various academic disciplines and different periods, Parker believes that terroir is instrumentalised by the governing elites to help form 'the taster's mental construct of the region in question' (Parker 2015: 3). Terroir is constructed as affecting taste and conveying a sense of specific regional identity savoured initially through words and poetry, and later through wine and food (Parker 2015: 36). The diversity of France is the key to this expansion of the concept and its regional deployment as part of the nation building process.

As discussed, the discourse on taste associated with place originally formed part of the regional wine literature, and if this discursive field can be seen as heterogeneous, fragmented and a-historical, it is nevertheless the case that it was the pillar of later writings about local wines. Anthropologically speaking, wine has always been a commodity that is not simply an item of consumption, but also valuable as a gift, a facilitator of exchange, a symbol of power, a religious ritual and a vector of sociability. The history of Burgundy wines as a commodity is a history of elites, power and prestige. Rulers, the Church and the most powerful of this world have all consumed or been given Burgundian wines. In order to facilitate the wine trade, the profession of *courtiers-gourmets* was created as early as the fourteenth century and their role was officially demarcated by a series of regulations enacted in 1607 (Morris 2010: 33). Interestingly, their job specification was first and foremost to regulate more and more strictly the wine market, especially the territorial and fiscal governance attached to the town of Beaune. Tasting was central to their appointment and at the time they had to prove their expertise by being able to recognise the same wine presented in two different cups (Delissey and Perriaux 1962). The *courtier-gourmet* needed to taste all of the wines from the same area of production to vet their belonging to the same *marque*, that is to say under the same place's name. Their venal office was clearly linked to the emergence of the first *maisons de commerce* or *négociants* such as Maison Champy in 1720. What is striking about their role is the obligation to guarantee that the wines were 'bons et loyaux' or good and authentic, and identifiable as coming from a specific place.

The concept of origin was later to become the key to French quality wine production. By the early eighteenth century, merchants from outside the region were coming to Burgundy to prospect for good wines and they naturally sought out the expert advice of the *courtiers-gourmets*. Before the French Revolution, Louis XVI's cellar contained prestigious wines including Clos de Vougeot 1774, Richebourg 1778, Romanée St-Vivant 1774, Chambertin 1774 and 1778, and La Tâche 1778 (Morris 2010: 26). Later in the century fledging *négociants* began to travel abroad to search for clients. In many instances wine was added to an existing commercial portfolio, frequently related to the cloth trade (Morris 2010: 35). If this profession, which still has an important role of intermediary in the contemporary local wine trade, can be seen as the first attempt to establish a tie between place and taste, it was nevertheless the market organisation and regulation, the fiscal context and the fight against fraud which were the primary forces behind the professional emergence of the *courtiers-gourmets*. The discussion of taste and place needs to be contextualised against the broader background of French wine production and consumption.

The historical constructions of place and taste in contemporary Burgundy have always been understood in the plural and they have played a major part in constructing the story about wines while offering a wide repertoire to choose from when honing contemporary strategies of engagement with globalisation. Yet this could not have developed into an economic strategy without the role of cultural mediators interacting in a complex fashion in this politics of scale. For generations there has been a rich range of specific discourses attached to wines from Burgundy and the particular grapes – Pinot Noir or Chardonnay – tasted. It is clear from historical texts that all the wines were always 'good' and specific *village* and *crus* had a particular *goût du terroir*. In Burgundy, more than anywhere else, the relationship between place and taste has been constantly emphasised in the regional discourse, presented through the plural evocation of villages and perpetuated as one of the powerful stories of the place, which have been constantly forged and reconfigured. It is a place which is synonymous with both diversity and continuity, past and tradition while engaging with the standardisation of the wine industry and the pressures of the market. The use and reuse of history is therefore central to Burgundy's definition of quality wines and tastes.

Regional literature has, since at least the eighteenth century, contributed to this construction of place, showcasing what has come to be seen as a global reference in the world of wine. Understanding the relationship between place and taste, in this context, requires the unpacking of the multiple ways in which they have been connected historically or of the strategies by which specific groups or individuals have used taste to engage with, and to adapt to, the changing global context. The permanence of the relationship between taste and place has been maintained through the constant reiteration of long-lasting references about each site as a unique sensorial field with its own singular authenticity and historical depths. Yet when analysed more closely, it is clear that the story of wine production is separate from that of the taste of place. Moreover, these two literary fields have emerged separately and were relatively heterogeneous. It is only recently in the light of the UNESCO application that they have come to be closely related, as if they were only one story, and that campaign illustrates the extent to which the close link between place and taste has been reactivated as part of a new strategy of rebranding Burgundy, its authenticity and its singularity in the changing world of wine.

To illustrate my point, it is helpful to explore in greater detail this global story and how it was reimagined in the context of the application for UNESCO World Heritage status. The region has been famous for its high-quality wines for nearly '2000 years' and superficially Burgundy appears to be stable and unchanging, a region arrogantly proclaiming to be a 'terroir béni des Dieux' or 'soil blessed by God'. Nowhere is this ideal better illustrated than in a YouTube clip promoting the UNESCO campaign.[7] It shows a gathering of local dignitaries, including leading members of the wine profession and politicians, standing in the vineyards and watching an actor dressed as a monk recount his tale.

> Have you asked yourself why and how? Why and how the *climats* or the terroir were born here? You're thinking about the Romans, aren't you? I am sure the Romans, but not the Benedictines, they arrived after the Romans, just to reorganise everything. They didn't know how to do it amongst the chaos and the ruins they found. They asked themselves, how could we do it? Let's think Greek, and they thought about the great Greek philosopher Aristotle who said that the world can be understood by following the natural lines. The Benedictines understood that and thought about it. They observed the soil and they tasted the soil. They said why does the snow stay here and not here, why does water stagnate here and not here? They asked themselves all these questions and above all they tasted the soil… (author's translation)

This picaresque scene is a perfect illustration of some of the most enduring clichés about Burgundy and its wines. As Burgundy was the site of Cluny and other great monastic orders, the figure of the monk is perhaps the most iconic. The monastic trope guarantees the historical authenticity of the region and its long-lasting search for quality and good taste. History, religion and the ties to the soil have all served as the guarantor of the place and its reputation. In contrast to viticulture in the New World, history here is used to claim a rootedness and uniqueness. This apparent timelessness seems to lie behind the decision in 2008 to apply for UNESCO World Heritage status, thus securing a global seal of approval for a unique local space and culture identifiable through the taste of Burgundy's wines. At the heart of Burgundy lies 'bottles which are rich in flavour, delightful, civilised and long – and certainly plural' (Morris 2010: 15).

The reiteration of the link between place and taste forms part of a broader articulation of history, folklore and culture in which regional writings on wine have always played an important part in telling the story. The French literary corpus of viticultural literature dates back to at least the eighteenth century, from the commercial and professionally orientated to more folkloric and literary styles, but they have all contributed in one way or another to the propagation of the terroir story. Most contemporary publications on wine can trace their origins back to these older literary genres and they seek to use history as a way of legitimising contemporary understandings of Burgundy and its wine. It might be best described as the cumulative literary edifice of terroir in which new local strategies need to be embedded by referring to the past. At the regional level, this is still dominated by a repertoire of essentially folkloric literature which constructs Burgundy wine and gastronomy as a complex sensory field, characterised by its tradition of hospitality and sociability, *bons goûts* and *bonne chère*. This is about experiencing an idyllic pre-modern sociability embedded in its terroir before the pressures of fast capitalism and modernity, and it is imagined as a return to a pre-industrial conception of place.

The writings of Jacky Rigaux[8] illustrate this re-invention of Burgundy as a place where terroir matters and where authenticity is rearticulated through a new politics of taste. Yet what he means by taste is not the sensorial characteristics of each plot or each wine, but the ideological engagement towards a specific conception of terroir, that is to say a sensorial field that reflects the gustative characteristics of place (see Chapter 7) and corresponds to the *air du temps*. For Rigaux, who is a passionate believer in Slow Food, terroir wines are to be judged in the mouth with our gustatory sense. It is an approach to evaluating wine that he calls 'Geo Sensing', or tasting the land, a phrase that recalls that of the monk described in the clip above. Tannin quality and persistence cannot be technically reproduced, they are the product of a unique place.[9] Indeed, his vision forms part of a recent shift in this regional literature that is inspired by broader ideological movements such as Slow Food and is marked by a greater preoccupation with environmental issues, a re-interpretation of place where terroir is directly translated through a non-interventionist stance towards the site of production in sharp contrast to the mechanised approach of the immediate post-war period.

This shift is echoed by the English-language literature on Burgundy wines where there has been an attempt to promote a better understanding of the region by publishing guides or descriptions of the sites of production. The Anglophone writers who are proficient in French also pick up on specific local discussions or debates and then relay them at the international level, testing their economic and marketing appeal to consumers. Recently, Jasper Morris has written of having the courage to do nothing (not working the land), which was inspired by a quote from one of the landowners in Meursault, emphasising this return to terroir (2011: 70). Several British and American writers have contributed to the retelling of the Burgundian story as engaging with the wines of the region is something of a *rite de passage* in the professional world of wine critics, a crucial step in their acquisition of a reputation. These publications also contribute significantly to the international commercialisation of Burgundy, ensuring the continuity of the Burgundian story and seeking to make its wines more accessible by unpacking the complexity discussed above. Anthony Hanson, Clive Coates, Remington Norman as well as Matt Kramer and Jasper Morris have all contributed to this repertoire where the descriptive dimension of the place of production is omnipresent and where place erases tastes. Their writings have contributed to the making of Burgundy, adding new stones to the cultural edifice represented by the terroir story. In the preface to *Inside Burgundy*, Jasper Morris posits that everybody tastes wines in different ways while his predecessors were more prescriptive in linking places to tastes (Morris 2010: 14).

The Politics of Taste

As we have seen, the politics of taste relied for several centuries upon the work of specific cultural and commercial brokers who spread the gospel about the wines of Beaune and its surrounding villages. Most of the discourse of taste at the time was dominated by *négociants* and wine merchants and by their commercial strategies which attempted to differentiate a wine, a particular vintage or a place of production from their competitors. While wine experts were neither willing nor able to assign specific descriptive characteristics to particular wines, a relatively durable set of flavour and bouquet categories were visible from early in the nineteenth century (Shapin 2012: 66). For Shapin, this way of talking about the tastes and odours of wines provided a pattern for much subsequent nineteenth-century writing. A description of Richebourg, one of Burgundy's most prestigious wines, for example, compared its colour and body to Romanée-Conti and judged it to possess 'a great deal of *sève* and *bouquet*', while Chateau Haut Brion in Bordeaux has 'a fine bouquet, a more aromatic *sève*, but less *bouquet*' than Chateau Margaux 1973 (Jullien 1824: 115). Such a rich and sharply focused discourse on place and taste characterised only a few reputed and emblematic vineyards where political and religious power resided and to some extent still does. These emblematic sites were situated within a sea of small and highly productive vineyards which were serving no other purpose than to quench the national thirst, but would later benefit from the construction of Burgundy as the paragon of excellence in wine production.

The systematisation and use of local names in commercial practices is relatively recent, probably corresponding to a new form of self-protection in an increasingly open economy (Fourcade 2012: 526). Labbé (2011) situates the beginning of the movement in the 1740s, when he identifies a shift from the generic denomination of Beaune (the main commercial city in Burgundy) to that of individual villages in commercial sales; the first organised protection of place names took place in 1766. As Fourcade (2012: 526) argues, the rigid system of geographically based qualifications that is characteristic of the terroir logic thus emerged progressively out of deeply rooted political conflicts over the economic advantages to be derived from the commerce of wine. Until the establishment of the AOC system, the *courtiers-gourmets* were in a dominant position, able to dictate wine prices and to claim a certain taste attached to a place. At the time of the 1855 Bordeaux classification, Burgundy relied on the *courtiers-gourmets* to regulate the wine economy. Lavalle (1855) explains that wine prices were officially fixed by *courtiers-gourmets* – often themselves brokers or growers – who were recruited by local mayors to taste the various wines produced in their commune's territory. For Colman (2008: 11), price was in fact the main factor in determining the producer's place in the wine hierarchy, although the brokers also performed several tastings.

The discussion on place and taste during this earlier period was above all about constructing places in economic and governance terms and the wine industry was seen as one that needed to be regulated more strictly than most others. Wine is an ambiguous product; on the one hand, it represented a jewel in the crown economically speaking, contributing to the nation's wealth, while on the other hand, it necessitated stricter social regulation due to the damaging consequences of alcohol abuse. In this context, taste can be seen as a cultural mechanism for controlling consumption and preventing social disorder. The politics of taste in France can therefore be read as a way of maintaining the balance between these different objectives. Here again, as is the case in other fields, culture has been used as a strategic tool to ensure that a social balance is maintained. Yet the politics of taste is also about the ways in which the local economy interacted with the national one at a time when there was a powerful political drive to construct the national identity. Burgundy illustrates the contradictions within this economic and political process as, it could be argued, the local economy was internationalised much earlier due to historical, political, social and geographic positioning.

Once the AOC system had been established, place names became formally recognised as the primary denomination for wines (as opposed to, for instance, grape varieties) and terroir acquired both a legal definition and a more positive connotation (Fourcade 2012: 528). This process protected place recognition through the idea of the origin and the development of a local quality charter. Yet, as Laferté (2006) has demonstrated, it came about as the fruit of a realignment of rural politics, the triumph of small and large property owners backed by radical and socialist representatives against the few capitalist businesses with conservative political allies. The governance of the AOC saw the emergence of the *appellation* as a collective name, not limited to one producer only, but officially recognising the products of local wine growers' associations called *syndicats*. In fact, the governance of quality wine making defies conventional interpretations of French law and culture because if the state played the decisive role in wine governance, most of the rules were imposed by the wine producers themselves (Colman 2008: 38). In Burgundy one of their main principles was based upon the notion that reduced supply creates value and this became the dominant commercial strategy of several domains from the 1970s onwards: 'One place, one producer, one vintage, and only a few bottles per year allocated to one consumer/buyer', commented a local wine buyer.

It was only between the two world wars that taste emerged as a matter of expert knowledge, especially in gastronomic circles (Karpik 2010: 136). Geneviève Teil (2012: 478) argues convincingly that regardless of whether terroir exists or not, taste, even protected from external influences, is so much a personal subjective phenomenon that it cannot generate 'a taste of the place' independently from the individual experiencing it. While the origins of tastes are usually objects-in-the-world, the experience of taste belongs to the individual human subject, and no other person can know just what it is that someone else tastes and smells. Teil's analysis is shared by a growing number of wine experts. Yet for the majority of producers something is happening between the place of production and the object 'wine' they have produced. The AOCs, which in the case of Burgundy constitute the heart of wine production, played an important part in enabling the establishment of a link between taste and place, but the profession was also helped by the role of cultural mediators and wine critics. The development of modern wine criticism, which emerged earlier in England and the USA, contributed to the building of a new world of wine from the 1970s onwards. As Fernandez (2004) has perceptively remarked, the style and logic of professional wine tasting depends, in part, on the taster's position vis-à-vis the dominant actors in the world of wine. Originally AOCs were suspected of not judging a result but only of indicating a 'potential' quality. Geneviève Teil (2010: 257) noted that it was not until 1967 that a yearly tasting of AOC wines, which was already quite common but not compulsory, was added to a series of constraints listed in the denomination decree. As they were considered the most knowledgeable experts, the producers were in charge of the official tasting which raised obvious questions about their objectivity, not least because they were also responsible for the definition of quality for their own sites of production, which suggests a clear conflict of interests (Teil 2010: 257).

The role of wine critics, specialist guides such as the *Guide Hachette*, American importers and wine gurus is not to be neglected in the edification of a performative sensorial field attached to Burgundy wines. The knowledge they disseminated through performative wine tastings and the writing and publication of their notes had an impact even if the engagement of wine producers towards this critical body might vary drastically, spanning everything from the traditional wine grower who will not consider any change, to the young and keen learner who seeks to sell his wines and respond to the market more actively. An excellent example of this was the sudden fad amongst wine producers in the 1990s who decided to use new oak barrels to create new wine styles suiting the market defined by their importers.

The chain of wine mediators or wine brokers constitutes the sensory field in itself, and in her analysis of this practice, Jung (2014) writes of the 'global taste knowledge' composed of a heteroclite and diverse, but hierarchised, group of sensorial fields in which a few landmarks dominate the world order but could also be the subject of reorganisation and renegotiation, a kind of 'field of action and for action'. In this constant process of adjustment, wine critics set the tone and choose whether or not to pick up debates or to push specific views over sites of production. Local and global actors are here arbiters of taste in the reproduction of a global wine hierarchy (Jung 2014: 27), and they contribute to the replication of the terroir narrative by legitimising, or questioning, the performativity of tastes in different settings as a central feature of the world of wine. What is happening at the global level is not only a replica of the local engagement of each individual producer with taste and place, but also a transnational negotiation, adjustment and continuous imbrication of some of the core values around which the global world of wine is constructed.

In this creative engagement with the global world of wine, which is characteristic of the most successful and innovative local wine producers, the AOC functions as a hegemonic and constraining framework which for some constitutes a 'sensory field' of alienation. Barrey and Teil (2011) have used the concept of authenticity to refer to some of the debates concerning this new generation of young wine growers who often get their wines refused by the taste agreement (the legal process by which a wine is given an AOC) organised by their fellow producers. Such reactions are especially acute in relation to so called 'natural wines', which even in Burgundy have enjoyed some success. In most cases, these wine growers seek to control their own active intervention and use as little SO_2 (sulphur dioxide) as possible. They claim that they are seeking a return to the roots of terroir; according to one of our informers, there was a case of a wine grower who saw his wines rejected and was told to empty the bottles in the sink, despite the fact that they were already prepared for delivery to a Japanese importer. Yet as Barrey and Teil (2011) have pointed out: 'it is wines that meet the strongest constrained specifications'. The approval procedure which enables producers to display the AOC is not a conclusive test; rather, it indicates the 'defects' so that the producer can correct them and rectify the wine. But these producers consider these prescriptions as a source of bad practice that can lead to the loss of a faithful expression of the quality of the soil. In Burgundy, the strong territorial and professional identity has facilitated the recognition of such wines through working parties organised by the BIVB and through AOC local committees, giving the collective a more active role in shaping the taste of place.

Tastings in Social Contexts: 'This is About a Philosophy of Wine and Life'

Taste has been deployed historically as a strategy to add more value to the politics of place. At the professional level, the aim was to guarantee the origin of wine and ensure that any external change or pressure to adapt the taste of place to consumers' needs would be mitigated, stopped or controlled. It was about preserving terroir and it is still about maintaining what Burgundy stands for. Until recently, the AOC system helped to fix the image of an a-historical terroir producing a wine with a taste unchanged since time immemorial. Through the definition of quality, taste and geographic origin, it was possible to ensure that existing social and professional hierarchies were consolidated to guarantee the status quo. In the world of wine producers, the concept of a taste belonging to a specific plot was not necessarily expressed and the emphasis was placed on the natural and geological characteristics of the vineyard rather than on the qualities of the final product. Taste was not articulated in a sophisticated way at the time of our first ethnographic fieldwork because there was no normative discourse on taste in the wine market, or at least not in an accessible and democratic way. Taste, and its definition, were first and foremost the prerogative of the *négociants*, who had control over the commercialisation of most of the wine production and the key markets. Wine producers had rarely tasted wines other than their own and it is only since the 1970s, when the *négociants* began organising local wine tastings, that producers have realised their wines were different from those of their neighbours. This was interesting considering that most of the producers were already selling part of their production directly to a local or international clientele, who, according to them, were increasingly keen to acquire more information about their products. Wine growers started to develop a greater understanding of the taste of the place when they began to compare their products with those of their neighbours under the same AOC. It is difficult to identify precisely when it happened as it was a progressive shift at the local level from the 1970s onwards. As the market competition increased, producers were increasingly keen to compare their products: 'It is only when we went to the wine fair in London that we really started to taste our colleagues' wines', was how one well-known producer explained matters.

It would not be fair to generalise this sociological point as the groups composing the rich social fabric of the Burgundian landscape are more socially diverse than has been assumed, which means that levels of education, landownership, wine knowledge and engagement towards the global wine economy reflect a wider range of positioning in relation to what producers would define as 'quality' and 'taste'. These different perspectives also define access to different sensorial fields with events, key actors, chefs, wine critics all helping to shape their own understanding of how their wines taste. This social and sensorial tapestry is characterised by the leading role played by a number of influential *propriétaires*, a handful of dominant *négociants*, and a majority of small- and middle-size domains who have established themselves in the market. Several commentators have noted that the Bordelais are merchants and businessmen, not farmers. Burgundy is the other way around (Pitte 2005). This impression has been shared by a number of foreign commentators who have encountered the folkloric marketing strategy analysed by Laferté (2006). But beyond the local culture and its display for international consumers, or the strong stereotype depicting the Burgundian *vignerons* as 'food loving peasants, whose hands are always calloused and deformed by manual labour' but nonetheless have 'large piles of money' that they spend on 'expensive cars like so many vulgar nouveau riches' (Pitte 2005: 6), local hospitality remains defined by sociability, reciprocity and generosity.

Over the years of fieldwork conducted in Burgundy, in the cellars, the vineyards or around the kitchen table of the wine producers, taste has rarely been the main focus of our discussions. Most of the direct encounters with the producers have been dominated by conversations about nature, climate change and wine production as a form of knowledge and understanding about life. 'Spending hours talking about wine, not only the taste of wines, but the overall experience, this is about a philosophy of wine and life', recalled one of my informers, a wine buyer with a great knowledge of Burgundy. The Burgundian ideal of hospitality and generosity relies on a specific form of sociability which is often experienced by the visitor and seems at odds with the reputation of the wines and their prices. This contrast between Burgundy as the region of great and expensive wines and of meetings with wine producers contributes to the distinctiveness of the place and its experience as an authentic site.

The symbolic or moral character of certain economic exchanges or transactions is a long-standing theme in anthropology and sociology.[10] As such, authenticity carries with it an almost sacred, cultural type of interpretation that conveys value (Frazier et al. 2009). A common sociological observation is that authenticity is not a 'real' thing or something that can be objectively determined, but rather a socially constructed phenomenon. Following this interpretation, certain specific aspects of a product, performance, place or producer somehow get defined and treated as authentic by audiences in a particular social context. Empirical studies of authenticity attempt to document the specific. Which aspects are highlighted and when? What stories are used to justify them? How do different groups interpret them and which interests seem to benefit most from these interpretations? The construction of authenticity in Burgundy is embedded in the social experience of the consumer, the meeting with the producer, the talks, the visit to the cellar and the ways in which wines are tasted and performed during the wine tasting. Sometimes, when the encounter is successful on both sides, the social experience will then be transferred into the domestic space of the wine grower and might develop into a regular commercial bond or even a lasting friendship.

The wine cellar plays an important role in terms of showcasing the wines of a producer and visits to it frequently follow a pattern involving a series of tastings, from the more recent wines to the oldest vintages, from the regional denomination to the most prestigious wines. The nature of this encounter forms part of a deeper Burgundian tradition of sociability and hospitality where wine and food play a prominent role and a specific performance takes place. This is not about a wine event, or a *foire aux vins*, or even wine competitions, this is about the direct encounter with the producer, which can take different forms depending on the level of engagement displayed by the visitor and the personality of the *vigneron*. This can range from the novice who wants to be initiated into the secrets of Burgundy wines, to the wine *aficionados* who have chosen to taste the wines from this particular producer and seek to establish a relationship with him or her. Whatever the aims of the social encounter, the wine cellar will be first and foremost the space where tastes will be displayed and experienced. Yet during my initial fieldwork, I was surprised by the absence of a specific discourse on taste. When I was invited to join my informers for a wine tasting in the cellar, the majority of them did not comment on the wines tasted; even when asked about them, the discussion rarely went beyond the description of the vintage or of specific meteorological factors relating to its production. The cellar as a social space was often characterised by a kind of quasi-religious, almost sacralised experience punctuated by tasting, spitting and a few comments or questions. Most producers remained discreet, almost shy in their own wine cellar, treating it almost as a temple or a religious site where wine is kept and preserved in contrast to its folkloric construction as a place for producing an 'authentic cachet of terroir'.

In recent years there has been a more visible emergence of the sensorial field on the part of the producers and within the wine profession. A study of contemporary websites clearly shows that taste is now one of the marketing tools used to showcase wine production and to position the producer more precisely in the sensory fields in circulation. Most producers have added wine notes to their descriptions of the range of products available on their websites.[11] One wine producer, whose work I have followed over the years, has recently developed a leaflet for his *vins primeurs*[12] which demonstrates the wide range of strategies of taste put in place around the sensorial field of Pinots Noirs. The leaflet which promotes his *primeurs 2012*, for example, is presented on a square sheet of high-quality, ivory paper, 22 x 22 centimetres; on the front cover is a series of shapes – two squares followed by two circles and then a long rectangle which is supposed to depict the evolution of the wine from the press to the second fermentation. Each of the shapes includes a special fabric with a particular colour, from a rough beige material to a more austere red linen, a silky but flaky pale red fabric to a dark red silk and, finally, ending in a soft red fabric. What is underlined in this presentation is a visual and tactile appreciation of the wine, which is presented as developing from a rough to a more refined taste. Terroir is therefore absent from the presentation and the notion of place becomes invisible through the commercialisation of *vins primeurs* to be taken over by red wines as a unique sensorial category representing the domain and its production. Interestingly, when I last visited the domain in the summer of 2012, the producer's son took the visitors to the cellar and gave us a tour, which was, from memory, more eloquently presented than those I had heard from his parents, but he remained silent in terms of the description of the taste of each place.

As we have argued, taste is at the crossroads between the objective and the subjective, the sensorial and the social. In the sensorial world attached to Pinots Noirs or Chardonnay in Burgundy, different strategies have been deployed by producers to engage with the challenge of selling their wines to an international clientele. Depending on their positioning in relation to the market, whether they sell directly to a faithful clientele or work with importers, their discourse on taste might vary drastically. For natural wine producers, a specific taste is promoted within the discourse surrounding the lack of SO_2 (sulphur dioxide), while, for a more traditional AOC producer, Pommard is about body, fruits and sharpness. In Burgundy, marketing remains based upon a personal and individual approach, even if things are slowly changing. However, the new generation of young wine growers choose to use more modern strategies of marketing. According to Fernandez (2004: 145), some wine makers are real wine experts, while others employ more commercial and local logic aimed at their traditional customers. Over the years, the majority of my older informers have produced a discourse

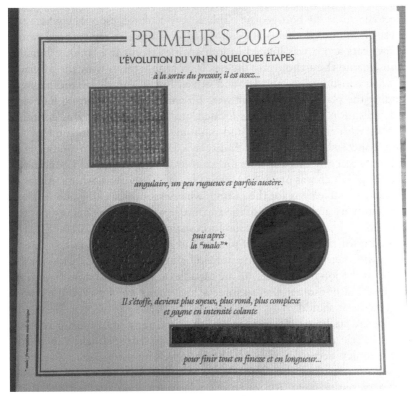

Figure 3.1 The Taste of Place? Author's photograph

on their wines as particular tastes, while the younger generation is less shy in describing their products. In the first case, the seller will multiply strategies to ensure that the product reaches the right people, enabling the cultivation of cultural collusion with players from the oenophile world, or the maintenance of good relationships with the press. These strategies are all part of a marketing culture based on the American model which is often more professionally articulated in the New World. Yet there are still some houses wedded to routine and tradition which favour the consolidation of traditional customer operations and develop strategies in that direction. Certainly, the history and formation of the wine grower and the image of his or her domain and lineage partly explain these different approaches in how to manage the reputation of their products.

In this global hierarchy of values attached to wine production and consumption, a few emblematic domains have deliberately sought to maintain a modest and humble image of themselves. This strategy has become part of their brand and of the product they sell. An image is constructed around simplicity, authenticity, discretion, modesty and *bon goût*: 'the discreet charm of the bourgeoisie'. This is very striking, especially where the most prestigious domains are concerned. I remember my surprise when, a few years ago, I was invited to join a wine tasting at a famous domain, whose name throughout my life has been synonymous with the pinnacle of wine consumption, and I found myself lost in the village incapable of finding the place. Indeed, there were no names on the door, no flamboyant indication of where it was located, no sign of wealth. This contrasts sharply with the ostentatious and monumental entrances to some of the highly successful domains which display coats of arms and majestic gates. It is only recently that the domain has moved into a renovated building in the village which was previously owned by the Cistercians, whose influence is still detectable.[13] As for the tasting, what was most striking about it was the simplicity and intimacy of the encounter with the wine manager of the domain. Following the felicitous formulation of Morris (2010: 13), 'we should resist the temptation of placing the growers on pedestals, investing them with hero status. They are human beings like the rest of us: some are better at the job than others, all are capable of making mistakes from time to time and of moments of sublime achievement when everything comes together as it should'.

Looked at from this perspective, the producers' relationship to taste relies largely on his/her positioning within the sensorial field and within the complex networks of critics, buyers, chefs and *négociants*. As several producers remarked, their attitude towards taste will depend on their own interests, engagement and questions relative to their production. Those producers who still rely on selling their vintage to the local *négociants* remain largely indifferent to the sensorial field as they do not control it, while other producers position themselves in very diverse ways in relation to it. A wide range of strategies are deployed and often this all comes down to the personality and professional trajectory of the producer. Some have worked closely with local chefs to maximise their visibility, others have sought to engage with the concept of performative taste and the ways in which they want to project their wines on the local, the national and the international stage. What seems to prevail is the wide range of sensorial engagement and the fact that it goes beyond the concept of taste to participate in a broader vision of life. In these networks around Burgundy and the sensorial fields of Pinots Noirs or Chardonnay, the notion of friendship is often articulated and emphasised, and producers and consumers find themselves related emotionally not only through the passion for the same products, but also through the sharing of the same philosophy of life. Countless times I heard in the course of my fieldwork references to wines and the special relationships established between individuals, stories about love, friendship, competition, envy, admiration and good food. It is also about pleasure, sociability, emotions and being true to oneself. These are some of the values that help to define wine appreciation.

Taste in a Transnational Context

According to Yuson Jung (2014: 27), the taste of place is not an attribute available to every wine producer, but is the product of a global hierarchy of value that gives preference to certain forms of sensory experiences and knowledge over others. The Burgundian example illustrates this point at the global level and pushes the argument further. In whatever forum, Burgundy is recognised as one of the main global players in the sensory fields of Pinots Noirs or Chardonnay and there is an assumption that specific domains, *vignerons* or *négociants* will be displayed or referred to, tasted or discussed as examples of 'the best' of what Burgundy has to offer. This discussion has, however, developed over the years and the global hierarchy of values on which it relies has also integrated new civic, ethical, political and economic concerns or processes. In the global hierarchy of values, noble vines are at the core of the concept of quality and it could be argued that a certain hierarchy of grapes and their expected tastes shape the world of wine. Indeed, Pinots Noirs and Chardonnay are prominent amongst that elite, and the wine profession and critics place great emphasis on the fine grapes which have been cultivated and preserved at the local level by *selection massale*.[14]

A striking example of the importance given to fine plants and their historical trajectory is provided by the DRC website:[15] 'The selection and propagation of "très fin" (very fine) Pinot Noir inherited from the old Romanée-Conti vineyard, an incomparable genetic legacy whose finesse and complexity determine the purity of the wines produced'. Jancis Robinson confirms on her website the supremacy of Pinots Noirs, noting the centrality of the grapes in the global hierarchy of values:[16] 'The character of Pinot Noir produced in newer wine regions can change enormously as newer, finer clones are planted. Much Pinot Noir produced in its homeland of Burgundy was disappointingly thin in the 1970s because the fashion then was to plant clones for quantity and reliability rather than wine quality'. Through the various wine tastings organised by the wine profession to display the vintage and comment upon it, as well as reflecting on the local hierarchy of producers with the newcomers or rising stars, a sense of the place and how it has evolved is integrated within this global hierarchy of values against which each region, producer and wine is evaluated and ranked.

In the global order of wine, the positioning of Burgundy is uncontestably hegemonic and historically rooted. Each wine critic who decides to engage with it chooses to do so within a longer historical sensorial narrative, as the example given by Jancis Robinson shows:

> The greatest Pinot Noir is the greatest red Burgundy, without any shadow of a doubt. In fact the *grands crus* of the Côte d'Or, the heartland of Burgundy, tower in my opinion much further above their counterparts outside France than Bordeaux's top wines do above the best Cabernet Sauvignons of, say, northern California. Other *grands crus* are on the most favoured, south-east-facing mid-slopes above the villages of Gevrey-Chambertin, Morey St Denis, Vougeot, Vosne-Romanée and on the famous tree-topped hill of Corton above Aloxe-Corton. The greatest concentration of vinous greatness is around Vosne-Romanée, with the world-famous likes of Romanée-Conti, La Tâche and, sometimes just as good, Richebourg. The first two in particular are produced in such small quantity that their prices have always been stratospheric.

Yet the global hierarchy of value might be reviewed or contested in the light of new rising wine regions that are now offering stiff competition. The recent arrival on the wine scene of Pinot Noir producers from New Zealand, through the Pinot Noir festivals organised in Wellington or Otago, demonstrates how the message of New World excellence has been relayed and communicated to different audiences. *Forbes*, the American business magazine, devoted a page in 2013 to the New Zealand wine industry and their efforts to produce high-quality pinots. Katie Kelly Bell noted in an article entitled 'A Global Tasting Proves New Zealand Pinot Noir is the World's Best Value' that 'Indeed, the historically famous contender Burgundy is finally enjoying some serious … competition.

Burgundy made an indisputably lovely showing but when considering value, well, the numbers don't lie. Burgundy will always be Pinot Noir royalty, but dynamic newcomers are set to take the stage and that can only be a good thing for the joy of Pinot for generations to come'.[17]

Yet at the local level, as argued before, each producer chooses to engage or not to do so with the sensorial spaces, from the local fair to the *foire aux vins* or the international wine festivals. Often this depends on his or her reputation, family trajectory, education and positioning within the international wine rankings. Most of the producers I have met did not have access to the big wine events and only a handful of highly reputed domains or *négociants*, who already dominate the scene, were present at these. In the Pinot Noir festival organised in Wellington in 2013 (see Chapter 7), one of the wine critics cited two of the emblematic Burgundian wine growers as his 'friends' and producers of great Chardonnay. Both names were tweeted thousands of times during the event even if their wines were not tasted on that occasion. It is a world that thrives on hypes, trends and buzz, on technological and marketing insights that come and go and on the influence of individual people who, for a while, have come to dominate certain segments of the market (Lagendijk 2004: 14). These major events are not the only fora where wine producers are tasted, evaluated, debated and ranked and the wine industry has several networks attached to the food industry, hospitality and restaurants as well as the professional and cultural world of wine associations, together with wine associations, trade journals, websites, wine experts and scholars through which and whom the circulation of knowledge – an essential part of the profession – flows. These fora all contribute to the multiple sensorial fields of wine in which reputations are consolidated, stories are repeated and newcomers establish their reputations. A great deal of competition is taking place between producers, styles of wines, regions and countries in the world of wine. Yet against this fluid and ever-changing background, we should not forget the dinosaurs of the wine industry who cultivate and try to maintain their dominant place in the political economy.

In the world of wine, taste is a multi-dimensional, multi-scalar and multi-sensorial experience that allows us to understand and interpret the complex and nuanced aspects of everyday encounters, thereby broadening the study of food and taste in exciting new directions (Jung and Sternsdorff Cisterna 2014: 4). The recent fashion for natural wines and more ecologically defined products is an example of how contemporary societies have become increasingly concerned about how their food and wine is produced. Producers too, even in emblematic Burgundy, have since the 1970s begun to engage with more ecologically defined practices (see Chapter 4 and 8). Organic, biodynamic and natural wines are becoming commonplace on wine shop shelves (Black and Ulin 2013: 242). In Burgundy, *biodynamie* is often associated with some of the well-known domains even if the term covers a wide range of practices and has a great deal of mysticism attached to it, while organic wines are only produced in a handful of domains. The work of some of these producers occasionally clashes with the local community in terms of the definition of tastes through the AOC commissions. Wine cannot exist without human intervention and the ongoing development of technology used in the vineyard and the cellar (Black and Ulin 2013: 243). Interestingly, the wine industry has largely escaped the intense scrutiny placed on other food products and agricultural activities, but in light of recent controversies, that is likely to change. Rather than reading on the label the description of the taste of the product, we might find that the information about its contents challenges the global wine culture and its sensory fields.

Conclusions

In Burgundy, the local discourse around taste is always about 'good taste' and I have never known a wine producer to state that his wine was 'awful'. Yet with the development of the profession of wine critic in France, and especially following the rise of wine clubs, a growing body of judgments about specific wines, written mostly by consumers and wine lovers, has transformed the field of wine culture. Yet at the local level and between wine producers, it is still not appropriate to state publicly that such and such wines are 'dreadful' to taste. Instead there is a resort to euphemisms – 'not yet reaching maturity' or 'still too young' – and it is interesting that it is only in contemporary discourses that old vintages are reevaluated. In the discourse on taste, time plays a major role in shaping the evaluation. Over the years, wine producers have increasingly engaged with the concept of taste, but their approach to it has also relied principally on public perceptions and evaluations. Taste was seen as a monolithic and largely externally defined evaluation of a product which was, first and foremost, consumed for social purposes. It then became an object of expertise and the basis for a growing social legitimacy for certain wine critics.

Historically, taste in Burgundy was associated with the role of intermediaries who were responsible for buying and selling the wines, as well as ensuring the conditions of their transport from one town to another, and often across frontiers and boundaries. Their role was to guarantee the quality of the wine during its transport. Price was intrinsically linked to that commercialisation, and ensuring that wines arrived safely and intact was a key challenge. Generally, it could be said that taste in wine was far from what it is today and palates were less refined, expectations less varied. When the glass bottle was invented in the eighteenth century, the conditions of transport became safer and taste more reliable as it was easier to guarantee that it was going to be drinkable. During that period taste became more normalised and a discourse started to emerge around specific crus or places such as Volnay *premier cru*. This discourse often relied on the colour, the nose and then the taste of the wine as well as its qualities in terms of its *longueur en bouche*. This helped the wine profession to guarantee the quality even if the actual origin of these wines was less precise than was later the case with the AOC system, established during the 1930s, in part, to combat the problem of fraud.

The ethnographic analysis of taste from the wine growers' perspective remains largely attached to an experience of pleasure, sociability and sharing, while the institutional stamp given to the *typicité* of the AOC (in terms of corresponding to the collective definition of how the wine ought to taste if it comes from this plot) is currently being challenged by an increasing number of wine producers. The recent example of a well-known producer who tried to oppose the local AOC system and was told to throw her wines into the sink is a telling example of the weight of tradition. For example, a Chambolle-Musigny *premier cru* is expected to display specific flavours and have a list of descriptors which will enable the consumer to recognise it. Yet as we have seen, taste has also transformed into a quest for individuality and for some of the producers it is a question of ethical positioning that is not always compatible with the authoritarian and normative framework proposed by the INAO (The Institut National de l'Origine et de la Qualité – previously known as the Institut National des Appellations d'Origine).

Taste in Burgundy today is central to the producer's definition of his or her engagement with terroir and the younger generation, in particular, engages more critically with the legacy of the AOC system. As one of my informers stated recently in a Facebook post: 'To produce AOC wines does not necessarily mean producing the wines that you like. Can we be more ambitious than our AOC?'

Notes

1. See, for example, Bessière (1998), Peace (2011), Pratt (2007) and Trubek (2008).
2. See also the Forbes article positioning New Zealand Pinots Noirs in relation to Burgundy: http://www.forbes.com/sites/katiebell/2013/10/07/a-global-tasting-

proves-new-zealand-pinot-noir-is-the-worlds-best-value/. Consulted on 14 July 2014.
3. http://www.lapaulee.com. Consulted on 11 July 2014.
4. For more information about this local tradition and how it fits into the local Burgundian folkloric repertoire, see Laferté (2006).
5. Defined as the understanding of a wide spectrum of cultural issues around tastes and other sensory modalities (Ritchie 1991: 192).
6. The fake wines were confirmed by government laboratory tests in Montpellier. They concluded that wines in the bottles were of mediocre quality, with 'very poor sensory qualities', and were a blend of several wines of indeterminate origin. See, for example, http://www.wine-searcher.com/m/2013/10/arrests-made-in--2-7m-romanee-conti-fraud-ring. Consulted on 3 July 2014.
7. See *La Marche des Climats de Bourgogne*, http://www.youtube.com/watch?v=VnFErwQlQtE. Consulted on 14 June 2017.
8. See, for example, Rigaux (2010).
9. See http://www.altoslashormigas.com/terroir/terroir-project/. Consulted on 30 July 2014.
10. See, for instance, Veblen (1899), Malinowski (1922), Geertz (1973) and Douglas (1966).
11. See, for example, http://www.chateau-de-citeaux.com/#/fr/content/chassagne-montrachet-village. Consulted on 14 July 2014.
12. By *vins primeurs*, the wine producers offer the chance to buy wine at a lower price and before the harvest. This helps with cash flow and it also favours long-term and established customers by giving them priority over the next harvest.
13. http://www.romanee-conti.com/#/Accueil. Consulted on 14 July 2014.
14. This means selecting the best vines and propagating them by crafting the original vine.
15. http://www.romanee-conti.com/#/ProfessionDeFoi. Consulted on 15 July 2014.
16. http://www.jancisrobinson.com/articles/jrs03402. Consulted on 15 July 2014.
17. http://www.forbes.com/fdc/welcome_mjx.shtml. Consulted on 15 July 2014.

Chapter 4
WINESCAPE

On 25 and 26 January 2014, the village of Saint-Aubin in the Côte de Beaune hosted for the first time the Saint-Vincent Tournante, to 'showcase their appellation rather than the domains'.[1] This traditional festival, created in 1938 by the Confrérie des Chevaliers du Tastevin[2] in parallel with the religious celebration of the local saint, rotates every year to one of the emblematic villages of the Côte. Over the years, the event has become part of the regional wine calendar. As Gilles Laferté (2011: 680–712) argues, it was not until after the Second World War that regional gastronomy became part of popular practices and that local people engaged with the commercial folklore initiated by the Paulée and then by the Confrérie des Chevaliers du Tastevin, and with the growing success of the Saint-Vincent Tournante, the aim of which was to find 'a folk for the folklore'.

More than any other event created between the wars by Burgundian landowners, the Saint-Vincent Tournante was first and foremost a form of folklore inspired by the religious confraternities and the cult of the patron saint of *vignerons* which aimed at creating images for the community. It progressively became the object of a strong territorial identification, not only articulating a sense of regional pride, but also challenging notions of collective belonging. The study I conducted in 1991 of the Saint-Vincent Tournante[3] revealed the attachment that local wine growers had for the festival and the extent to which it formed part of the way in which they wanted to project the image of a collective and united 'community'. Key events originally selected by the Confrérie des Chevaliers du Tastevin, such as the procession of eighty-five confraternities around the AOC area of production as well as the church service and the opening of cellars, accentuated the popular folklorisation of Burgundy and its wines.

Yet the analysis of this model created by the local elites in the 1930s and headed by the Confrérie des Chevaliers du Tastevin, opens an interesting window onto the ways in which wine production could be anthropologically analysed. Wine encompasses symbolic processes that point beyond the commodity itself (Black and Ulin 2013: 6). Neither fitting the ethnographic analysis of the world of marginalised Greek artisans so well-described by Herzfeld (2004), nor that of the French *chocolatiers* and their worldviews (Terrio 2000), wine producers are unique in ethnographic terms as they are difficult to categorise and are often described as artisans or even artists. They pose a challenge to ethnographic analysis, frequently belonging to the world of economic elites largely underrepresented in the discipline of 'anthropology at home', rather than representing the field of peasant studies which has benefitted from a long tradition of investigation in French anthropology (Rogers 1987). Anthropological research on wine as an exclusive topic of inquiry has been relatively rare over the past twenty years (Black and Ulin 2013: 1). There has been, however, a venerable European tradition of ethnographic and folkloric research conducted in the regions and often promoting local museums or political interests. In France, for example, the work of folklorists such as Charles Parrain or André Lagrange, and much later of ethnologists such as Claude Royer (1980), notably his *Les Vignerons: usages et mentalités en pays de vignoble*, offers an illustration of the enduring regional literature devoted to the wine grower. These works often focused on material culture, folklore and traditions, portraying the image of a timeless agrarian culture rooted in the soil and in the hard work it encapsulated. The painting of Charles-Francois Daubigny, entitled 'The Harvest in Burgundy', which is now exhibited in the Musée d'Orsay in Paris, offers an enduring visual image of an idealised world.

Vigneron, propriétaire, viticulteur, négociants, travailleurs de la vigne:[4] these are a few of the contemporary terms used today in everyday French conversations about wine production in Burgundy. In his *Dictionnaire universel du vin de Bourgogne*, published in 2010, Jean-François Bazin (2010: 715) defines *vigneron* as 'someone who is personally in charge of the vineyard, winemaking and domain', pointing out that his/her work has changed considerably over the last few decades. Interestingly, this definition draws our attention to the socio-economic structure of the place as well as the idea of how it has changed and how the management of nature is differentially organised between wine growers who control the production from vineyard to glass while *négociants* traditionally deal with the buying and blending of grapes. The relatively recent emergence of the wine grower as the prime figure in local wine culture, with a strong emphasis on production rather than commercialisation, is a now a key feature of the Burgundian vineyards.

From the phylloxeric crisis onwards, Burgundy has witnessed the progressive rise of the small and medium landowners, most of whom originally combined polyculture with viticulture, who have become the new wine growers as defined above by Bazin (2010: 715). As discussed in Chapter 3, wine growers, following the establishment of the AOCs, became wealthier and have expanded by stages their portfolio of vineyards. The group itself has acquired a clear sense of identification through the commodification of its products and their construction in the public sphere. Today they form, with the landowners and the *négociants*, one of the three major social categories more or less precisely defined as being in charge of wine production and commercialisation. Yet there have been constant cross-overs between these groups and the boundaries of each social category has always been fluctuating and porous. Indeed, a few wealthy wine growers decided in 2000 to open a wine shop in Beaune. Yet each of these groups has its own rules, its own cultural identity and shared values, ways of defining themselves and others. This chapter focuses on the wine growers, analytically defined here as workers of the land, and their relationship to their productive environment as well as the anthropology of care.[5] Their control of the key stages of production, from the vineyard to the glass, is at the core of the theory of how people and place, cultural tradition and landscape ecology are mutually constituted over time. Yet the economic dimension attached to the selling of their own products renders more complex the analysis of this highly successful group. In the food landscape, they present unique characteristics: they cultivate the land, produce grapes and transform them into wines that they then sell globally for prices varying from a few euros to tens of thousands of euros for a single bottle.

Wine Growers

At the heart of the Burgundian economic and social edifice, the wine growers occupy a hegemonic position as they have been able to define the AOC rules of production and to take over the commercialisation of their products. According to the recent agricultural survey, Agreste,[6] viticulture in the Côte d'Or has remained stable over the years, marked by a strong specialisation. In the last ten years, despite an increase in terms of the wine surface cultivated in Burgundy, around a quarter of domains have disappeared. The remaining units have generally expanded, employing a growing workforce, an additional 16 per cent compared to 2000 (see Agreste survey). This restructuration has gone hand in hand with the development of new societal forms to the detriment of individual units. For example, the number of EARL (Exploitation Agricole à Responsabilité Limitée, or limited liability companies) has seen a rise of 36 per cent compared to 2000, while the SCEA (Société Civile d'exploitation agricole, or farming corporation) are favoured by the big domains. Interestingly, the workforce is becoming less family orientated despite the fact that the head of the wine estate remains the pillar of the workforce.[7] It is also observed that there are less young wine growers taking over than previously, with the average age of the head of a domain being around forty-nine. Yet women are becoming more involved, with 21 per cent of domains having a woman in charge. Unlike the *chocolatiers* described by Terrio (2000), it is the nuclear family that provides the pool of possible successors – including daughters, even if the sons usually take priority – and there is no attempt to recruit outside it. In 90 per cent of cases, the successor belongs to the same kinship group, demonstrating the hegemonic, patrimonial nature of the wine industry. This can also be explained by the financially lucrative and symbolically emblematic dimension of the profession. Another distinctive element of the landscape is the important part of the production which is directly transformed and commercialised by the domain, with 72 per cent of the overall production of Burgundy sold directly. Selling bottles is now the norm for most producers.[8]

The gentrification of Burgundian *vignerons* has come about as a result of the largely favourable economic climate dating back to the *Trente Glorieuses* (a period of economic growth in France, from 1945 to 1975), and has been reinforced by the remarkable internationalisation of the wine market. For the outsider, Burgundy is characterised by the wine growers and their domains and is represented by a family name. According to Laferté (2012: 9): 'It was a model of business dynasties where the family was above all a brand image. The strategy of these family-brands of the *Côte* was to appropriate aristocratic trappings with the construction in the nineteenth century of châteaux and manor houses, the acquisition of coats-of-arms through marriage, or the design of heraldry from scratch'.

Signs of these phenomena can be clearly seen in the local architecture of villages such as Meursault or Vosne-Romanée, with some families buying a pedigree and seeking to ennoble themselves through an ostentatious performative culture. The family name constitutes a reminder of the social mobility experienced and of the enduring relationship to the land or vines. Most domains have kept, from one generation to next, the name of the lineage as a commercial marker and have also kept the same clientele of faithful consumers. Others followed a different route and sought to take advantage of the monopoly rent attached to the AOC by developing new international markets, adopting a more modern outlook and, in some cases, moving to Beaune to open a wine shop or buy properties. A strong collective rhetorical stance on ecology, which can now be seen on the websites of producers, has also emerged in recent years.

Behind the term 'wine grower' is a wide range of socio-economic positions and a constellation of different attitudes and values which characterise the two or three generations who have successfully established the reputation of the domain. What they have in common is that the domain represents the household around which each generation gravitates. In some cases, grandparents, parents and children still share their meal together on a daily basis during the week or at harvest time. The name of the domain frequently reflects the strategies and struggles that have arisen with regard to the transmission of land. 'Père et fils' (father and sons) is the most common expression coined to designate the domain, while 'père et filles' (father and daughters), if still rare, is now occasionally seen. A patriarchal system of filiation dominates the social transmission of properties. When I was conducting fieldwork in the 1990s, the issue of transmission was a recurrent theme in conversations with my informers who were all in a position of crisis on account of it. Two of my informers suffered because their inheritance was blocked, which meant that nothing could be done without parental consent. In both cases, when they became independent, they kept the family name, but changed the Christian name to impose themselves. Another informer inherited the domain following the sudden death of her father and had to pay a substantial lump sum to her sibling as well as starting everything from scratch with her husband. They opted to keep the name of the domain. Finally, the last of my four informers faced a similar dilemma and an identity crisis, but the domain is still named after his father today.

Years after this work, I was contacted by a professional accountant who was keen to talk to me about issues of inheritance and how they affected the local wine growers. However, after we had exchanged a few emails, he confessed that there was a kind of taboo and although he felt it was important to open a debate, most of his clients refused to engage with the subject. The 2015 Amplitudes plan presented by the BIVB (Burgundy wine board) endorses the importance of discussing inheritance as a professional priority: 'They want to keep their lands until the eve of their death' was described by several commentators as the normal way of doing things in Burgundy. Land prices have made inheritance more complex and economically challenging with the value of plots varying from just 30,000 euros per hectare to as much as 2,760,000 euros per hectare for the best locations.[9] In the Côte d'Or, prices almost invariably rise annually (+4.5 per cent in 2015), mainly driven by the *grands crus* and red wines of the Côte de Beaune. In 2012, the market value of vines with an AOC status rose by 3 per cent in relation to 2011.[10] Land ownership is therefore a key issue in any discussion on terroir.

For many *vignerons*, land ownership means not only ownership of a range of plots but also those they have acquired through rental or sharecropping and which are managed as part of the domain. Working the land, whatever its legal and productive status, is central to their sense of identification. The majority of the cases analysed in this study combined the three types which are often transmitted with the domain (owning, renting and share-cropping). What most of them are aiming at is to establish a portfolio of a wide range of AOCs, with a few *grands crus* or *premiers crus* leading the way and other less emblematic AOCs enabling them to keep diverse economic strategies open in case of hail or economic hardship. What emerged from my ethnographic investigation was a clear sense that wine growers did not differentiate markedly between the different types of land use. The story of each of their plots mattered more than the fact they owned it, rented it or shared it. This was about the specific relationship they established with the plot as a 'site of experience', and as one informer described matters: 'the emblem of the domain, it is *les Tessons*'. As I have argued elsewhere, even if wine producers in their discourse claim that they are behaving in exactly the same way on all of their plots, they nevertheless engage in different ways technically with each of them. This has been even more the case following the vertiginous rise in prices brought about by the global demand for those wines. What is striking is the accumulation of differentiated knowledge and experience in relation to individual vineyards. Moreover, some emblematic plots, often but not always with a higher AOC status, benefitted from more sustained attention compared to others: 'I pamper that one!'. Twenty years later this is still an integral part of how they think about their vines. There is a hierarchisation which goes beyond the AOC system and the commodification of the products attached to the plot. Each domain ends up having a specific 'champion' in terms of the range of wines they produce, and an emotional relationship characterises their engagement to the land.

From Taskscape to Winescape:
'After a While You Know What You Are Doing'

Burgundies are often presented by journalists and professional commentators as having been there for 2000 years, incarnating the quintessence of wine production. History is an integral part of the local story about wine production and several classic texts are cited to illustrate its birth in specific sites, such as the famous *Pagus Arebrignus*. Many commentators place the emphasis on the long-lasting historical establishment of the vineyards and the continuous quest for quality which can, it is said, be read by selecting key episodes from the past, such as the role of the monks or the edict of Philippe Le Bon banning the cultivation of supposedly inferior Gamay grapes. In contemporary discourse about landscape, the place is defined as eternal, quintessential, historically charged with intrinsic qualities, a soil of excellence and of religious resonance. This understanding of place is shared by wine professionals and also the wider community and remains largely the result of a recent historical construction. Yet both professionals and the public are also influenced by the ways in which individuals experience the vineyards as a site of production, consumption, pleasure or leisure. For the wine growers landscape offers one way of better understanding what terroir embodies. Terroir for them is rooted in the range of geographical locations in which their plots are expressed through the wines produced. Following Ingold (2012: 434), to understand materials is to be able to tell their histories – of what they do and what happens to them when treated in particular ways – in the very practice of working them. When applying this definition to wine production or wine as an artisanal product created by humans from a landscape, the socio-historical context of the site becomes the prime lens through which to unpack the history of the product. Wine growers here have just begun to take control and to develop narratives around their products while emphasising the terroir story as the foundation of quality wines.

The cultivation of vines is the most enduring characteristic attached to the local community of wine growers and '*aller à la vigne*' (going to work in the vines) is still at the heart of who they are as individuals and communities. The emphasis is placed on direct contact with vines, the hard labour and the micro-knowledge wine growers have acquired of their plots. The experience of many years of intensive fieldwork makes it clear that the majority of wine growers agree with this definition. The calendar of their activities is organised around regular visits to their plots, checking the impact of meteorological conditions, controlling how specific operations have been conducted by the workers they employ and just having a look to see if everything is in order.

The landscape is crafted to such a degree that it is almost comparable to an ornamental garden. The skills and actions involved in the creation of the site naturalise the site of production. Yet to the attentive observer, it is easy to spot the tiny variations in terms of ownership or methods of cultivation. The expression 'beautiful vines', commonly used by traditional producers, illustrates this visceral engagement with the land which was seen by producers as a sign of quality, despite the fact that it was previously characterised by intensive mechanisation and use of pesticides. The vineyards needed to be clean and beautiful, cleared of any unsightly debris. For the new generation of producers, the notion of 'beautiful vines' lies not only in the aesthetic of the landscape, but above all in the amount of work invested in looking after the plot, tidying it up, pruning it and making visible the direct quantity of work done. Today as practices have become more ecologically friendly, for example with the use of horses, the expression 'beautiful vines' has taken on another meaning, yet the producer needs more than before to maintain control over the vineyard during the annual climatic cycle.

As in the case of the artisan cheeses discussed by Heather Paxson (2010: 445), environmental conditions influence the development of wine and the taskscape of its production also alters landscapes – social as well as natural ones. The discussion on taskscape, defined by Ingold (2000: 195) as 'connected practices of daily life within a given environment that congeal to form landscapes', needs to be framed in relation to the social life of things, that is to say here, wine. Critics of Ingold have pointed out the absence of the political in his approach to landscape (Uchimayada 2004) and the refusal of a distinction between self and others (Brereton 2004). The example of wine permits us to go further in the discussion on taskscape. Wine growers traditionally produced small quantities of wine for their own consumption, with most of their grapes being sold to local *négociants* who actually produced the wine by blending the same crus together. That situation has been transformed, and considering the historical transformations of the Burgundian wine region, it is easy to see why wine growers emphasised work on their land as a central element of their self-identification and social differentiation. As previously noted, I met several wine growers who were unable to produce a specific discourse on their wines when tasting them. Terroir was figuratively evoked, but there was no direct connection between soil and tastes. The link was established later through the emergence of the wine experts and guides in the literary field. Wine growers have, however, become increasingly aware of the politics of taste and have tried to engage with it in different ways.

The sensory qualities attached to terroir are de facto a contemporary invention and the result of the commercial and cultural visions of the profession and wine critics as part of the internationalisation of the French wine market. The discourse on wine and taste can be seen as a product of our modernity, illustrating the necessity not only to create meanings between place and taste in an otherwise industrialised and standardised world of food, but also to justify the AOC system in the context of an expanding group of discerning global amateurs and wine lovers eager to understand the foundations of quality. Against the background of these changes, producers themselves were in need of clear signals and a language to present the gustatory and aromatic profile attached to their products, especially when competing on the international stage as they were increasingly asked to present and comment upon their wines. The definition of taste attached to specific grapes is the key to the globalisation of the wine market and to the positioning of wines in international settings of food consumption. The AOC system, reinforced through the normative definition of taste by the various AOC committees, can be seen as the relics of a narrowly and self-professed corporatist worldview which increasingly clashes today with the realities of wine consumption.

With regard to the relationship between man and his environment, wine growers in Burgundy have had to reengage with terroir in a more critical fashion. Terroir as an ideology implied a specific model of viticulture that is routinised, standardised and embedded in the wine landscape. Yet a critical approach to it requires generating thoughtful actions for bringing-into-being the site in line with what the producer seeks to achieve. In this context, the notion of winescape can be interpreted as a constituted site of an enduring record of – and testimony to – the lives and labours of past generations who have dwelt upon it, and, in doing so, have left something of themselves (Ingold 2000: 189). It can also be envisaged as a modern experimental site of constant adjustment between economic value, taste and place. As Heather Paxson argues for cheese making, reverse engineering[11] terroir offers a new way of locating value. Interestingly, it is in the place where terroir was first born and in the most traditional of wine regions, Burgundy, that wine producers wish to create a new signification of place through environmental stewardship and the crafting of history through *climats*.

In a recent article published in *Sociologia Ruralis*, Anna Krzywoszyncka (2015: 305) speaks of an anthropology of care which relies on the centrality of situated expertise providing a better understanding of the nature of vine growing: 'The centrality of situated expertise to care … suggests that a practical recognition of uncertainty flexibility and adaptation as characteristic of care and of expertise in farming, merit further attention by scholars and policy-makers alike'. In her article, Krzywoszyncka, using auto-ethnography and the acquisition of a new competence in the field such as pruning as 'enactment of cares', illustrates convincingly how variable viticultural practices are and how they rely on local adaptation, tinkering to enable the social reproduction of the wine estate. In the work I conducted in the 1990s in Burgundy, not only it was clear that a certain degree of uncertainty and tradition ('I do the same as my Dad') dominated the anthropology of care of three of the four domains I worked in, but it was also the case that their personal stories were about differentiating themselves from the past and learning from scratch as a consequence of a major crisis of professional transmission caused by bereavements or other serious matters (Demossier 1999). Over the years I also observed this care becoming more situated, more self-reflexive and more embedded for them in their engagement with both the natural cycle of the plant and the wine produced from one vintage to another.

The anthropology of vine care is therefore partially rooted in the accumulation of a working experience over several generations of growers with different expectations about their products, the politics of the place and its commercialisation. It is also characterised by a complex and highly fragmented series of caring activities which punctate, often independently, the management of the whole vineyard, providing various situated challenges to the wine grower and ultimately culminating in the wine making and processes of fermentation transforming the grapes into wine. Establishing connections between knowledge and practices in a specific embedded locale and in the context of a particular climatic year is particularly revealing of the challenges attached to the profession. Transforming these juxtaposed operations into wine through a process of fermentation adds another stressful dimension for producers. It is therefore easy to understand why stories, rituals and beliefs matter when one is facing the uncertainty of the outcome.

Differentiated Social Engagement and Embodiments: 'The Big Ones Plow'

In this context, *climats* exemplify the shift described above from the geological argument to the recognition of the wine grower as the mediator in the expression of terroir. While terroir remains the trump card at local, national and global levels, the campaign for UNESCO recognition, by using the *climat* argument (historical depth of the place combined with a micro-identification and a wine grower), introduces a new set of values and meanings which embrace international preoccupations and ensure that the heritage factor will add further value to the place and the product (Chapter 8). After the success of the UNESCO bid it seems reasonable to conclude that the 'natural' connection between place and culture will remain at the core of what defines Burgundian wines in an international context. Yet the winescape will be impacted as it will oblige the producers and the wider communities to act upon it. On several occasions, one of my informers reminded me of the importance of using the term 'vigneron' although he was mostly defined within the community as a landowner. Yet when we were tasting wine in his cellar, it became clear that he was not involved directly in the cultivation of his vines. The key issue in terms of social stratification and discourses produced here is that of land ownership and economic positioning in an era of intense European and international debates. Following Robert C. Ulin (1996), in Burgundy, as in Bordeaux, work and labour are fundamental values underpinning the self-identification of wine growers in a world where both are becoming contested by 'flying wine makers', capitalism and the standardisation of technologies.

The discussion on winescape cannot be separated from the socio-economic and political configurations. The engagement towards the product is also conditioned by the social life of wine. As discussed previously, the social organisation of production was traditionally defined by the *vignerons* who produced and sold their grapes or grape juice directly to wine merchants. Until the 1970s and in some instances later, only the wealthy landowners were masters of the whole of the production cycle. The landowners were defined by their social status and their connections, and every village counted, and still counts, a few of them. By contrast, the wine merchants focused on the end product and the mass market. By blending different wines from the same AOC, the *négociants* were able to produce a more stable and reliable product for their clientele. Many years ago, Pierre Poupon, a reputed buyer for one of the *négociants*, who was also a wine writer, told me: 'Yes it is true most of them have never tasted other wines than their own and it is only since I began organising local wine tastings in the 1970s that they realised their wines were different from those of their neighbours'.

Despite this apparently patronising comment, most of the wine growers were indeed separated from the commercial side of their activity and produced their wines in association with local *négociants*. Thus, until the 1990s taste and its expression were largely absent from definitions of terroir and quality. If a few pioneers were already engaged in bottling their wines by the 1950s, it did not become the norm to sell wines directly to a clientele until the 1990s. It was during the intervening period, especially from the 1970s onwards, that the relationship between taste and place became stronger, especially with the work of the wine critics and the proliferation of French wine drinking culture.[12] Yet it is worth noting that this process was far from homogeneous and there were still striking differences between domains at the local level. When I first engaged in fieldwork, it was common to hear examples of landowners who had inspired the local producers to become involved in the commercialisation of their products. For example, one reputed domain in Puligny-Montrachet was cited as belonging to a pioneering landowner who established the reputation of the white wines from the village in the American market. As competition has increased, discussing business matters is now a more private affair.

As a result of the increasing take-over of the commercial sphere by the wine growers and their recognition in the global wine industry, making a difference has increasingly become a key issue for success. Following the growth of the wine market and due to the impact of generational changes and the development of wine education, more wine growers wanted to make their own wine, bottle and sell it. As a result, they began to be open to the idea of taste, engaging more actively in the making of better quality wine and contesting more openly the role of geology in the definition of quality. Wine making was thus competing with viticulture, and this led several domains to divide tasks along these lines across the generations: 'C likes to go out and work in the vineyards while P is very good with the cellar and meeting visitors'.

Historically speaking, for wine producers making wine represented another stage in their social emancipation as they were able to produce and sell their products directly to a clientele they had inherited or built up. By the 1990s wine making was a major area of debate amongst local producers and making a difference mattered. The acquisition of oenological competence and the development of a strong oenological culture coincided with the emergence of a wine discourse on taste. Interestingly, it is only in the last two decades that AOCs were, gustatively speaking, not only defined by wine producers but also by wine lovers trained at the local level. Landscapes of tastes emerged strongly and started to play an important role in promoting products and defining them at the territorial level. A Chardonnay from Meursault became distinct from a Chardonnay from Puligny. Taste became the foundation of this new performative culture of tasting (Chapter 3).

The experience of years of fieldwork has convinced me that in terms of wine making competence, knowledge and skill, the situation is extremely heterogeneous. Each individual story is unique in its own right. Yet there is also clearly a common technical culture of looking after your vineyards and making wine. Perhaps, surprisingly, wine growers in Burgundy, as in Bordeaux (Ulin 2002: 700), were initially reluctant to embrace oenology, and many refused to abandon their traditional methods and were suspicious of the outsiders who were held up to them as a source of modern scientific expertise. The first generations of wine growers to be trained at the local *lycée viticole* of Beaune exemplifies this traditional group, which was initially very wary of the rising power of the oenologist. When interviewed in the 1990s, most of my informers thought of the oenologist as 'the wine doctor', who was called upon only in case of a specific problem or to check the final stages of vinification (fermentation during the wine making process). For these wine growers, maintaining control of the work process was crucial, especially in the context of their recent development of the commercial side of the domain. However, amongst this same generation it was becoming increasingly common to attend training courses at the local university in order to obtain the *Diplôme National d'Oenologie*, which was perceived as the most valuable scientific diploma at the national level.

These wine growers are now in many ways the leaders in the field and they also occupy a central position in local viticulture. They are very well connected to different segments of the wine industry, and are generally the most willing to experiment, and they are firm believers in the concept of terroir, as well as being actively involved in local matters contributing to the regional dynamism of Burgundian viticulture, maintaining links to the university in Dijon, and travelling to different wine producing countries, especially the USA, Australia and New Zealand. A wider process of negotiated social differentiation and distinction has occurred, although viticulture is the field of action in which different professional practices define the wine maker as artisan and the guarantor of the true expression of terroir. In this context, taste became a crucial factor in establishing the normative framework for deploying the highly hierarchised range of AOCs. It also recently became an area of contestation between different visions of terroir, that of terroir seen as a gustative norm dictated by the AOC and rooted in a traditional way of making wine, as opposed to a more engaged, alternative vision of taste claiming to be closer to nature and the soil.[13]

Another major change in terms of the wine landscape is the role of women, who have become an important feature of local viticulture in the last two decades. Several leading domains are now headed by women and their presence in the field is defined by innovation coupled with a high level of wine education. They are young, willing to question tradition and happy to engage with professional associations. I remembered visiting a well-known female wine grower in the 1990s as part of a study devoted to women in the industry and was surprised by her approach to wine making, which was highly unusual in the Burgundy landscape. Terroir was at the centre of her viticultural approach, albeit not in a traditional sense. Instead, she was prepared to test and experiment, even to the extent of combining grapes from different AOCs or locations. I was taken to the cellar of a house built in the 1960s and tasted a wide range of wines which were presented as 'the products of my experimentation with terroir'. Today 26 per cent of managers in viticulture in Burgundy are women. Their visibility is demonstrated by the multiplication of websites devoted to them. According to the website of *Femmes et Vins* (Women and Wines) created in 2001:[14]

> In the old days, women were restricted to a role of secondary importance. Here they are now! Playing the main roles, using their assets to build businesses and defend their values. They have been here since the beginning, and they have often been overshadowed by man. They were restricted to the most unrewarding tasks, that they were only entitled to be the 'wife of' ... The 21st century woman is emancipated. She holds the reins on her own, with her husband or in family. At Vinexpo or at other professional fairs, on the web... they are everywhere. Journalists started to depict the coming of feminine wines, usually, in a disrespectful way. Nevertheless women refute this idea and prefer speaking of their feminine contribution to a rather masculine, not to say male chauvinist

sector. If woman is the future of mankind, she must necessarily be the future of viticulture. Since the end of the 90's, women are taking their future in hand and forming groups.

Their high profile in key professional organisations reflects their growing recognition. There is also another less visible, but no less crucial, group of women involved in viticulture, employed for some of the tasks such as pruning, cutting or harvesting. They belong to the viticultural workforce and account for 40 per cent of employees, a rapid increase from 18 per cent in 2000.[15] They are also less qualified, in most cases have been attached to the same domain for decades, and are often presented as part of the family.

In the discussion of skills, ability and work, the engagement of each of the social groups identified above can often be detected. Donna Haraway (1988) advocates the recognition of location, that is, non-equivalent positions, in a substantive web of connections. The emphasis on location accepts the interpretive consequence of being grounded in a particular embodied standpoint (Csordas 1994: 2). A romantic discourse of the local, the traditional and the authentic has become commonplace in regional viticulture, articulated around the wine grower as the paragon of quality and the historicisation of specific places. The image of *vignerons* as working the land is almost existential and their bodies, especially their hands, face and back, speak of terroir for themselves and I have often felt impressed by this visible corporality. The traditional image of the *vigneron* has prevailed for decades, despite the intense modernisation of French agriculture and the pressures of globalisation, which threatened the concept of terroir. Thanks to their new prosperity, they increasingly leave the work in the vineyard to their trustworthy workers. Thanks to their new-found prosperity, they increasingly leave the labour in the vineyards to their workers. Yet as their actual presence in the vines has diminished, the symbolic and folkloric value of the association between producer and labour has, if anything, increased. Even if modernity has become the key element of the wine industry, the emphasis is nevertheless on the imagined, idealised and seemingly enduring links with nature. The ideal of authenticity associated with the wine grower is widely promoted by the various actors of the wine sector, and marketing practices refer to it as one of the main elements marking the specificity of quality French wines. The prevailing power of persuasion of this iconic image of the wine grower is something which is widely used by other categories of actors. One of the leading wine producers featured on the covers of several French and international wine magazines was presented with his vineyard in the background, dressed as a peasant, bending over the vines and looking like a monk. The image, which was widely circulated, demonstrates the borrowing of cultural idioms by other social actors in order to create a sense of authenticity and a meaningful experience of terroir. In the milieu of consumer culture, with its multiplicity of images that stimulate needs and desires and the corresponding changes in material arrangement of social space, the body/self has become a means of performing and of display and image (Featherstone 1991: 187 and 192).

Learning Never Ends!

As we have seen, it is very difficult to conceptualise the sheer complexity of the interrelations established between different areas of viticulture which were historically separated and became progressively part of a flow in which every stage – from plantation to growing healthy grapes and to producing good wines – contributed to the transformation chain or winescape. In this process, 'to follow the matter-flow as pure productivity' (Deleuze and Guattari 2004: 454) required the wine grower to learn how to master the overall cycle of production. Learning how to connect place and taste presented a real challenge to the new generation of wine growers. This did not happen overnight but was the result of long and repeated experimentation with nature and the market. The notion of winescape therefore offers an interesting example of complexity at stake in producing, making and selling wine. The example of J.P is quite telling. Interviewed twenty years after our first encounter in the context of my PhD, A.M made a point in telling me immediately how he 'did not recognise the practices he had described to me twenty years before' and that he was 'sure that they were truthful as he remembered that I used a recorder'. This comment illustrates something commonly mentioned by my informers, which is the fact that the learning process attached to viticulture and wine making never stops. 'This is a job where you constantly learn. From one meteorological cycle to another, you keep learning', was how one of my informers described matters and that holds true for the majority of the profession, not just the most qualified and educated. Each producer has to create a wine under a specific set of constraints which directly impact upon the final product. They start with a vision or a philosophy which they aim to implement in the way in which they approach their production. 'I always wanted to make wines like these, I have learned a great deal especially from *stagiaires* coming from all over the world', remarked A.M during our interview. Then this philosophy has to take into account a wide range of factors, whether it is defined as more terroir driven or as more interventionist or traditionalist or even experimental.

A female wine grower explained to me that she wanted to make more natural wines and distanced herself from the wines her father use to make. In contrast to the post-war generation of her parents, she rejected 'chemical' agriculture, and went back to pre-industrial traditions of vine cultivation and winemaking, producing organic wines. She was interested in natural wine and sought to limit the use of chemicals, including sulphur dioxide. Yet the issue of the market and also the recognition by the AOC agreement committee posed problems that she needed to address: 'This wine was sparkling, they did not like it, it did not correspond to their expectations in terms of the tastes of the AOC in this area. But you see I thought it was nice, you could drink it with a picnic on a nice summer's day'. Over the years, ecologically driven practices have developed and this has meant that a larger workforce was often needed. So the issue of taste became, in some cases, a point of disjuncture or a break with tradition for the local community and an area of increasing tensions between the state and the wine profession.

The majority of producers agree that as far as more ecologically friendly techniques are concerned, more work and more money are needed. This explains the fact that landowners are more likely to follow the *biodynamie* route than the average wine grower. If there has a been a growing recognition of the need to address environmental issues, local viticulture is still dominated by a group of traditionalists who, while espousing the rhetoric of environmental concerns, continue to follow what they were taught by their predecessors. This group can be defined in educational terms as those who had a traditional training at the local viticultural school and are content to hide behind their financial success. They have not faced serious economic problems as they rely on their portfolio of *grands crus* and *premiers crus* to ensure their financial security. Yet their economic position is far from secure in the long term, primarily on account of the cost of inheritance which threatens successive generations. When training their successors, however, they have demonstrated a willingness to push them towards a more educated pathway rather than 'just staying in the cellar'. Some of the trajectories encountered today are interesting as they illustrate the growing importance of foreign travel especially to the New World to learn the job, but it is often the most educated who go. The more traditional group, who remain on the domain, is often identified by the local decision-makers as a 'major obstacle in changing things' and in making sure that quality constantly improves.

The last two decades have seen the emergence of a number of small formal networks or groups of producers who have resolved to use different strategies to ensure their viability or to market their differences more strikingly. They often have in common a particular vision of their products, or share a particular segment of the market, or they have similar issues that they wish to address, for example in relation to the commercialisation of their wines. Often the connections between them were established through education and beyond the confines of the village which traditionally served as the place for exchanging knowledge and ideas. Several new websites have recently been created such as *Bourgogne: de vigne en verre*, dedicated to the promotion of the authenticity of Burgundian wines. The group includes several producers from different areas of Burgundy including Côte de Beaune, Côte de Nuits, Chalonnais and Macônnais. They present themselves as 'the wine growers who come together to strengthen the identity of the wine and claim to be dedicated to their profession: working the vineyard, making their own wines and selling them independently. Their energy goes towards a single goal: quality'. The main aim of their group is 'to enrich our differences and to cultivate our authenticity'. Another example of a grouping around the '*École du vin et des terroirs*' illustrates a different but increasingly popular facet of Burgundian wine culture. The group is more esoteric in nature and includes seven well-known leading producers with substantial fortunes; its founders offer a bold definition of their school: 'Its goal is to broaden the knowledge concerning vine and wines by offering new points of view, with an ecological, environmental and humanistic approach. This flowering of new initiatives and new poles of knowledge confirm the more open nature of local wine culture'. Yet as several commentators acknowledged: 'It is not always easy to educate the other producers. Most of them do not attend or are not interested. They have a particular idea of who they are and if they sell, they do not ask questions'. One of my informers mentioned the fact that even in the same AOC or village they do not always dare to ask each other questions, even if encouraged:

> I organised a seminar on markets and I discussed the fact that within the same AOC there were huge variations in price and the issue of commercialisation was the prime factor in price differentiation. They were all aware of for how much I sell my wines, four times the price of the average price in the AOC, but they never asked me how and why…

This is something which was echoed by key experts when conducting seminars on different issues. The local winescape is therefore characterised by a strong social polarisation.

Behind the wide range of stories and trajectories encountered on almost an individual basis lies an extreme heterogeneity of practices in wine production.[16] Yet the legacy of education and personal experience impacts on the trajectory of each wine grower and the ways in which he/she engages with the final product and thus taste. Wine experts and wine critics emphasise the importance of a new generation of talented young wine growers who are helping to transform production, but not all have the same level of engagement and commitment and, as far as quality is concerned, heterogeneity and personal trajectory play an important role in shaping the approach to viticulture. According to a survey on organic viticulture,[17] those who have a level of general education above the *baccalauréat* and who own less than 20 hectares of vines are more likely to be organic producers. Adopting this mode of viticulture seems to be generational. In Burgundy, a reluctance to resort to chemicals is also more common among young producers who make wine and sell it. Harvesting manually rather than with a machine and limiting yields are two qualitative factors that increase the likelihood of a wine producer choosing organic viticulture. This wine has a cost and the price of wine is an important factor.

During our recent ethnographic investigation, the issue of innovation rarely came under discussion. Innovation was, according to several informers, not typical of the AOC landscape. According to Susan Terrio (2000: 11), traditional groups associated with rural pre-industrial France focused less on the dynamics of change. This is particularly true in the case of Burgundy. There are many examples where terroir is presented as fossilised, the result of a long history of inertia and traditions showcased. Lionel Gratian[18] has recently argued that innovation is limited by the AOC system and the AOC decree does not mention the possibility of any innovation. What have been coined as 'local, fair and traditional practices' define the environment in which producers relate to their winescape. Moreover, any entrepreneurial innovation is often presented as 'natural' especially in the context of the *climats* discourse. Yet when we look at more closely at actual viticultural practices, small innovations become visible and help us to understand differentiation and accentuate the singularity of the domain in economic and marketing terms. Some producers decided to focus on wine making while others sought to improve viticultural practices by improving the quality of their vines. *Biodynamie* also contributes to this reframing of the AOC system in a more innovative fashion.

The example offered by the emblematic domain of the now deceased Anne-Claude Leflaive in Puligny-Montrachet illustrated this shift towards innovation when compared to the earlier generation of her father and uncle. In a recent PhD on the work of precious commodities such as perfumes and wines, the sociologist Anne-Sophie Trébuchet-Breitwiller (2011) discussed the trajectory of Anne-Claude Leflaive and her engagement with the concept of quality and environmental well-being. Her choice to opt for *biodynamie* rather than conventional, organic or *viticulture raisonnée*,[19] is explained by a number of factors. The productivity of the plot is the prime factor, with the quality of the must and the improvement of the soil conditions also playing a part. At the heart of her trajectory was the ambition to make a difference by focusing on the vines and the conditions of the soil, differentiating herself from previous generations which had concentrated on wine making and oenology. What defined the domain was the engagement of Anne-Claude towards the quality of the vineyard and how she saw it as 'making a difference'.

The work of several experts in the 1990s, such as Claude and Lydia Bourguignon, was instrumental in drawing Annie-Claude's attention to viticulture as an area of differentiation in qualitative terms. This has been echoed more recently with the work of Maarten Van Helden,[20] a scientist champion of biodiversity. The choice of converting a domain to *biodynamie* is also part of a global shift taking place in the world of wine. Wine is a unique example of a product that thrives in a globalised environment because of its attachment to particular places of origin and associated methods of production (Overton, Murray and Banks 2012: 278). *Biodynamie*, to some extent, reframes the terroir strategy by pushing further the relationship between place and taste. But it is also reflected in a growing segment of the market which is looking for a radically different type of consumption and also has the means to finance it. Wines from all countries and regions strive, to different degrees, to establish their place in the highly competitive and increasingly liberalised world wine markets, by identifying and emphasising their geographical characteristics (Murray and Overton 2011). While there is certainly a significant bulk wine market that competes on the basis of price and consistency of product, the wine industry as a whole, especially at the middle and upper levels, has progressed by stressing its origins, traditions and internal differentiation (Overton, Murray and Banks 2012: 278).

The Global Political Economy of Wine

The political economy of wine is the background against which each domain competes and tries to ensure its survival. By taking over the different steps between wine growing, wine making and wine selling, the producers faced a new set of challenges. In the past, selling directly to the *négociant* was a means of getting money quickly and of avoiding keeping a costly stock in the cellar. The various operations that producers have added to the management of their domain have increased the economic weight they carry. A few domains have been unable to manage these investments and are still dependent on the *négociants* for their harvest. When discussing the commercial dimension with my informers, I have been surprised by the lack of knowledge they generally have of the circuits their wines follow. Often domains present their commercial spread with percentages in terms of the French market, direct sale and exports. When questioned about the type of consumers they cater for, responses remain vague and are not always clearly informed.

The mention of specific names such as Berry Brothers or the Pantheon Caves or a specific country is characteristic of the descriptions encountered in the course of my fieldwork amongst the most prestigious producers. The story of the economic side of the wine industry, because of its competitive nature, remains generally untold. Not all of the producers, however, are representative of this trend and the well-known and established wine leaders have been noted for their extensive knowledge of their market. Two distinct groups can be identified as a result of my more recent fieldwork: the first, a more traditional group, which is not in control of the commercial process and either works with its traditional clientele or expands it by acquiring importers; and the second, a more innovative group, which has studied the market and knows exactly where it wants to go in commercial terms. In order to develop its strategies, the latter group will control every step of the commercialisation of their wines and will ensure that it controls the circulation of its commodity by using different marketing and advertising techniques. These producers will also keep an eye on speculation and fraud by trying to guarantee the origin of the products and by knowing where they are sold and consumed. Speculation is one of the challenges affecting their products. For the most valuable wines, their sale is similar to that of works of art, and the emphasis is on the originality and uniqueness of the product. A wine lover commented to me:

> I know how X works, he has a faithful clientele of a few buyers who use the same merchant (there are only a few in the world) and there is a contract signed between the merchant and the client in order to guarantee the non-circulation of the product within the economic sphere. It is all about control, authenticity and quality. The client that I know well orders every year only a few boxes of 12 bottles, anyway there is not a lot to buy.

For a few young producers, the commercialisation of their products was essential to ensure their economic viability and to develop their reputation. By creating a rupture with what the previous generation was doing in terms of wines, they sought to position themselves in market terms and to develop in parallel the different components of their winescape. The establishment of a new clientele while keeping their faithful customers happy was a key priority which enabled them to rethink their overall strategy and the product they wanted to offer. Yet the new segment of the market they sought to target also influenced the ways in which their wine was made and played a crucial role in creating a market niche for specific products. As one of my long-term informers explained: 'This is the case for me. I have agents in Paris and in Japan, they like my wine, they encourage me to develop, they buy and pay well, this is encouraging … Behind this they create your reputation and it has a snowball effect'. Other producers reflected back on their strategy, commenting: 'When you work hard and you aim at producing better wines, in one way or another it costs more, then you logically have to increase your prices and then your clientele changes as a result' (one of the VTFP producers).

Interestingly, a few producers, who are leading the way in terms of quality or innovation, confirm the importance of knowing your buyers and consumers as it is an area where you can make a difference: 'I must confess that when I took over the first thing I looked at was the market for the AOCs I produced'. Another informant cited the example of a well-known organic wine producer who, in 1993, following a poor harvest, decided to go to the United States with her bottles and organise tastings with clients and the press. It was a great success, and she not only increased her prices tenfold but also sold her entire stock. The originality of the model was that it places the emphasis on drawing back the consumers to the original site of a culturally mediated experience through the connection to the grower. However, her co-owner thought differently and it resulted in the division of the domain due to 'incompatibility of character', reflecting the different views they had of the commercialisation of their products.

Selling to visitors represents another important aspect of the Burgundian economy. Most of the domains have an established clientele that they have looked after over the years, some even becoming close family friends. A wide range of strategies have been put in place to keep this clientele happy. One of my informers for example, offered his wines as *vins primeurs*[21] every January with a reduced tariff, ensuring a welcome cash flow. The long-established reputation of Burgundy as the source of some of the best wines in the world relies on the connections made between different imaginative discourses and experiences, which promote place, producers and consumers in a quasi-religious encounter. The taste of place here takes on its full meaning, but is passed on in different ways from the knowledge about the place to the taste of a particular wine. For some wine lovers, this visual, gustatory and sensorial experience, constituted through the encounter with this bounded culture, is conducted by meeting with wine growers and their families, descending to the cellar, learning about the grammar of the *grands crus,* and memorising social and emotional experiences. Embedded in a specific place usually defined at a gustatory, an emotional and a sensorial level, the encounter encapsulates a distinctive social experience of a cultural form that could be easily disseminated, translated and shared worldwide.

Many wine lovers compete to access these stories as social experiences and dream of having visited and tasted the object of their desires. This evocative and powerful construction of the place as a natural site protected from any external changes has progressively been consolidated in response to the increasing internationalisation of wine supply and the growing competition in the market. It offers a counter-story to that of globalisation, standardisation, and industrialisation as, increasingly, the taste of place is seen as a challenge to the vast array of anonymous, mass-produced foods and beverages now available to the consumer.[22] If quality was not explicitly spelled out as being at the core of this social edifice of Burgundian wines, it is because the main story was one of a historically stable terroir defined as an imaginary discourse about the historical relationship between a specific place, one acquired with difficulty and through hard labour, and a specific wine grower and his family.

Another way of experiencing Burgundy as a wine region is defined by the expansion since the 1930s of its folkloric marketing through the work of the Confrérie des Chevaliers du Tastevin and more recently through the work of specific 'technicians of globalisation', as defined by Bestor (2003). The figure of Daniel Johnnes, Wine Director for Daniel Boulud's Dinex Group, which includes Restaurant Daniel, DB Bistro, Cafe Boulud, Bar Boulud, DBGB and Boulud Sud, is remarkably telling. Johnnes joined Chef Boulud after spending twenty years as the Wine Director for Montrachet and the Myriad Restaurant Group. He is also an author, an importer and the founder of La Paulée de New York, based on La Paulée de Meursault, established by Jules Lafon, one of Burgundy's most respected wine growers. In 1923 Lafon's aim was to revive the traditional medieval grape harvest celebration to which Cistercian monks invited their vineyard labourers and he held his first Paulée at his Meursault domain, inviting thirty-five of his friends to a small banquet in the vat room. Neighbouring viticulturists decided that Lafon had come up with an excellent idea, and over the next few years La Paulée de Meursault expanded rapidly. By 1932, it was officially established as an annual event. La Paulée de New York is Daniel Johnnes' homage to La Paulée de Meursault and the traditions of Burgundy. It is his attempt to transport the ideal of generosity and camaraderie to an enthusiastic and passionate Burgundy loving American clientele. The first Paulée de New York took place in March 2000. Since then La Paulée has been celebrated in San Francisco, New York and Aspen, Colorado. In his review of La Paulée, Robert Parker noted: 'Any Burgundy enthusiast who doesn't jump at the opportunity to attend this event is crazy as it is a dinner/tasting of a lifetime'.[23] As we can see, the Burgundy wine trade is made up of integrated social systems that connect production and consumption through tightly coupled linkages across great geographical distances. These linkages are constructed around specific ideas of terroir seen as a folkloric and idealised construction of Burgundy as a wine region. An object of consumption, it aims to re-establish a cultural encounter between different categories of social actors, consumers and producers in a less formalised atmosphere. What is constantly emphasised is friendship, good humour, conviviality, gift and exchange which are supposedly amongst the lost values of our modern age.

Conclusions

As we have seen, the concept of winescape offers an interesting platform from which to discuss ecologies of production as well as the extent to which men and women engage productively with their environment over a long period. The discussion needs not only to focus on the site of production and the soil, but also to integrate the broader process of transforming grapes into wine and marketing the products. If we have been able to investigate in detail the ways in which wines are created, it is because we wanted to focus on the 'production as a process of life' and show how things and persons are joined by their differences. Collective practices and worldviews of wine producers are supposedly well-adapted, yet when one looks more closely at the history of the site as well as the wide range of practices adopted by successive generations, it is clear that this romantic view can no longer be sustained. The *climats* rhetoric is about reinvesting the place as it was imagined to be during pre-modern times, erasing the work of specific groups on terroir and emblematising the virtues of history in preserving quality and ensuring isomorphism. My contribution lies not in providing a counter-story, one that which will tarnish the lustre of the place. It is, first and foremost, about understanding the extreme complexity behind the eternal story of Burgundy, and by the same token, rendering justice to the long engagement of a few producers in crafting and shaping quality.

While the dominant myth of Burgundy ensures continuity and the reputation of wine production, the reality is of successive generations of wine growers working the land and attempting to create a meaningful tie between terroir, taste and quality. The winescape as a discontinued, reflexive and lively engagement with the land needs to be seen by consumers as a holistic process by which a producer engages with a site and produces its wines. Yet from one producer to another, this process of engagement is far from standardised and homogeneous; it remains a very personal story which needs to be told. Yet the very differentiated human dimension of this experience is likely to be silenced by the monolithic cultural *mise en héritage* of Burgundy. Ultimately this is this incredible heterogeneity which ends up being masked by the historical and social construction of the region as 'God given'.

Notes

1. http://www.tastevin-bourgogne.com/fr/index.php?rub=5. Consulted on 17 July 2013.
2. The Confrérie des Chevaliers du Tastevin is an international and exclusive bacchanalian organisation of Burgundy wine enthusiasts which was created in 1934 and inspired by the Ordre de la Boisson (Order of the Beverage) founded in 1703. It has its headquarters at the Château of Clos de Vougeot in the Côte d'Or region of France. For more information, see Laferté (2006: 6).
3. A film was made by Georges Nivoix about the Saint-Vincent Tournante of Puligny-Montrachet in 1991 entitled 'Jour de Fête en Bourgogne' and an exhibition was prepared by the *Musée du Vin* in Beaune. See, for example, Demossier (1999).
4. Translated, respectively, as wine grower, landowner, wine merchant and land worker.
5. For a definition and analysis of anthropology of care in vine work, see Krzywoszynska (2015).
6. http://agreste.agriculture.gouv.fr/IMG/pdf_R2611A14.pdf. Consulted on 18 July 2013.
7. This can be explained by the decline of social endogamy (marrying within the same social group) since the 1990s, as with modernity, marriage follows less traditional lines as was previously the case. Even until the 1990s, wine growers preferred to marry within their social geographic group. However, these last two decades have seen more marriages within the social group, but crossing different wine regions. There has also been a market decline of social endogamy.
8. http://agreste.agriculture.gouv.fr/IMG/pdf_R2611A14.pdf. Consulted on 18 July 2013.
9. Agreste Bourgogne, *Valeur vénale des terres 2007 en Bourgogne*, 95 (July 2008), p. 4.
10. http://agreste.agriculture.gouv.fr/en-region/bourgogne/. Consulted on 18 July 2013.
11. By reverse engineering, Paxson means thinking 'backward from European ideal types suited to the environment of their fabrication, of communities centered around foodmaking to fashion innovative models of cheese, and terroir, suitable to the nature–culture of U.S. agricultural and culinary landscapes' (2010: 445).
12. See Fernandez (2004) and Demossier (2010).
13. See Chapter 5 and 8 for more details.

14. http://www.fevb.net/en/the-association/women-and-wines.html. Consulted on 22 July 2013.
15. http://agreste.agriculture.gouv.fr/en-region/bourgogne/. Consulted on 18 July 2013.
16. See Chapter 3.
17. http://www.agreste.agriculture.gouv.fr/IMG/pdf/primeur294.pdf. Consulted on 23 July 2013.
18. See Lionel Gratian, 'La qualité dans les appellations contrôlées viticoles: Une notion problématique appliquée à un concept "performant"? Regard critique sur l'innovation, la gestion et le développement des AOC viticoles'. Document given by one of my informers, February 2013.
19. For more information about these different terms, see Teil et al. *(2011)*.
20. Maarten Van Helden interviewed by *Bourgogne Aujourd'hui*: 'Parti pour durer', *Bourgogne Aujourd'hui*, p.14.
21. They have not yet been made and they will be collected only in July of that year, but the customer is offered the advantage of a reduced price which comes in handy for the wine grower in the middle of January.
22. For more information, see Bessière (1998), Peace (2011), Pratt (2007) and Trubek (2008).
23. http://www.lapaulee.com/history. Consulted on 23 July 2013.

Chapter 5
BEYOND TERROIR

From the Wine Board campaign of the 1990s, 'Bourgogne: Un terroir béni des Dieux' (Burgundy: A terroir blessed by God), to the recent application for UNESCO World Heritage status, Burgundy's claims to excellence lie in its unique terroir, presented as a model of reference to the global world of wine. Terroir here is translated in the plural, rooted in the historical legacy of the monastic orders and in a peasant culture of 'working' the land which has imposed itself under the impact of the progressive change of land ownership over the last two centuries. The landscape is highly crafted, inhabited and hierarchised, exemplifying the extreme diversity at the heart of local culture. It forms part of the narrative about the place and its history, its people and its products. Its cultural boundaries are elusive, but for most contemporary commentators the essence of Burgundian viticulture is to be found in the Côte d'Or, this 'petite colline sèche' (dry little hill), as Stendhal described it. Terroir offers a representation of space as a place of continuity, isomorphism and a site of harmony and of shelter from harsh economic realities. But terroir is also about the story of generations of wine producers for whom the legacy of the system of AOC (denomination of origin) was one of social transformation of the balance of power between different professional groups (Jacquet 2009). One only has to visit the rich villages of Meursault or Puligny to witness the wealth and economic success. Prosperity, competition and individualism characterise contemporary village life, against the background of a nostalgia for more collectively defined forms of mutual aid and reciprocal assistance. One of the paradoxes of local society is the juxtaposition of this quest for global economic recognition and the down to earth generosity of traditional forms of economy illustrated by the gift culture which is particularly noticeable during the various regional wine fairs or other social interactions. The local professional culture is built upon this principle of giving and exchanging wines, as demonstrated by the Paulée de Meursault or the Saint-Vincent Tournante,[1] where wines are distributed free of charge.

In Burgundy, human agency plays a role in guaranteeing the permanence of the terroir story at a time of major changes in the global wine industry and in negotiating the complexities of power. For the outsider, terroir is presented as, among other things, harmonious, coherent, respectful, original, natural, threatened, a setting in which people, space and time are organically connected (Filippuci 2004: 79). Yet at the local level terroir is itself the product of thoughts and tensions within the context of a highly globalised commodity culture and increasing competition. As Overton, Murray and Banks (2012) have argued, wine is an industry that exemplifies the complex and contradictory elements of globalisation. As globalisation unfolds, restructuring in the wine industry is leading to the increasing economic and social differentiation of rural space. As I have argued elsewhere,[2] 'scale-making projects' and the emergence of new landscapes of wine cultures and tastes contribute to major contestations of terroir at local level. Following Michael Herzfeld (2004), this chapter seeks to question the wine 'hierarchy of value' by using terroir as an ethnographic vignette to understand what is at stake in this rescaling of Burgundy as a wine region in local and global terms.

While my initial doctoral research of the 1990s focused on traditional knowledge, skills and practices, my more recent ethnographic fieldtrips covered less focused examples and benefitted from a long-term investigation of the site. Appearances can be deceptive and Burgundy has never been an easy place to conduct fieldwork, despite the many glib comments made to me over the years about 'drinking wine' and 'staying in nice places'. There is something of a wall of silence protecting local knowledge, identity, skills and know-how and these are rarely talked about explicitly. Discussing your wine and the way it is produced and sold remains a local taboo. An insight into that culture can be gleaned from the account of one of my informers who spoke about a conversation he had had with a fellow wine grower:

> 'How do you do it to have white wines like that'... so I said to him, 'I bring back the grapes, I press them and there is fermentation and it works like that' and he got angry and he said 'yes, but what is your secret?'... I did not have a secret, but with wine growers the more you go into details the more you will learn, he will know if you hide something, then he will realise that he cannot go further in the discussion. But that one did not understand.

Unlike New Zealand producers, who are very happy to talk openly about what they are doing among themselves and with the anthropologist,

Burgundian wine growers, for different reasons, feel that this type of conversation is intimately bound up with their own identity not only as a producer, but also as a human being belonging to a collective. It was only many years after completing my PhD that I realised that for many *vignerons* to discuss openly their know-how was almost a form of heresy. Several informers interviewed more recently have mentioned this as a cultural feature of the place and as a possible obstacle to any innovation and collective re-evaluation. It also became clear during my contribution to the UNESCO bid that this side of the dossier would not be articulated in the public sphere. The bid was first and foremost about the vineyards and its aesthetic dimension as a new heritage good. Yet terroir and its complex deployment at the local level help us to acquire a better understanding of the group and its own contradictions, heterogeneity and tensions. Following Herzfeld (2004: 2), the question 'how might we, observers of these tensions, discern in them any sense of engagement with those contemporary forces that seem to suffuse the entire globe with an increasingly homogeneous set of cultural, moral, aesthetic and political values?' is one that I would like to explore further in what follows.

Conceptualising Terroir

There can be little doubt that terroir has become the most commonly referenced and controversial concept in both popular and academic discourse and literature on wine (Black and Ulin 2013: 11), and, depending on the discipline, emphasis will be placed on the physical, cultural, economic or social dimensions of the commodity. It would seem that the enrichment of the terroir concept is a strong signal of its social importance (Deloire et al. 2008). Having initially emerged as a European concept linking locality and quality, the notion of terroir has become globalised and has expanded as an idea around quality and place to other food and foodstuffs to include such diverse commodities as Bresse chicken, Puy lentils or American cheese. European agriculture, which is one of the oldest areas of policy making in the European Union (EU), has entered a post-productivist era which is defined by the buzzwords of multifunctionality, rural development, heritage and environmental concern. At the heart of the process of European integration, agricultural modernisation has been characterised by the emergence of a growing interest in quality foodstuffs and agricultural products which are protected by what are termed legally as Geographical Indications (GIs), or more imaginatively, the concept of terroir. More recently the discourse of terroir has been applied to issues of local development and territorial definition and it has also been widely adopted by food producers at the global level as a commercial and economic strategy (Trubek 2008). Terroir is recognisable as the productive outcome of market capitalism and trade regulation while simultaneously speaking to the intimate, sensory appreciation of, and semiotic significance given, to being-in-location (Escobar, cited by Paxson 2010: 445). Yet terroir in Burgundy has a much greater historical depth than might at first be assumed. Thomas Parker (2015: 155) has convincingly argued that from the Renaissance onwards, inhabitants of France discovered, essentialised and developed a national and regional existence in relation to terroir and the local geographical features of the place. Burgundy epitomises this terroir ideology, but with a different regional flavor. With no less than 100 AOCs, it exemplifies the terroir ideology first in its initial form, but also in its evolutive and adaptative dimensions. France is also the country with the longest experience and the greatest number of AOCs.

As wine is, first and foremost, the sector in which the concept was originally developed, my analysis will remain within the boundaries of its deployment as a specific commodity. The literature is broadly speaking divided between the extensive fields of enquiry represented by the geographers,[3] the historians,[4] the French sociologists, especially the work of Geneviève Teil (2001, 2004, 2010, 2011), and a growing group of anthropologists.[5] If it is a difficult task to do justice to the vast amount of innovative research inspired by terroir, it is nevertheless important to start from a working and broad definition. Heather Paxson argues that 'terroir offers a theory of how people and place, cultural tradition and landscape ecology are mutually constituted over time' (2010: 444). As such, it is an idea which evolves, but at the same time, contains the possibility of creating an isomorphism between space and culture. Capitalism itself is a disorganised rather than consistent and uniform social process (Lash and Urry 1987) and its impact on localities can disrupt any perceptions of equilibrium or continuity. I argue here that terroir is used as a local governance tool leading to homogeneity and rootedness, while supplying a means for individuals and localities to respond to globalisation (Demossier 2011). Terroir, as Amy Trubek (2008: 18) has rightly pointed out, has become a 'folk category through which people understand their relationship to the land'. But it is also a model for practice, a way of redefining artisanal production as in the case of the USA's cheese industry (Paxson 2010: 445) or the California wine region. Moreover, terroir is also a philosophy, even an ideology, an engagement with the product which can take many different forms from the most traditional wine producer attached to the AOC to the well-travelled wine newcomer endorsing the virtue of history and nature. Terroir has therefore acquired a historical, philosophical, social and geographic complexity and it is only by using an ethnographic gaze that it is possible to gauge the social depth of the concept.

Over the years, and despite the vast literature produced on terroir, geographers, especially French geographers, have continued to privilege the physical manifestation of terroir, that is to say the land, the vineyards and the quality of the soil. Their contribution still dominates any discussion on quality wines to the detriment of an economic or technical approach to them. Wines are almost invariably defined as 'good or excellent' and their economic trajectory is often silenced. The geologist, James Wilson, in his seminal book *The Role of Geology, Climate and Culture in the Making of French Wines* (1998), illustrates the extent to which the definition of terroir in Burgundy has shifted, but has also remained the story of a place. Taking Burgundy as his case-study, Wilson asked why the great vineyards of France are located where they are, and why one site produces a superior wine, while an adjacent plot that looks the same yields a lesser one. Most of his argument is founded upon a geological interpretation which emphasises the natural conditions of the soil, and, as a result, the role of the *vignerons* in recognising differences between them is generally marginalised. He argued that: 'It was in Burgundy that the realisation came to me that it was not the surface geology alone that decides the better vineyards, but the combination of the elements of the vineyard habitat. I quickly learned that the natural history of wine would be a complex study, but the key factor would be geology' (Wilson 1998: 5).

The recent bid for UNESCO World Heritage status was developed along the same lines, with a refined argument in relation to terroir. In the application, culture was again silenced and the human dimension of terroir was hardly discussed. History and the landscape, presented as a 'geo-system'[6] (an extension of terroir which incorporates the historical dimension attached to the place and to the geological interpretation), are the stars of the show.[7] The social dimension is rarely cited, and the last three decades of intensive mechanisation and non-environmental practices have been conveniently forgotten. Within the UNESCO application itself, terroir was presented throughout as an ideal of environmental sustainability illustrating a clear attempt to shift the agenda and local meaning about terroir in the new global wine hierarchy. This new strategy represents a way of preserving the equilibrium between people and place and of mediating globalisation at the local level. It aims to create a prescriptive category for thoughtful action for bringing into being (Paxson 2010: 445). This is illustrated by the ambitious regional agenda Amplitude 2015[8] led by the Burgundy Wine Board which aims to reposition the wine region in the global hierarchy of value.

Over the years, terroir has progressively become, in the French context, a vehicle for social and regional territorial development, a tool for change. For some commentators, such as Jean-Pierre Deffontaines (2005: 38), terroir requires a rigorous definition because of the dangers of the abuse of the term. André Micoud (2004) describes the politics of rural heritage as a new way of linking local to global change, nature to culture at a time of major transition. As a result, terroir and its analysis have gone beyond the physical dimension of the place to encapsulate the collective or 'group'[9] of producers attached to the place and the product. So the question is how does it make sense in Burgundy? How can we as anthropologists analyse a complex concept such as terroir? As we have seen, it is possible to focus on the ways in which terroir is experienced and used by wine producers, a concept with which they have long engaged professionally and one that has been institutionalised through the AOC system. The anthropologist, Sarah Daynes (2013; 16-17), has drawn our attention to the conclusion reached by the experts of the viticulture section of the International Organisation of Vine and Wine (OIV) who recently drafted a definition of terroir which was passed as a resolution:

> Vitivinicultural terroir is a concept which refers to an area in which *collective knowledge* of the interactions between the *identifiable* physical and biological environment and applied vitivinicultural practices develops, providing *distinctive* characteristics for the products originating from this area. Terroir includes soil, topography, climate, landscape characteristics and biodiversity features. (Organisation Internationale de la Vigne et du Vin, resolution OIV-VITI 333-2010, author's italics)

What the definition emphasises is the relationship between a collective of producers, a place or a specific area of production and distinctive characteristics. These three elements constitute the basis of how regional wine production is organised and institutionalised. It is the framework within which Burgundian wine producers and their products are legitimised and recognised.

The decree of the AOC, which was made legal decades ago,[10] serves as a guarantee of quality wine production. However, the *syndicat de l'appellation*[11] (AOC committee/union) and the management of the AOC have been almost completely overlooked by earlier scholarship. Specific controls have been put in place, but their credibility is sometimes questioned. The territorial dimension of terroir is rarely discussed in political and socio-economic terms. Yet in Burgundy this is a crucial factor in deciding whether or not your wine is typical of the AOC to which it belongs. These discussions take place at different levels and the complex political configuration is sometimes difficult to grasp for the outside observer. As underlined by most of my informers, the village and the *syndicat de l'appellation* still play a major role in shaping what the AOC is about. As one Vosne-Romanée producer said to me, 'the village is still very important in terms of debate and each village has a distinctive way of dealing with things. Here we are pretty engaged with the discussion on the AOC. We have lots of charismatic leaders'. Other producers have noticed that their *syndicat d'appellation* is controlled by a 'bunch of traditionalists' which means that nothing can be changed. As one of my informers commented: 'Burgundy is difficult to manage because of its diversity and the social complexity of the region. You cannot compare two villages such as Vosne and Meursault'. Paradoxically, Burgundy benefits from a strong social and cohesive image as a wine producing region. This institutional and collective framework is an intrinsic part of the terroir equation and therefore needs to be brought back into the discussion in all its historical and social complexity. It is also defined against the ways in which wine producers collectively distinguish their products in a highly differentiated market.

Terroir in Historical, Political and Social Contexts

The historical development of terroir in France is undeniably associated with its use as well as its deployment by different academic disciplines, especially geography. According to Deloire, Prévost and Kelly (2008: 2), terroir became established as a geographical term during the seventeenth and eighteenth centuries when it was employed to describe the characteristics of a homogeneous physical milieu. These authors claim that the word came into socio-cultural usage from the Middle Ages onwards and it was used to describe a social unit at the village level. It was only in the nineteenth century that the meaning came to describe a rural provincial region considered to exercise an influence on its inhabitants. Interestingly, the local is still the principal focus for discussion about the nature of the AOC. Various semantic shifts have often led to confusion in relation to both the use of the word and definitions of it (Deloire, Prévost and Kelly 2008: 2). I want to focus now on how terroir has been more precisely historically conceptualised and deployed at the local level through a particular social configuration, that of the representations and discourses of wine growers, landowners and *négociants*.

The literature on terroir in Burgundy has recently benefitted from the work of historians such as Gilles Laferté (2006, 2011) and Olivier Jacquet (2009) as well as Christophe Lucand (2010). Laferté and Jacquet have demonstrated that in the inter-war period Burgundy wines went through a fundamental shift in terms of their 'social image' and 'affiliation'. Focusing on either the 'republican control of the market' or on the 1919 statute on AOCs, they argue that 'bourgeois vineyard owners understood the need to break with the wine merchants, who were suspected of fraud through the marketing of a regionalist ideology, highlighting the central role of the winegrower ... images ... that were brandished as guarantees of the quality and authenticity of wines' (Laferté 2011 17). Unlike in Champagne (Guy 2003), where the countryside forms one of the mainstays around which modernisation was achieved through France's economic specialisation in craftsmanship and the luxury goods market, in Burgundy, a good product was defined as a traditional product from the terroir (Laferté 2011: 1). The works of these historians demonstrate the power of regional alliances and national political networks across the social spectrum linking regions to Paris. The nineteenth-century model that portrayed luxury goods as aristocratic was superseded by one in which luxury products conveyed conservative values. The shift in the balance of power in the wine market away from *négociants* and toward vineyard owners can be understood only in the light of the political and cultural networks that vineyard owners managed to develop:

> The négociants, who initially controlled the entire wine supply chain (through complete control of commercialisation, labeling of wines, and commercial networks; through the near monopoly of the vinification facilities, since most owners sold their grapes to merchants; through their family fortune in a world where self-financing was near exclusive), finally yielded some of their positions to vineyard owners, who began to benefit from their political lobbying. (Laferté 2012: 18)

The local social configuration, especially the relationship between wine growers, landowners and *négociants*, is still the key to understand contemporary strategies around terroir, especially in the light of the UNESCO bid. Olivier Jacquet's argument (2009) goes further in asserting the role of the wine growers in making sure that the AOC status of 1919 (known as law of 6 May) enabled them to push their agenda at the national level. Jacquet sees in the debate around this law the signs of a 'republican control of the AOC' which favoured the wine growers rather than the *négociants* or wine merchants. He argues: 'The principle of the rule of origin and local, loyal and constant, the very idea of a dominant *typicité* relative to the notion of a substantial quality standard becomes effective in the first third of the twentieth century. Quality associated with the land is a recent legal construction'.[12]

Following his analysis, it becomes clear that terroir needs to be conceptualised as an 'historical object that is constantly being reconstructed' (2009), an analysis which has been recently reasserted through the work of Thomas Parker on the history of terroir as an idea (2015). Yet if the social dimension of terroir is addressed by the French historians, it remains unclear what the social categories 'vineyard owner' and 'wine-grower' entail. Their analysis of local society would benefit from a more precise discussion in economic, social and political terms. As Robert Ulin (1996; Ulin and Black 2013) has argued, this is a crucial area for the understanding of the deployment of terroir.

This body of historical work confirms how the anthropological analysis of terroir needs to be approached from a variety of perspectives, including the socio-cultural, political, local and national. Secondly, it argues strongly for the powerful role played by landowners, notables and wine growers in asserting their agenda on the international scene against the background of growing economic competition and increasing frauds originating from the *négociants*. This goes back to some extent to the role of the INAO (Institut National des Appellations d'Origine) and its original institutional status in the French political landscape. Indeed, the INAO is in charge of regulating the AOC for wine and other food products. The Appellation d'Origine Contrôlée identifies an unprocessed or processed agricultural product, which derives its authenticity and *typicité* from its geographical origin. This status guarantees a close link between the product and the terroir, which is a clearly defined geographical area with its own geological and climatic characteristics as well as particular disciplines which are self-imposed by the landowners and *vignerons* in order to get the best out of the land. This notion of terroir encapsulates both natural and human factors, and means that the resulting product cannot be reproduced elsewhere. The purpose of the AOC is thus to protect an established reputation.[13] The conditions of production are also the result of a culture and a history: they include local, loyal and consistent customs and are included in the decree. Finally, products with the AOC status must be submitted for approval under the authority of the INAO, and undergo an analytic and organoleptic examination conducted at the local level. A specific *cahier des charges* (list of criteria), which could be defined as a consensual agreement for each AOC placing limits on the yield of fruit per hectare or deciding on the date of the harvest, was historically established at the level of the village by the producers from the 1930s onwards and has been regularly amended. Flexibility in the interpretation of these criteria remains the key feature of the collective management of the place. For example, in 1999 levels of production from Burgundy yields were allowed to rise as high as 40 per cent above the level stated in the syndicate's charter document (Rovani 2001). The AOC is therefore managed by the collective and all practices are theoretically identified and regulated at the village level by the wine growers themselves.

The issue of *typicité* (typicality), and the debate surrounding it, illustrates the role played by local actors, and especially wine growers who are members of the AOC, in managing the ideology of terroir. Historically, efforts have been made at the national level to emphasise the product's regional characteristics in the face of expanding competition nationally and internationally. Defining the AOC with a list of organoleptic characteristics forms part of the process of creating and legitimising a direct relationship between place and taste. The terroir concept lies not only in the site itself, but also within the relationship that exists between the vineyard and those who have tended it over generations. Producers tend to emphasise, through experience, observation and countless iteration, a particular grape variety or an individual genotype thereof, on a particular rootstock, on a particular soil type which produced a wine that has its own unique, special quality (Deloire, Prévost and Kelly 2008: 3).

Despite the seemingly precise definition, matters are far more contested in practice. According to a public document issued by the INAO in November 2006,[14] it was felt necessary to contextualise *typicité* in relation to broader global changes, acknowledging the need to provide a definition that would include consumers and other actors in the debate. The document is of interest as it defines *typicité* as being related to the properties of a product belonging to a particular category, built over time on a soil that helps to identify and define a taste, linked to a particular 'geographic origin'. Human factors can play a part in the construction of taste through the power of memory and the influence of practices and techniques of both individuals and the wider community. Both origin and quality therefore become categories of prescription. *Typicité* for terroir is understood here as a property which creates a distinct value and taste compared to other similar products. The human reference group that identifies and defines the *typicité* related to land includes not only the community of producers or what is coined as 'memory carriers' who built the soil, but also stakeholders, operators and 'French' (I underline here) consumers whose opinion is taken into account. In its conclusion, the document, however, seeks to open the door to more flexibility in the local definition of taste, arguing that in some cases, sensorial analysis is not sufficient, especially when there is no sharp difference between the definitions of particular wines.

Having presented the institutional framework, it becomes clear how little Burgundy has changed since the 1950s in its attitude to terroir and the socio-political configuration of the place. Most of the literature on terroir, at whatever level, has until recently neglected the social and political dimension of its emergence as a collective narrative. Burgundy is often presented by commentators as a traditional wine producing region which takes advantage of its historical reputation and presents 'a homogeneous territory that is endowed with a very strong identity which is characterised by a specific range of natural (soil, climate) and cultural resources (historical, social)' (Ditter 2005: 35). Combining variety with quality and a strong territorial identity, it has contributed to the success of the French wine industry. In an article published in 2000, Marie-Pierre Cerveau (2000) argued that in a more competitive context marked by regular cases of fraud, wine producers have since the 1970s tried to produce better quality wines and to address the criticisms of wine experts and journalists.

Yet the professional community which is heterogeneous and individualistic in its approach to wine has not always responded collectively to these external challenges. A wide range of attitudes and trajectories in relation to wine production continue to characterise local culture. During the early 1990s, specialists of terroir such as Claude Bourguignon argued in *Bourgogne Aujourd'hui* (the regional wine magazine) for the need to look after vines in order to produce quality wines. It was during the same period that the wine sector decided to organise a series of conferences on the issue of soils and their management. Fieldwork conducted at the time confirmed that there was an emerging discourse in the wine profession emphasising the need to use fewer pesticides and other chemicals and return to more natural and ecologically friendly techniques. This emphasis upon traditional methods was presented as a flagship for some of the most renowned vineyards in the Côte d'Or, such as the Romanée-Conti.

Yet the majority of wine growers knew little about these innovations and the discourse of terroir provided a façade for a heterogeneous and constantly evolving professional wine community, which relied on a modern technical culture dominated by intensive agricultural methods and viticultural experimentation. It is also worth noting the lack of a clear consensual and collective technical culture, be it in viticultural or wine-making terms. The school of viticulture in Beaune played an important role in the diffusion of wine knowledge among wine growers, but the level of wine education remained limited. This interpretation was confirmed by the Lebanese consulting oenologist, Guy Accad, who during the 1990s was employed by several well-established domains to make their wines. Accad, often described as the 'wine guru', advocated the use of very high levels of SO_2 in red must prior to the commencement of fermentation. I vividly remember some of the wine tastings organised in the Côte de Nuits in 1995 where a veil of magic and surrounded the vertical tasting experience, in which different vintages from the same plot are sampled one by one. Using a specific fermentation technique, he produced wines in which the taste of terroir was obliterated to magnify the vintage effect. His influence did not prove to be long-lasting, although his wines remained part of the local story about the place.

Throughout the 1980s and 1990s, most innovations and experiments conducted in Burgundy were carried out in the cellar, and included Guy Accad's maceration trials, the adoption of roto-fermenters[15] and an increasing percentage of new oak use. Another interesting example is that of the GJPV (Young Wine Professionals Association), created in the 1990s, which played an important role in providing a forum for the new generation who were defining themselves against their elders by trying to gain more knowledge through their involvement in the association as well as through education and travel. The GJPV is today less visible in the landscape while terroir as an ecological site has come back into fashion and some once fashionable practices are now being questioned. A new innovative generation of better educated and well-travelled wine growers has also recently emerged in the local landscape.

'A Folk Category'?

Rather than adopting a sociological approach defined by a set of pre-determined questions, a more anthropological, comparative and critical scrutiny offers a window onto how the world of wine is experienced by Burgundian wine growers. We have just discussed the institutional framework in which wine is defined; we now need to consider what is really happening in the vineyards and the cellar. Following Trubek (2008: 18), terroir will be analysed as a way of thinking, 'a folk category', but it will also be unpacked in a more structural fashion as a historical, national, regional and local framework in which questions of origin, quality and *typicité* are debated and negotiated against the background of globalisation. This is about what people want to do with what they have and what they imagine they could do within a specific constrained historical, legal and cultural environment. What matters here is not only what they perceive and understand, but also what they say and actually do.

In order to engage with the concept, it is necessary to go back to the work of geographers. For most, wine terroir is defined as encapsulating a wide range of factors, from the particular climatic and micro-climatic conditions, soil, underlying geology, topography, aspect and even landscape, as well as the cultural and historical dimensions of wine-making traditions and techniques to imbue wine that is produced in a certain place with unique characteristics.[16] More broadly, this is about distinct ecologies of production generating distinctive sensory qualities in handcrafted agricultural products (Paxson 2010: 44). As far as wine is concerned, the equation between soil, origin and cultural practices is crucial for an understanding of the product. The economic approach to the market also needs to be taken into account. Most wine growers start their story from the vineyard, describing the meteorological year up to the end of the process – the glass – but the economic trajectory of the product is rarely explored. That said, when we are approaching terroir as an ethnographic window, it remains essential to separate discourses from the actual practices of the wine producers. Actions do not always match the theory and that is where a long-term ethnography can make a difference.

In Burgundy, the ecology of production could be defined as a culture of gardening with a large number of extremely diverse small plots, now commonly defined as 1,247 *climats*,[17] which have been historically hierarchised through their reputation and their economic recognition as luxury commodities. Each plot, each product and each wine producer bring their uniqueness into the equation, adding another level of difference to an already highly differentiated landscape. The vintage adds another layer of complexity to wine. As a result, the issue of *typicité* associated with place is far more complex here than anywhere else. As we have seen, the recognition of a product's *typicité*, its belonging to a given 'type', is evaluated by a panel of trained and experienced individuals. In Burgundy, the wine board and its technical committee have trained a panel of tasters[18] over a long period to be able to discern the *typicité* of each appellation. The identity of a category is established by a group which is essentially the repository of knowledge and expertise. Socio-cultural developments, combined with technological advances, necessitate regular updating of this knowledge base (Deloire, Prévost and Kelly 2008: 3). However, internal conflict can occur when the majority of the panel disagrees with the perceived organoleptic properties of the product. The application of expertise in knowing 'how to establish' and 'how to evaluate' requires the use of analytical techniques. Tasting, or, more precisely, sensorial analysis, is the only tool currently available that enables the above 'know-how' to be established. This system was put in place in Burgundy in the last two decades and it is still open to contestation in relation to the AOCs.

More recently, a new generation of highly educated wine growers has started to question their own practices and thus AOC categories. Their concerns have often met with strong opposition across the range of key local actors, and this has forced them to seek justification in their viticultural choices by pushing their agenda further. Most of the controversies have emerged following the rejection of their wines by the AOC wine-tasting committees. The VTFP (*Vins à très forte personnalité*, or wines with strong personalities), which were the centre of controversy during the *vinosciences*[19] of 2011, are an example of this conflict. These wines have been promoted by a new generation of ecologically minded wine producers who have decided to opt for a technical improvement of their own products;

one of the VTFP producers argued that: 'When you work hard and you aim at producing better wines, in one way or another it costs more, then you logically have to increase your prices and then your clientele changes as a result'.

Behind their approach is a willingness to produce the best possible wines on the basis of a technical evaluation and a personal interpretation. In this category one might find natural wines, but also wines with very long period of maturation or wines from sulphite macerations. As one producer remarked: 'I make wines with a small amount of sulphur, but not systematically from organic grapes. One of my colleagues from Champagne is in the same boat'. Most of the producers in this category are associated with biological wines and/or the *biodynamie* trend, which is increasingly popular in French viticulture (Barrey and Teil 2011). There is a sense that these products appeal to new consumers interested in ecological or environmental issues who are seeking other strategies to differentiate themselves from more traditional wine consumers.

Another distinctive feature of these wines is that they, yet again, underline the singularity of their wines and provoke a negative reaction from experts, wine growers and other wine lovers already used to the taste of place (taste of terroir). Often the VTFP are perceived in wine tastings as having defects and containing technical flaws: 'This one was sparkling, they did not like it, it did not correspond to their expectations in terms of the tastes of the AOC in this area' pointed out one of my informers. In our globalised era, the wide range of cuisines now available nearly anywhere in the world has had an impact on tastes in wines. As a result, several merchants and intermediaries saw it as a promising niche market and encouraged the producers to continue their quest, as illustrated by the example of the Panthéon *caviste*, located in Paris, who sells these products. The first *vinosciences* organised in June 2011 were dominated by the issue of VTFP. The audience in the room were quite critical and suspicious, as they perceived the VTFP as denying the role of terroir. This episode could be read as a disjuncture in relation to the terroir story, but it is also about different strategies coalescing to respond to greater differentiation in parallel with the consolidation of the terroir and the *grands crus* story worldwide. As one of my informants explained: 'If you are working very hard and you like your product and it sells, the AOC system becomes meaningless. What matters is quality…'.

This episode reveals some broader changes in the French AOC wine landscape and questions to some extent the concept of quality and its definition by the wine profession. It could be said that in order to embrace economic competition and the quest for quality, wines which are selling well, especially internationally, need to be emulated. Some of the innovative and ground-breaking producers are often the most highly qualified and the most vocal about terroir in terms of their level of education and their approach to the product. Following the rejection of one of the AOC wines by the syndicate and its possible requalification as 'table wine', the producer concerned set up a specific working group through the Wine Board in order to debate the future of these vintages. Interestingly, the producers concerned were generally respectful of the concept of terroir. They were the ones claiming to be using more environmental techniques that are closer to the terroir concept. After several meetings it was concluded that the panel of tasters needed to accept the marginal difference offered in terms of taste by these products. They belong to the same category as they were produced in the area, and, even if they did not conform to the taste expected, they had a number of points in common with the AOC definition. The main issue was therefore the expectations of the panel of tasters and the variability of tastes covered. One of my informers defines the wines produced as wines with a strong personality or with strong added value. He uses the expression 'innovative and integrated technological itineraries' to characterise these products which are adapted to the market. The emotional dimension of their consumption becomes an integral part of the act of consuming. In a recent note published by the Scientific and Technical Committee for the wine sector,[20] these types of products have been identified as a subject for its future research strategy.

In their seminal article, Barrey and Teil (2011) argue about the difficulties of designing a wine-tasting procedure capable of judging whether or not a wine really does express its terroir. They show that the 'authenticity' of terroir wine is neither objectively measurable nor merely an illusion, but comes from everything that has gone into making it. What their argument suggests is that there is a cultural friction in the wine hierarchy of value between terroir, on the one hand, and, authenticity, on the other hand. The traditional framework opposing Old and New World wines has come to be questioned in the light of the increasing globalisation of wine as a commodity. The debate on tasting and judging quality, as defined by the AOC and some of the French social commentators, misses the important point attached to wine as a good consumed globally. This is about pleasure, sociability, status, imaginings and discovery rather than a pseudo-scientific approach to the quality of the product through wine tasting. The artificiality of these wine agreement committees, which put the emphasis on the scientific approach to quality wines, contrasts with the world of consumers which is more diverse, more evanescent and more volatile than assumed, and asks relevant questions about stories, authenticity, environmentally friendly products and ecological statements. These questions, however, in the case of wines have not been yet properly addressed or discussed.

Decades of intensive use of pesticides and other chemicals sprayed on vine-yards rarely make the news, even if in terms of public health they might one day become an issue.

What emerges strongly from a transnational approach to consumption is how imaginaries of wine are central to the act of consumption. By consumption, I mean the more subversive and creative readings of the significance of drinking wine to the lives of individuals and the re-appropriation of meanings from that act by different cultures, groups or individuals.[21] What the producer or consumer engages with is this core set of articulated and reiterated values that tie a place to a product through its constant deployment and circulation. Learning the grammar of the site and the language of its products can thus become integral to the experience of drinking and to the social forms and shared sociability underpinning it. Individuals engage in different ways with the place and product. In their encounter with wine, most consumers and wine lovers place great empha-sis on the personal story behind the producer, and wine production and its ethnography are marked by the wide range of stories encountered. As my earlier ethnographic fieldwork demonstrated, each producer is unique in terms of their personal trajectory, their engagement with their vineyard, and their approach to wine making. This is a constant learning experience for some while for others it is just a question of replication.

If some of the cases I examined were located at the margins of the group, they were nevertheless highly revealing about access to knowledge, know-how and competence. Heterogeneous practices and experimentation characterised them because they were all engaged in a quest for quality. Returning to meet those producers many years later, I realised far more clearly how wine production is rooted in annual meteorological challenges in which a relationship is established with the soil and above all with the vine. Challenges are interpreted as learning experiences and the complex journey from the vineyard to the glass makes the work of the wine grower an embedded creative process (see Chapter 4). As one of the producers remarked: 'I cannot believe we did this! Things have changed so much since! I did not know anything at the time'. In contrast to that open-minded approach stands the group of more 'traditional wine producers' who have been in the same village for several generations and are just routinely reproducing what their predecessors did: 'Dad did it so I do it as well'.

During the 1990s, for example, Burgundian wine production was dom-inated by a growing scientific and technical discourse. Terroir was widely acknowledged and used to explain the individuality of different plots of land, even when they were located only a few metres apart. Terroir was systematically cited by wine growers, landowners and wine merchants as the result of the primary influence of geology, which explained the reputation, the location and the price of fine wines. There was a general consensus which recognised the supremacy of nature in determining quality. Most of the wines sold very easily and therefore the terroir strategy was not questioned. When conducting fieldwork in the 1990s with a group of wine growers, all of whom were landowners of fine wines, I was struck by the fact that they never directly used the expression 'traditional', but they always claimed to have seen techniques or actions practised, referring to generational transmission or to inter-group knowledge. Most of their know-how was reproduced by imitation rather than by empirical observation or personal decision-making. Quality, for them, resulted primarily from the established hierarchy and the discourse on origin and soil. Moreover, 'traditional' meant reproducing what had been done in the past without questioning it. These personalised techniques designed to improve quality did not always produce consensus and the issue of productivity remained central to the debates on quality.

The absence of a specific discourse on taste was even more striking and when I was invited to join my informers for a wine tasting in the cellar, the majority of them did not comment on the wines tasted; even when asked about them, their description related to the vintage or specific meteorological accidents. When asked during one of the tastings about the specificities of a particular wine, I was told that the year had been cold and that September was rainy which created problems when harvesting. The concept of a taste belonging to a specific plot was not expressed and the emphasis was placed on the natural and geological characteristics of the vineyard rather than on the qualities of the final product. Taste was not articulated in a sophisticated way at the time because there was no normative discourse in the wine market. Taste and its definition were first and foremost the prerogative of the *négociants* and later the wine critics. This was interesting considering that most of these producers were already selling their wines directly to a clientele who, according to them, were keen to acquire more information about their products. It is worth noting that producers have relied over the years on a faithful clientele that was progressively built up. It was only at the end of the 1990s that taste became normalised at the local level and, through the work of various experts and *négociants* as well as emblematic wine growers, that place and taste started to be linked and institutionalised.

One of the domains I studied in the 1990s waited until 2012 before producing a small brochure about taste for each of the crus produced, comparing in parallel the different stages of wine making with different types of red fabric, from silky to more cottony or linen. This is to some extent a way of 'creating' difference in the discourse on taste, but also a way of avoiding the traditional critical narrative on wines or referring to wine critics. Today most wine growers have acquired a broader wine education and 'the son who has never left the cellar' is increasingly rare. My recent informers, most of whom travelled extensively in their youth, are happy to present their wines internationally during wine tasting, competitions or directly to their clientele. Their discourse on taste has become more sophisticated, relying on both wine critics, comments from clients and also their own impression of the quality of the vintage. Often they will taste their wines directly from the barrel during the maturation process and will have a less refined and normative discourse on their products.

Naturalising Terroir or Reverse Engineering Terroir

Terroir cannot be fully grasped without contextualising it in relation to recent French debates which have developed from 2000 onwards around wine and the environment. A number of key official reports have been published discussing either sustainable agriculture, like the Paillotin report (2000) or the Grenelle Environment report[22] (2007), the Berthomeau future of French viticulture[23] or the *Referentiel national pour la production intégrée de raisins*.[24] What all these publications have in common is an attempt to reposition French viticulture in the global landscape against the background of EU wine reforms and the debate on TRIPS (The Agreement on Trade-Related Aspects of Intellectual Property Rights) (Josling 2006). As part of the French strategy, an emphasis has been placed on the agenda of environmental and sustainable farming. Several commentators have underlined how viticulture is traditionally a high consumer of phytosanitory products.[25] Yet very few wine labels mention exactly which products have been used in terms of viticultural practices. An increasing number of French wine growers have, however, begun to turn towards a more ecological form of viticulture, prompted by a popular demand for more healthy products and the need to have an agriculture that respects the environment (Boulanger-Fassier 2008). The global environmental agenda has also been more prominent since at least the Rio summit in 1992. The recent publication of a volume entitled *Le Vin et l'environnement: Faire compter la différence* (Teil, Barrey, Floux and Hennion 2011) confirms the growing interest in biological wines amongst both the public and the French government. What emerges strikingly from this volume is the wide range of practices and 'engagement' (to be read here as 'commitment') from wine producers with what could be defined as 'sustainable viticulture'.

Underpinning the concept of sustainability are a wide range of viticultural practices that fall under the category 'bio', including *biodynamie*, environmentally friendly and other sustainable forms of wine production, which are faced with the difficulties of ascribing and creating categories of 'visible and recognisable quality' attached to their wines. Perhaps not surprisingly in such a context, there is little consensus about what constitutes an environmentally friendly wine: 'This is not only about the diversity of interpretations of what "bio" means, or terroir, or sustainable farming, but the debate is also about the signs themselves and the uses producers and consumers make of them' (Teil, Barrey, Floux and Hennion 2011: 281; my own translation).

Different visions of what constitute 'quality' in sustainable wines are themselves objects of debate between the producers, the state and consumers (Teil, Barrey, Floux and Hennion 2011: 281). The protection of the environment is not a simple monolithic notion. It deploys a multitude of uses and interpretations. If the shift has occurred in four regions (Languedoc-Roussillon, Val-de-Loire, Paris and Jura), it is nevertheless telling of a major change which has occurred in other wine regions as well. Burgundy has not escaped this trend and it has gone even further in embracing the environmental agenda set by the government. Indeed, the regional plan Amplitudes 2015, adopted by the BIVB, aims at positioning Burgundy as the world model of viticultural sustainability.[26]

The anthropologist, Bruno Latour, who was born in Beaune to a family of prestigious *négociants*, has certainly inspired his fellow Burgundians with his work on Pasteur and the concept of engagement: 'Engaging around the environment is to gather around this cause, support the development of ever more sustainable practices, draw more attention towards them, contribute to the overall picture each time a little more and in doing so, step by step transforming the world' (Teil, Barrey, Floux and Hennion 2011: 297; my own translation).

When attending one of the sessions of the Association pour la Reconnaissance des Climats de Bourgogne in 2010, I was reminded of Latour's work by the former estate manager of the Domain Latour in Aloxe-Corton: 'We are related to the famous French sociologist, you know'. The former manager remains an important local figure in the world of wine and he has played a crucial role in developing the environmental agenda in Burgundy. He was also instrumental in setting up Amplitudes 2015 and was behind several local environmental projects such as Colline de Corton.[27] He was decorated with the Chevalier de l'ordre du mérite agricole (national recognition for his work in agriculture) in 2012. His work is part of a constellation of individual and collective initiatives which have mushroomed in Burgundy since the 1970s, but have only acquired a critical mass of supporters in the last decade.

When I conducted my initial fieldwork, environmental issues were still largely dormant and there was a handful of committed biological wine producers who were visible at the local level. They were not always taken seriously, but it is undeniable that, over the past few years, more and more wine growers have joined their ranks. While conducting fieldwork in 2004, I witnessed several signs of a growing environmental preoccupation at the regional level. Environmental issues were becoming a site of tension and debate amongst producers. But it was also part of a broader fashionable discourse. This growing interest was, however, driven more forcefully by the elites and was becoming an important card in terms of territorial strategy for the local players.

One of my informers recently stated that Burgundy was one of the first wine regions to support environmentally sustainable and organic wine growing. The observations I made in the 1990s as well as recent interviews about past practices made me aware that sustainable viticulture here, as well as elsewhere, is still a contentious area of debate. Several statistics corroborate a rise in the number of vineyards without herbicides, that is to say 30 per cent compared to 20 per cent in 2006.[28] Yet in 2010 it was reported that herbicides were more commonly used because of the difficult meteorological conditions. The surface of vineyards cultivated biologically represented 2,160 hectares in 2011 and 7.5 per cent of the overall surface. Similarly, Teil et al. (2011: 316) cite 1.3 per cent of active agricultural surface in bio (certified and in conversion) in 2001 as opposed to 2.5 per cent in 2006 for Burgundy. Most of the Côte d'Or is reported to use more ecologically friendly practices because of the economic value of their wines. According to Agreste Bourgogne (July 2012),[29] 'for four out of ten hectares of vines, weed growth is controlled by a foliar herbicide in winter, followed by a two-pass adapting molecules post emergence to the flora present and alternating'. This practice may involve undisturbed ground (natural grass control), be combined with mechanical maintenance, or be applied to the largest grass plots. In 2006, this practice involved 35 per cent of the area. Similarly, in the Côte d'Or only 20 per cent of the surface was mechanically harvested and this figure remains roughly the same today.

The environmentally sustainable profile of the region cannot be assessed solely on the basis of these statistics as producers have a tendency to provide local authorities with a rosy picture without any hard evidence.[30] The profile also focuses on certain practices, while avoids discussing others. For example, a number of local producers have raised concerns about the treatment of winery effluents. In 2012, sixteen areas of collective washes had been set up and a dozen more are under discussion, while 85 per cent of the wine effluents are now treated (Chamber of Agriculture, cited by Amplitudes 2015). Yet there is no clear identification of the areas under threat nor of the environmentally unfriendly practices that may exist. In another report, written by the CRECEP (Coordination of Research on Chardonnay and Pinot 2006-2013) in 2006, the authors acknowledged in their introduction that the consumption of phytosanitary products has not significantly decreased in Burgundy in the last six years and that the problem of pollution of soil, water and air all need addressing urgently. To conclude, the profile remains patchy.

If the environmental picture for local viticulture is difficult to evaluate especially due to the density of soil occupation, it is nevertheless clear that a collective awareness of the issue has emerged. During one of my fieldtrips in the autumn of 2013, I was taken aback by the sight of a number of plots in the Côte de Nuits being ploughed by a horse, a practice which was not even mentioned in the 1990s. According to the local employment agencies, a larger workforce is now required. Yet the assessment of sustainability cannot be understood without going back to the discussion of the people who are making the place what it is. Looking at the social configuration of the vineyard, it is easy to understand why the most educated, well-travelled and wealthy have chosen to opt for more environmentally friendly practices. By contrast, some of those who engaged with more environmentally friendly practices in the 1990s did so for ideological reasons. Since then, the rhetoric around terroir has clearly shifted from a clear emphasis on the land and on its productive and established system of hierarchy to a more ecologically minded approach to 'let the terroir speak'.

The application to UNESCO formed part of the strategy of putting environmental issues on the local agenda.[31] Nature comes back here disguised as something for producers to be guided by, rather than something to control and manage. In this new discourse, the role of the wine grower is paradoxically silenced, but is strangely more omnipresent than before: 'it requires being more attentive than before, you need to be in your vineyard all the time and to act when and if necessary'. These changes are set against a paradigm shift in French national and local discourses, from an explanation of terroir based upon natural geography to a recognition of the key role of the wine grower in the production of quality wines. This shift has blurred some of the issues contributing to the definition of terroir and has led to a romanticised and essentialist approach to wine culture, in part, as a defence mechanism against the impact of globalisation. Yet the different conceptions of terroir nevertheless share an appeal to notions of unchanging place and of permanence which are used to justify claims of authenticity and to consolidate established reputations by emphasising the local and even the micro-level of production.

The growing influence exercised by a more ecologically aware generation of wine growers could be read through the wide range of stories created around terroir. The role of the wine elites, mostly owners of the best portfolio of *grands crus* and *premiers crus* in the Côte, is illuminating. The same list of names constantly recurs, sometimes punctuated by the arrival of newcomers whose wines have acquired a global reputation. The example of *biodynamie* in Burgundy helps to illustrate these stories of terroir. Out of eighty-six members of Biodyvin, the international union of biodynamic wine growers, four are registered in Burgundy, with Anne-Claude Leflaive in 1995, followed by Anne and Pierre Morey in 1998, and more recently Jean-Louis Trapet in 2000 and Louis-Michel Liger-Belair in 2010. The term 'biodynamic' is, however, more widely spread as several iconic domains have also opted for *biodynamie* without joining Biodyvin.[32] A few others have also tried experimenting without publicly acknowledging it. In 2008, Anne-Claude Leflaive, director of Domaine Leflaive in Burgundy, collaborated with six other highly respected Burgundy vintners to establish the École du Vin et des Terroirs in Puligny-Montrachet: Michel Boss (Vinium); Pierre-Henri Gagey (Louis Jadot); Dominique Lafon (Domaine des Comtes Lafon); Jean-Marc Roulot (Domaine Roulot); Aubert de Villaine (Domaine de la Romanée-Conti); and Antoine Lepetit (Domaine Leflaive). With the goal of broadening wine professionals' knowledge and understanding, the *École du Vin et des Terroirs* is an educational programme that focuses on vine growing and wine making using an ecological, environmental and humanistic approach. The first school of its kind, the *École* had been in gestation for many years. In 1991, Domaine Leflaive began experimenting with biodynamic viticulture, which initiated inquiries about its effectiveness and benefits. Rather than respond to every individual inquiry, the *École* provides a forum for biodynamic enthusiasts to share their experiences with a broader audience.

This specific example of *biodynamie* needs to be understood in relation to Burgundy as a wine region where creating micro differences matters. Over the years, Burgundian producers have pursued a dual strategy, highlighting both place (Burgundy) and specificities including the village (Pommard, Meursault or Volnay), individual plots (Corton Charlemagne) or even domains (DRC). A broad range of highly differentiated and diverse trajectories characterise the terroir strategy. Each wine grower has a story to tell and innovation is certainly associated with the most successful examples of wine production and wine commercialisation. As Jean-Guillaume Ditter pointed out: 'The Burgundians also knew how to play with scarcity by maintaining strict AOC regulations and products with high added value positioned (*Grands Crus, Premiers Crus* and local names) to create a situation of monopoly rent' (2005: 48).

Individual and corporatist strategies have thus always been favoured especially at time of crisis. Professional organisations have, however, found it extremely difficult to engage wine producers around specific common goals. As one of the wine growers I interviewed noted: 'Have you seen the total research budget devoted to research in Burgundy. This is peanuts! It is very difficult to engage colleagues around issues which do not necessarily concern them directly'. Professional organisations are acting like public relations organisations and defenders of the common good while being the bearers of change (Ditter 2005: 48). This is inscribed in the conservatism of terroir as a majority of wine growers, particularly those in a favourable economic situation, hide behind the AOC and stop asking questions. A closer look reveals a segmented market (Colman 2008: 35), separating high-end producers from the low-end and the middle tier. The traditional-ist group, which was until recently in a hegemonic situation, now faces a growing internal contestation on the part of a wide range of social actors: the élites éclairées (enlightened elites), the newcomers and an increasing significant group of young female wine growers.

While terroir remains the trump card at local, national and global levels, the campaign for UNESCO recognition by using the *climat* argument introduces a new set of values and meanings which embrace international preoccupations and ensure that the heritage factor will add further value to the place and the product. This is about a new scale-making project. Yet the wine profession, even if not actively engaged, was divided by the campaign, and for some wine growers, UNESCO World Heritage status risks fossilising and 'disneyfying' the landscape. Three decades of intensive mechanisation, the use of tractors which was once seen as a sign of social emancipation, degradation of the environment as well as transformation of the landscape have all left their mark. I have discussed elsewhere how the concept of 'beautiful vines' played an important role in terms of professional representations and social belonging (Demossier 1999: 136). In the 1990s, 'beautiful vines' meant intensive use of herbicides and high intervention to control the vegetation. The use of tractors was also seen as a sign of serious professional commitment. The discourse on terroir today, which could be read through the UNESCO application, is about reversing this process, 'letting the terroir speak' as I have been reminded on several occasions. Yet the new rhetoric needs to be able to convince the tradition-alists that in order to compete globally, Burgundy needs to move beyond terroir. The success of the UNESCO bid will undoubtedly ensure that the 'natural' connection between place and culture remains at the core of what defines Burgundian wines in an international context. In Burgundy this has been pushed to the extreme as the notion of *climats* represents a further step in claiming distinctive quality. Yet it is likely that terroir management and discourse will mainly benefit the wealthy elites which will in return increase the monopoly value of their already enhanced plots.

Conclusions

Terroir offers a window onto the modernity of our societies with all their paradoxes. Moreover, its analysis is about the relationship between nature and culture in Western societies. The complexity of the concept as a 'scaling project' illustrates convincingly that both the local and the global need to be integrated into the study of this transnational object that is wine, produced here and consumed there. Somewhat paradoxically, globalisation has added lustre to the distinctiveness of Burgundian wines, highlighting the *savoir faire* of the wine grower or the uniqueness of the vineyard, while at the same time exerting great pressure for the standardisation of wine production by promoting grapes such as Pinot Noir and Chardonnay. The greater standardisation of wine techniques and viticultural practices has led to the negation of terroir and an awareness of this broader context is essential to an understanding of the strategies deployed at the local level. Terroir is about protection, but it is also a tool to engage constructively with a global market and its literary, economic and legal manifestations. What the example of Burgundy convincingly demonstrates is the power that specific projects and individuals or groups can generate in the game of globalisation. The constant questioning of the enduring historical relationship between place and taste by wine producers is retrospectively reactivated in the light of the new global wine hierarchy. At the same time, terroir reflects a conscious and active social construction of the present by various groups concerned with rural areas in France who jostle for position in their efforts to recover and promote elements of the rural past to be used in asserting a new vision of the rural future (Barham 2003: 132). Values such as authenticity, ecological engagement and provenance attached to quality become translated at the local level through a politics of scale which aims at maintaining the past while adjusting to the present.

Like perfumes or jewels, wine might be compared, in some cases, to precious commodities. But it is also something that is shared between friends around a meal. While terroir has expanded as an idea and as a legal concept at the transnational level, it has also become more complex and contested in its birthplace. Several disciplines have joined the debate on terroir, but the discussions have remained largely clustered. Much has been written on terroir as a spatial and ecological concept that links together the actors, their histories, their social organisations, their activities, and, most importantly, their agricultural practices (Bérard et al. 2005, cited by Bowen 2010: 226). What is missing from the analysis is the dimension of the political economy of terroir as well as a more informed discussion of practices, skills, know-how and competences.[33] Moreover, the hidden face of terroir ought to be fully integrated into a wider discussion about the unwrapping of food and wine. Do we really know what we are consuming?

The study of the wine growing elites, who through diverse strategies have attempted to redefine their products through an emphasis on the soil, more ecologically and environmentally friendly production methods and an intimate relationship with their own consumers, seems to be a successful attempt to engage with globalisation. What they seek to emphasise is minimum human and technological intervention and an appreciation of nature/terroir as mediated through the wine, which contrasts with the global and uniform technical approach promoted by oenologists and mass-produced New World viticulture. Yet, as we know, more intervention is often needed if you chose that technical path. Nature is constructed as the paragon of quality to contrast with the technical domestication which dominated wine production after the Second World War with the intensive use of pesticides and other chemicals. The example given by this group of wine elites, recognised as producers of excellence, provides a fascinating insight into the relationship between nature and man in the context of resilience – defined as the ways in which Burgundian communities have coped with the location of the vineyards and thus the difficult nature of growing wine at its climatic limits.

By focusing on the emergence of the discourse of 'Nature' since the end of the 1990s, I have discussed the power relationships at stake at the local and international level. The debate on wine as a 'natural' product defined through the taste of place in the long historical traditions of the Nature/Science opposition is still topical. Case-studies of well recognised producers demonstrate how the nature discourse resonates with new markets of wealthy consumers looking for authenticity and distinction through wine consumption. At the same time, the hegemony over definitions of terroir exercised by the more traditional wine growers is increasingly contested at the local level. There is a tendency to use terroir as a local governance tool leading to homogeneity and rootedness, while supplying a means for individuals in localities to respond to globalisation. This new shift in the construction of terroir could be read as a disjuncture relative to the traditional *grands crus* story, but it is also about different strategies coalescing to respond to greater differentiation in parallel with the consolidation of the terroir and the *grands crus* story worldwide.

Notes

1. See Chapter 3.
2. See my contribution to Black and Ulin (2013).
3. See, for example, Moran (1993) and (2001), Banks and Overton (2010), and Overton, Murray and Banks (2012).
4. Stanziani (2005), Laferté (2006), Guy (2003) and Jacquet (2009).
5. See Black and Ulin (2013).
6. See the work of Jean-Pierre *Garcia* (2011).
7. See in particular Chapter 7.
8. https://www.bourgogne-wines.com/home-press-room/release/gallery_files/site/289/1910/17904.pdf. Consulted on 20 November 2017.
9. By 'group', I emphasise the collective sense of belonging to a group of producers sharing the same ideas about their product and how they want to define it. This issue has over time become contentious in several local projects (see the work of Bérard and Marchenay) where rules of production have been fixed and can no longer be contested. The discussion on what is meant by 'collective' is in itself contentious.
10. The court judgements started in the 1930s and lasted until well into the 1970s and later in Burgundy.
11. Voluntary associations have taken the lead in governing the production of quality wine –both origin and control – in France following the 1930s, characterised by the upsurge of frauds in wine (Colman 2008: 39).
12. See his online article: http://revuesshs.u-bourgogne.fr/territoiresduvin/document.php?id=125. See also Jacquet (2009).
13. See for example a decree of AOC: http://www.inao.gouv.fr/public/home.php?pageFromIndex=produits/commune_index.php~mnu=348. Consulted on 14 June 2017.
14. See INAO Commission technique, 2007, 'Terroir et typicité: la typicité liée au terroir'. Personal communication.
15. A roto-fermenter is a fully automated red fermenter that is best suited for the wine maker seeking to get optimum fermentation and extraction of colour from red grapes (particularly through hot maceration). This tank can also be used for the cryomaceration of white grapes, the carbonic maceration of whole or crushed grapes, and finally as a de-juicing tank.
16. See, for example, Wilson (1998), Vaudour (2002) and Barham (2003).
17. See Chapter 7.
18. They are mostly formed of local wine professionals including wine producers, journalists, wine lovers and chefs. The gender balance is in principle always respected.
19. The *vinosciences* were the first professional conference organised by all the producers of Burgundy as a wine region under the leadership of the BIVB. They aim at defining new directions, opening debates and presenting the results of recent research projects.

20. See 'Note d'orientation de la recherche, de l'expérimentation et du développement destinée à la filière vitivinicole. Proposé par le Comité scientifique et technique pour la période 2014-2020'. Personal communication and document.
21. See Chapter 6. For more on consumption, see Miller (1988, 1997, 1998).
22. The Grenelle de l'environnement is an open multi-party debate in France that brings together representatives of national and local government and organisations (industry, labour, professional associations, non-governmental organisations) on an equal footing, with the goal of unifying a position on a specific theme. The aim of the Grenelle Environment Round Table (as it might be called in English), instigated by the former President of France, Nicolas Sarkozy, in the summer of 2007, is to define the key points of public policy on ecological and sustainable development issues over the following five-year period.
23. Berthomeau (2001); Pomel (2006).
24. ITV 2000. This is a two volume report which can be accessed at http://www.vignevin.com/publications/brochures-techniques/production-integree-de-raisins.html. Consulted on 20 November 2017.
25. See Boulanger-Fassier (2008), Barrey and Teil (2011).
26. The recent propositions for the sustainable development of Burgundy wines can be consulted online: https://www.bourgogne-wines.com/home-press-room/release/gallery_files/site/289/1910/17904.pdf. Consulted on 10 July 2013.
27. See, for *example, https://www.bourgogne-wines.com/home-press-room/release/gallery_files/site/289/1910/17904.pdf (consulted on 20 November 2017) and http://ec.europa.eu/environment/life/project/Projects/index.cfm?fuseaction=home.showFile&rep=file&fil=BIODIVINE_Rapport_Corton_FR.pdf (consulted on 10 July 2013).*
28. http://agreste.agriculture.gouv.fr/IMG/pdf/R2612A15.pdf. Consulted on 10 July 2013.
29. http://agreste.agriculture.gouv.fr/IMG/pdf/R2612A15.pdf. Consulted on 10 July 2013.
30. http://agreste.agriculture.gouv.fr/IMG/pdf/R2612A15.pdf, table on p.2.
31. See Chapter 7.
32. Biodyvin is the union of wine growers who apply biodynamic techniques throughout their property, and have received Biodyvin approval. For more information, see http://www.biodyvin.com/en/home.html. Consulted on 10 July 2013.
33. See Chapter 4 on 'Winescape'.

Chapter 6
TRANSLATING TERROIR, BURGUNDY IN ASIA

The *grands crus* story offers an ideal opportunity to examine not only the commodification of wine in transnational terms, but also the sites of its cultural deployment against the forces of globalisation. Rather than focusing only on the site of production, sites of encounters between production and consumption bring a more dynamic and thick description of the cultural forces at stake and of the complex processes of translation. Translating wine cultures and especially the terroir story takes different forms and involves different settings, protagonists, plots, contexts and characters. It is about both conspicuous consumption and the heightened value of authenticity within global capitalism, especially with regard to how producers and consumers link cultural production to particular times, social experiences and places as a way of understanding authenticity and of generating new forms of individual and collective identification. What is interesting for the anthropologist is to follow these multiple deployments in which new cultural experiences, values, discourses and encounters are formed, shaped and negotiated to become part of a process of cultural embodiment.

Through the concept of terroir and its globalisation, the *grands crus* of the Côte d'Or offer a classic example of a geographically and historically stable site and a fluctuating, but strongly culturally defined group of producers working in a particular ecological milieu characterised by diversity and complexity.[1] Like the tuna industry analysed by Bestor (2003), the Côte d'Or *grands crus* story acts as a form of cultural marker for the world wine industry, and is perpetuated, disseminated and transmitted through various networks established between agents and brokers constructing linkages. The technicians of globalisation, as Bestor (2003: 60) defines them, play an important part in essentialising the story and connecting the producers and consumers to the original experience, but it is also about bringing new stories to life. Yet these technicians of globalisation also influence the ways in which wine is made and play a crucial role in creating a niche market for specific products as explained by one of my long-term informers: 'This is the case for me. I have agents in Paris and in Japan, they like my wine, they encourage me to develop, they buy and pay well, this is encouraging... Behind this they build your reputation and it has a snowball effect'.

The material difficulties of following wine, from the vineyard to the glass and beyond regional or even national geographic boundaries, risks becoming a quest for the Holy Grail in the context of a product constructed and studied as a closed object in professional, regional and national terms. Through the ethnographic study of discourses and practices, anthropology has the ability to collapse a number of potentially troublesome dichotomies, such as the local and global, the virtual and real, the bounded and unbounded, the universal and the particular. The *grands crus* thus offer an ideal opportunity to examine not only the commodification of wine in transnational terms, but also the sites in which they are deployed against global forces. As Phillips has argued (2006: 43), food and wine have been, and continue to be, central to the production of a global imaginary. In the flow of ideas and people inscribed in this global imaginary, production and consumption remain two sides of the same coin. The terroir story offers a new insight into the social construction of quality not only at the local level, but more specifically at the global level and its circulation as an iconic discourse of the negotiated relationship between culture and nature, taste and place.

Wine is a powerful symbol of Western capitalism and it has contributed to the production of a mythical, idyllic representation of rural society in the context of an increasingly urbanised global world where cities have become the pole of a modern lifestyle. French wines, especially those from Burgundy, which have long been associated with terroir, origin, tradition, know-how and authenticity, have served as one of the means by which French gastronomy and culture have been repackaged at the global level through, for example, UNESCO's Gastronomic Meal of the French. Yet in the fragmented world we live in, translating specific heritage concepts requires cultural adjustment and much coming and going between different contexts. UNESCO's adoption of the Gastronomic Meal of the French, the *climats de Bourgogne* or the *paysages* de Champagne offer interesting examples of these processes of cultural translation in the global and more specifically Asian context where cultural differences could be perceived as more polarised.

The deployment of wine culture across several continents, often historically led by waves of Europeans migrating to the New World, is a story about shared core values such as resilience, social mobility and community, but it is also paradoxically one of elitism, prestige, differentiation and power. It is an illustration of fast capitalism, commodification and distinction in the context of an increasing gap between the fortunate of this world and those left behind. Yet sharing a glass of wine, whatever its economic value, has the power to erase social cleavages and to provide a forum for human interaction and exchange, communication and pleasure, experience and understanding. French commentators have used the expression social lubricant to describe the drinking encounter and the particular social forms it creates. Burgundy wines which have become economically highly valued are nevertheless the object of exchange and often intense social rituals which means that they become accessible through specific and shared social experiences of consumption. By examining three ethnographic examples – manga, two American women acting as cultural brokers with their 'French weekend', and the UNESCO translation of terroir in China – of how idiomatic cultural icons circulate, are translated and experienced, it is possible to demonstrate how wine culture plays an important role in shaping social landscapes and transforming patterns of consumption. By creating new ways within which cultural shifts can take place, wine culture facilitates individual and self-reflexive social imbrications. The focus on Asia provides an interesting ethnographic example of how local and global values, imaginaries, representations and know-how circulate and are by the same token negotiated. Asia constitutes an emerging market in terms of wine production and consumption, which it is characterised by a massive expansion of wine consumption and the rise of a new wine culture associated with the emergence of a wealthy middle class as well as a growing differentiation between segments of that market. Burgundy in this context has taken advantage of these changes and has tried to position itself in relation to its chief competitors, notably Bordeaux.

Grands Crus in Asia

Following the product in its contemporary cultural forms and deployment requires an ethnographic encounter with Asia in all its diversity and complexity. As far as wine culture is concerned, the majority of global wine experts agree that Asia has witnessed a major transformation of its wine drinking culture as well as, in the case of China, for example, of wine production. In 1973, the French scholar, former minister and close advisor to de Gaulle, Alain Peyrefitte, wrote a landmark book entitled *Quand la Chine s'éveillera* (When China Wakes Up) which became a point of reference for French understandings of China in much the same way as literary classics of Custine on Russia or Tocqueville on America had done in the past. Since then China has undergone a major economic revolution and the Chinese have become in general richer, more travelled and better educated and they have been attracted to wine as a product and a luxury commodity. Since 1997, the former British colony of Hong Kong has played a major role in this recasting, being both the bridge between East and West and a vibrant and major global financial centre well known for its culinary scene and its shopping malls. For the anthropologist Björn Kjellgren (2004: 13), 'as grape wine tries to sell its way into the standard culinary repertoire of China, it is more than simply a process of a global culinary flow from the centre to the periphery'. Changes in wine production and consumption in this part of the world need to be read against the broader geographic, economic and political context involving a patchwork of local economies as well as the great divide between rural/urban society. In Asia, these processes form part of redefining the nation be it in China, in Japan or in South Korea where there has been some debate and tension arising from the need to preserve what are perceived as traditional and historical values. Modernity can often appear paradoxical on account of what Kjellgren has described as an 'apparent willingness to embrace the new and foreign which supersedes the hitherto predominant Sino-Western dichotomy' (Kjellgren 2004: 13). Both Japan and China in their own intrinsic complexity and specificity illustrate this paradox at the heart of their respective political projects. Wine is a product that is strongly linked to modernisation and Westernisation in China (Kjellgren 2004: 13), while in Japan can be seen as both an evocation of the past and a quest for the present as we shall it see in due course.

Since 2000, China has experienced a 'wine fever' with a strong development of both production and consumption as well as the rise of oenotourism (Giroir 2015: 1). Coming to wine culture later than Japan and with a different perspective, China is still characterised today by a lack of infrastructure which might, in the case of wines, become highly problematic as far as delivery and safety are concerned in a sector not yet fully professionalised. As one of my informers from China recalled: 'The problem in China is that wines are not always delivered and they can be left for ages in a van under the sun without anybody noticing. The importers and sellers are not as rigorous as they are in Japan and the market is not always reliable'. Yet the proliferation of foreign companies and expertise since the turn of the century have started to transform both wine production and consumption, as this chapter will illustrate. Burgundy as a wine producing region has not escaped this trend. Over the last decade it has benefitted from growing interest which has triggered more collaboration between Burgundy and China, especially in the context of the UNESCO listing. In

2013, the BIVB described China as the 'new locomotive of its commercial strategies'.[2]

For the anthropologist Boris Petric (2014), the presence of wine in China can be traced back through different commercial routes and influences established over centuries. Yet this space is far from being homogenous and continuous in historical terms. The historian, Christophe Lucand (2015: 155), has recently argued that in Burgundy it was in the context of the wine crisis associated with frauds and the renegotiation of what was meant by quality at the end of the nineteenth and beginning of the twentieth century that wine merchants began to consider the possibility of expanding their commercial markets to the East where a rich European clientele of expatriates might be found. Chinese trade concessions at that time were seen as a possible route for such an expansion. Wine thus became a cultural, political and economic vector of the Republican project for Burgundian wine merchants which dovetailed with colonialist ambitions to disseminate French civilisation (Lucand 2015: 156). Yet the experience described by the historian is one of failure, resulting in part from a lack of translating skills, something which is confirmed through the Burgundian archival records. Ultimately, this republican model of viticulture, based on a French historical culture rooted in a national metropolitan vision and convinced of its unique qualities, failed to adapt to other cultural contexts (Lucand 2015: 156).

Today, a different picture has emerged with an increasingly affluent and diverse Chinese population numbering over 1.3 billion, with a booming economy which potentially is the world's largest future market for imported products. Living standards have improved greatly since China adopted a market economy. In this context about 211 million Chinese are middle class in terms of income, more than 300 million could be defined as middle class according to their consumption patterns, and over 400 million consider themselves as middle class (Fewsmith 2007: 1). Wine in Chinese society is, first and foremost, about prestige, social status, distinction and gift. The wine economy in China, as elsewhere in Asia, has followed recognisable paths starting from Bordeaux wines and gradually progressing to Burgundy, following the various fashions and wine crazes associated with those areas. Speculation was at the heart of some of these commercial transactions. Yet each segment of the French wine market presents itself as radically differently to Chinese consumers, who are primarily attracted by the brand or reputation. If Bordeaux was in the 1990s the subject of a gold rush driven by a massive expansion of demand and exemplified by the large quantity of wine imported and then speculated on, Burgundy, because of its limited production and size, was never the object of a similar craze. The soaring price of Bordeaux wines and the contagious nature of its growth created a bubble which was soon to burst following the economic downturn. As a result, China was left in 2015 with major stocks of wines bought at astronomical prizes and kept in far from perfect conditions.

Burgundy, on the other hand, presented a different and more humble picture as its wines were more difficult to buy, especially as far as *grands crus* were concerned, and also conditions of commercialisation meant that the level of production was kept to normal levels. Rarity in this case became the keyword of the Burgundian experience and meant that the rarest bottles saw their price increasing at a rapid pace following intense speculation.

Interestingly, a number of Chinese wine commentators have played an important role as technicians of globalisation and they have disseminated French wine drinking culture across and beyond China. The example of Jeannie Cho Lee, Asia's first Master of Wine, is telling of this cross-hybridisation not only between different geographic regions, but also between the culinary and the oenological side of gastronomic culture. I met Jeannie Cho Lee in New Zealand during the Pinot Noir festival in 2013 and she had just joined the prestigious journal *Decanter* as the contribution editor for Asia located in Hong Kong, confirming her key role as a global cultural broker. She spent two years visiting major Asian cities including Hong Kong, Shanghai, Beijing, Taipei, Tokyo, Seoul, Bangkok, Kuala Lumpur, Singapore and Mumbai, sampling dishes and trying out different wine combinations. Her book *The Asian Palate* (2009) offers a reinterpretation of food as place-driven and terroir is used as a way of relating place and taste, food and wine and refining what she has described as the Asian palate.

In her discussion of the pairing of wine and Asian food, she acknowledges the difficulties in trying to match wines with Asian food flavours which are dominant in taste. She describes the attempt as more a question of finding a less vocal wine which will accompany the food rather than lead the taste. For Cho Lee, each culture has its own palate and its own patterns of sociability and the process of translating one to the other is more a case of imbricating when it is possible different culinary or taste features, giving a balanced structure to a set of tastes which might otherwise clash. As she argues, Asian taste is about 'the love of chewiness of intestines, the gelatinous and chewy texture of chicken feet and to appreciate jellyfish, you need to love that very soft mushy texture of sea cucumber and sea urchin' and 'You can't tell someone to like that'.[3] This taste landscape that she articulates so clearly offers an interesting and challenging space which questions the traditional pairing associated with the Burgundian *boeuf bourguignon* food landscape. Regional cuisine in Burgundy still relies on a reinterpretation of the idiomatic dishes of snails, *jambon persillé* and Burgundy beef, all chewy and gelatinous in their own way.

From *Kami no Shizuku* to *Les Gouttes de Dieu* (Drops of God): Translating Wine Culture

Amongst Asian sites of encounter, the wine manga or wine comic books played an important role in the circulation of the Burgundy story. First produced in Japan and then translated into different languages and cultural contexts, they offer a window onto the processes at stake when translating wine cultures back and forth. Here both the original Japanese wine manga and the French translation will serve as anthropological lenses to unpack the Burgundy terroir story and its translation in different cultural traditions. What remains central to this story is the idiomatic pillar of French wine culture: Burgundy, a plot, a grape and its producer. Following the deployment of the terroir story through the sites of cultural encounter provides a useful ethnographic vignette for an understanding of the imbrications of cultural processes. As is argued by Jason Jones (2015: 18):

> though the wine manga covered [here] goes through great lengths to educate the reader on matters of French wine culture through the sommelier, when read within a larger context, we can argue that wine manga has at least as much to tell us about Japan and how the transnational narratives serving as the scaffolding for the popular consumption of wine and wine culture fit within the framework of pre-existing national narratives.

The wine manga and its ethnographic deployment both provide an interesting window onto the cultural transnational processes at stake.

During the opening of the first *vinosciences*, launched in June 2011 in Beaune at the Palais des Congrès, several local wine producers drew my attention to the recent publication by Shin and Yuko Kibayashi of a cartoon strip translated into French and originally published in Japan in 2006 under the title 神の雫 – *Kami no Shizuku* or *Drops of God* – which showcased a few Burgundian wine producers and the Burgundy terroir story. Further investigation revealed that in July 2009 the *Decanter* publication of 'The Power List', which ranked the wine industry's most influential individuals, had placed Shin and Yuko Kibayashi at number fifty, citing their work provocatively as 'arguably the wine publication of the last twenty years'. A few years earlier, a delegation of the BIVB (export managers of the Burgundy Wine Board) went on a visit to Korea in 2007 to discover that the manga phenomenon had put Burgundy on the map of Korean consumers, and they had to face forty companies and more than 900 people making enquiries about Burgundian wines in just twenty-four hours.[4] These examples illustrate the extent to which the Burgundy *grands crus* story takes on different forms, but it is almost invariably about a plot, a wine grower, a grape and a taste.

Manga are comics created in Japan which are inscribed in a long historical and complex tradition of Japanese art and culture. The wine series was
first published in November 2004 in *Weekly Morning* magazine in Japan.
In Japan, there is a tradition of the manga first being circulated through
cheap magazines (less than 230 yen or two euros) which are read during
journeys on public transport and then thrown away. Traditionally, these are
published in black and white on recycled paper and they typically include
a dozen chapters drawn from different manga. In Japan, people of all ages
read manga. The medium includes works in a broad range of genres: action-
adventure, romance, sports and games, historical drama, comedy, science
fiction and fantasy, mystery, suspense, detective, horror, pornography and
business. Although this form of entertainment originated in Japan, manga-
influenced comics exist in other parts of the world, particularly in China,
Hong Kong, Taiwan (*manhua*) and South Korea (*manhwa*). Many manga
are translated into other languages, especially into English. If successful,
they become rapidly transformed into comic books with glossy print and
colours. They are published more frequently than European comic books,
despite their 200-page format and the large number of volumes in a series
that can go up to forty volumes or more. Following the success of *Kami
no Shizuku*, a live action television adaptation was produced by Nippon
television in January 2009.

That wine would eventually become the subject of manga was almost
inevitable (Jones 2015: 2), following what has been described as a series of
wine booms in Japan spurred on by the popularisation of the drink by the
media, especially with the role of celebrity sommeliers (Dobronauteanu
2014: 6). The appearance of the wine manga coincided with the first
Japanese sommelier being recognised in 1995 by the Association de la
Sommellerie Internationale (Normand-Marconnet and Jones 2016: 164).
Although the luxury wine market has also expanded due to favourable economic policies enacted by the Abe government in 2013, the quality-price
ratio remains extremely important to consumers from all income brackets
(Dobronauteanu 2014: 8). A wine culture fever seems to have gripped
Japan and, more generally Asia, with sales hitting record levels especially
when they are cited in the manga. The growing body of Japanese literature
as well as its increasing media presence points to the increasing solidifi-
cation of wine as a staple at the dinner table and as an idiom of Japanese
culture (Jones 2015: 3). But it is also about the Westernisation of Japan
through its culinary and drinking culture.

The trend hit the most famous wines of Burgundy in striking fashion.
The example of several producers cited in the manga is revealing as they
had to face thousands of fax and phone orders of their wines after they
appeared in *Kami no Shizuku*. A similar thing happened in Taiwan and

South Korea when the comic appeared there, with wine merchants rushing to distributors for whatever they could get to meet a boom in demand for Mont-Pérat, and for other wines cited in the book, and ultimately for any wine at all (Musolf 2008: 218). It is worth pointing out that in the case of Japan, culinary and gastronomic culture, with its attendant rice wine, were traditionally inscribed in a politics of Western food which played an important part in creating a civilised, modern image for Japan abroad, helping to win recognition as an equal of Western nations (Cwiertka 2006: 134). Moreover, drink and drinking in Japan is a serious business (Moeran 2005: 25) and one may wonder if the new Western wine consumption threatened to undermine the traditional saké culture and, by the same token, Japanese national and cultural identity by recasting certain social relationships along gender, age and class lines.

With the publication of *Kami no Shizuku*, the Japanese manga tradition and the world of wine met, addressing at the same time a new and specific segment of the market, that of young male and female food and wine professionals, *aficionados* and wine neophytes. A similar trend towards democratisation has developed in France thanks to the popular impact of TV series as well as crime fiction books devoted to French vineyards, where family affairs, friendship, business, tradition and love all feature amongst the ingredients of this new genre, from *Margaux interdit* to *Sortie en primeurs*. The process of translation back and forth with the original version in Japanese and then the French version followed by an English edition offers an interesting platform to discuss wine encounters through transnational connections as well as issues of cultural translations. In Japan, the term manga is restricted to cartoon strips while in the Western world it refers specifically to Japanese publications. Specific idioms are worth mentioning as they give a sense of how the Burgundy terroir story is articulated and transmitted in a wide range of guises. In Japan, the main characters are at the centre of the story, facilitating a greater identification with the reader. It is not uncommon to have the female author calling for attention in one of the corners to talk about work or hobbies. The English and French translations – *Drops of God* and *Les Gouttes de Dieu* – of Yuko and Shin Kibayashi's *Kami no Shizuku* both fail to convey the double entendre that lends the Japanese title its appeal: Shizuku refers to drops of wine, but also the name of the protagonist, Kanzaki Shizuku (Jones 2015: 4). Moreover there is 'an established tendency for manga on drink and drinking to refer to the protagonist or the protagonist's work or workplace thus providing the central character with a platform to legitimise and rationalise discussions on alcohol' (Jones 2015: 4). Yet the French version refers back to *Drops of God*, putting more emphasis on terroir and its God-given nature, thus proposing a more esoteric interpretation which coincides with the new emphasis given to terroir through the *climats de Bourgogne*.

Manga are therefore frequently experienced not in their original version, but in a translated one, in which elements of the source and target language and culture meet and rearticulate words and images (Zanettin 2008: 1–32; Normand-Marconnet and Jones 2016). This process of translation allows the reader to navigate the multifaceted world of comics and the complex systems of social, cultural, economic and power relations in which the genre is inscribed within both Western and non-Western traditions. It was only in 2008 that the French company Glénat decided to publish the first five volumes of *Kami no Shizuku*. The Glénat publishing house has an established reputation as a leader of the manga market and it published the first Japanese manga in France in 1992, which primarily targetted teenagers and young children. Manga such as *Akira*, *Dragon Ball*, *Pokemon* and later *One Piece* or *Bleach* are good illustrations of the success of these series. Similarly, there has been a long tradition of cartoons in France, epitomised by *Bécassine*, *Les Pieds Nickelés* or *Tintin*. Since the 1990s, the repertoire has expanded and has succeeded in attracting not only young professionals as readers, but also more mature adults. The sociologist, Evelyne Sullerot, relates the comic's success to France's broader context, pointing out that the form has enjoyed the strong support of some of the most distinguished members of the cultural elite, citing Picasso and Cocteau (Horn 1991: 33). The popularity of comics has increased and its readership has widened and diversified, helped by the impact of festivals such as that of Angoulême. On the Glénat webpage, devoted to the history of manga as a genre,[5] Jacques Glénat traces his interest back to a trip to Japan in 1988 and to the immediate storm following his decision to publish *Akira* in 1990 and later *Dragon Ball* which would sell over 17 million copies.

The wine manga *Kami no Shizuku*, which features Burgundy wines, was created and written by Tadashi Agi, a pseudonym employed by the creative team of sister and brother Yuko and Shin Kibayashi, with artwork by Shu Okimoto. The story is about the world of wine, its critics and Shizuku who is summoned to the family home, a splendid European style mansion, to hear the reading of his father's will. He learns that, in order to take ownership of his legacy, he must correctly identify, and describe in the manner of his late father, thirteen wines, the first twelve known as the Twelve Apostles and the thirteenth known as the Drops of God (*Kami no Shizuku* in the original Japanese edition and *Les Gouttes de Dieu* in the French translation). He also learns that he has a competitor in this, a renowned young wine critic called Toomine Issey, who his father has apparently recently adopted as his other son. The story sounds very much like a quest to find the lost values of Japanese society amidst the mythical rural idyll of Western society. This is about family, commensality and authenticity.

The Japanese original version targets a specific readership as you must be over twenty years of age, and economically affluent, to buy alcohol in Japan. Interestingly, France and Japan have in common a vibrant and dynamic post-war society and they have both experienced the growth of the middle class, and more recently rising unemployment and a 'crisis' in their respective education systems. It is noteworthy that people work on average more than sixty hours a week in Japan, while in France the thirty-five-hour week is the norm. The global economic context, the sense of isolation and loneliness which has grown up in Japanese society incarnated by the *Hikikomori* (a term that's also used to describe the young people who withdraw) and, finally, the transformations affecting the family unit have all impacted on the ways in which drinking and gastronomic culture might be defined today. Increased international mobility has fostered a partial Westernisation of Japanese society with the arrival of new idioms deemed worthy of translation such as French gastronomy and wine. As Theodore Bestor (2014) has argued when discussing Japan's *Washoku*,[6] traditional Japanese cuisine which has joined the UNESCO list, it is the very idea of historical continuity and heritage that is pitted against globalisation and Westernisation as part of the defence of its traditional cultural heritage and cuisine. France, with the Gastronomic Meal of the French, shared similar concerns and Burgundy wine has recently joined the picture.

Yet both respective wine cultures – Japanese and French – share mythologies that represent major obstacles to the democratisation of wine drinking which is still on one level defined by snobbery, competition and connoisseurship. This partially explains the success enjoyed by the manga in both cultural settings. In Japan, it offers a way in which Western wine culture could be progressively learned and understood, helping the process of initiation through fun, humour, love and philosophy, while in France it contributes to the demystification and democratisation of gastronomy and wine. As Shizuku learns, the reader learns with him (Musolf 2008: 221). According to Jason Jones (2015: 4), the central characters who serve as sommeliers, professional bartenders, winemakers and sake producers allow for manga on drinking culture to establish and maintain a didacticism that lends itself to the legitimacy of the theme. These are not graphic novels extolling the perceived benefits of drinking for drinking's sake. Instead, they establish the consumption of alcoholic beverages as an endeavour the full enjoyment of which is to be found in cultural and even linguistic fluency.

The background attached to wine consumption in Japan merits more careful attention. Traditional alcohol drinking culture was defined first and foremost by saké and it is only relatively recently that wine has entered the drinking market. Wine consumption in Japan has been growing over the last three decades, even though there has been a long period of economic recession. The wine boom in Japan took place in the late 1990s, spurred on by the popularisation of the drink by the media, especially celebrity sommeliers. The principal demand was for red wine, however sales of white also increased progressively. During the short history of the Japanese wine market, it has been overwhelmingly dominated by European wines. However, wines from the countries which have more recently entered the Japanese market, such as Chile, Australia and the USA, are becoming popular. According to wine market tracker Vinitrac,[7] annual wine consumption in Japan has increased steadily, with both men and women consuming it on a regular basis. In 2010 there was a sharp increase in consumption which might be explained by the introduction of cheap quality wine. Over 50 per cent of the population drinks wine at least once during the week, with 7 per cent doing so every day; surprisingly, women constitute the largest percentage of wine consumers and buyers: 55 per cent compared to men's 45 per cent. In terms of grape preference, red wine is the most popular amongst regular wine consumers. Of those who expressed a preference, 50 per cent chose red wines, compared to 38 per cent who prefer white. Japan is seen by the Burgundy Wine Board as a traditional, mature market worth investing in alongside the new Asian market represented by China and Hong Kong.[8]

French gastronomy and wine entered Japanese culture together, and it is interesting to note that the gastronomic landscape played an important role in fostering wine culture. The sommelier Shinya Tasaki, who became the first Japanese person, as well as the first contestant from neither France or Italy, to win the Association de la Sommellerie Internationale contest in 1995, was also extremely important, supplying the impetus for the wine boom of the same year. During an interview broadcast on YouTube,[9] Shinya Tasaki recalled the magic of wine in French and provided a fascinating account of his own trajectory. Tasaki decided to go to France when he was nineteen to learn about wines and during nearly three years there he learned the job even if 'the language is still very difficult'. He started his career in a French restaurant in Tokyo as a *cuisinier* and noted that more and more customers asked him for advice about wines. At the time, in the 1990s, there were very few books on the subject and wine culture was still embryonic so it was not easy to learn about wines. For him, becoming the president of the Association de la Sommellerie Internationale presented the challenge of understanding fifty-five different wine cultures: 'we all share the same kind of approach, the same spirit, always learning for the client'.

It is perhaps because of the frequently, complex, elitist nature of wine culture that manga have proved to be so effective in democratising wine culture in Japan. The popularisation of wine in Japan is, above all, about the Westernisation of Japanese society with all the ambiguities and paradoxes attached to it. But it is also about a segment of society which can afford to drink wine and dine at a time when the problems of economic recession and social exclusion have worsened, affecting the young and the educated as is illustrated by the Japanese 'Have-nots' movements (Humbert and Sato 2012). The access to wine consumption and to the terroir story remains exclusive and exclusionary, benefitting mainly young professionals and the established middle and upper classes.

Wine manga epitomise Western values of social climbing, democratisation, meritocracy and individualism in a changing context of societal norms where traditional and modern values struggle in an attempt to preserve what remains as quintessentially Japanese. Different graphic styles are often mixed and combined, illustrating how Japan has been westernised. For example, a number of authors borrowed from the American comics of the 1950s or have found inspiration by copying the 'big eyes' of Walt Disney characters. The protagonists in these tales overcome prodigious obstacles to attain the foremost position in their fields. As stated by Schodt (1983: 106), 'More often than not, the heroes are young men from disadvantaged backgrounds who enter a profession and become "the best in Japan"'. As argued by Jason Jones (Jones 2015: 55), the protagonists have all become sommeliers through a life of insecurity and toil. All of the characters have therefore been deprived of their childhoods. This utter lack of 'traditional' grounding forms the mechanism upon which the narrative structure relies. Moreover, the characters are allowed complete freedom to travel and possess an insatiable intellectual curiosity that provides structure to an otherwise restricted or underprivileged life. They have overcome adverse circumstances to reach the sommelier echelon, the caveat being that they find it difficult to connect to others outside the world of wine (Jones 2015: 55).

In this journey and through the quest for the Twelve Apostles, the hero, who has often lost his identity, uses wine as a medium to root himself. Wine serves as the leitmotiv that gives the character's life meaning in a world that deprived him or her of the basic sense of grounding that might otherwise have been provided within the familial unit or through Japanese terroir (Jones 2015: 55–84). Yet this quest for a lost identity is mediated through the role played by the sommelier, offering the keys to knowledge and remembering the past. In volume five of *Kami no Shizuku*, both Kaori and her husband, the doctor Mizusawa, recall through the drinking of classic French wines – from Burgundy and Bordeaux – their memories of traumatic past events to rediscover a forgotten sense of happiness. The journey echoes Japan's anxiety in its attempt to modernise and still remain traditional. Wine throughout the series is presented as a medium to reconcile the past with the present, collectivism with individualism, traditional gender roles with societal modernisation and, finally, Japanese culture and globalisation.

Kami no Shizuku by Tadashi Agi also features an ambiguous protagonist who refers back to the figure of the wine grower as a barrier to globalisation, close to nature and true to human values. Family tradition, father-son generational conflicts and fetishism are all ingredients of these modern wine stories. The décor seems French and the characters reveal very French feelings, but with a Japanese twist. Kanzaki Shizuku rebels against his father, internationally-known wine expert Kanzaki Yutaka, by becoming a 'salaryman' at a beer company – a particularly pointed slight because beer is the drink of the proletariat. His rejection of wine culture that threatens the family line demonstrates the deep-seated resentment Shizuku holds toward his father. The characters are central to the story and Kanzaki Shizuku acts as a cultural broker in the various dilemmas facing them. Commenting on a painting, Skizuku, the main character, notes 'For a human being, the past is where you have your roots and live the present' (p.26). As Kaori, the female artist, states, 'without wine, I am no more than a vine uprooted from the earth ... and who will never bear fruit!' (p.75).

The journey is punctuated by the learning of French wine drinking culture, through the processes of decanting, tasting and drinking, and national vineyards are explained in all their complexity. Burgundy, in volume five of the story, is presented via Vosne-Romanée and its emblematic crus and producers which are both deployed through a geography of taste. Several pages are devoted to the identification of the First Apostle and the manga takes us on a tour of Vosne-Rosmanée, Chambolle-Musigny les Amoureux, Romanée-Conti and Bonnes-Mares, while commenting on the array of wines and their producers. In these pages, wine is not only named and geographically identified, it is experienced through different senses, from colour, smell, taste to texture and touch as well as through the emotional journey; the drinking experience is presented as an encounter with nature in the context of post-nuclear Japan. Tasting a good wine is a way of liberating the self through an encounter with nature, trees, flowers, water, the sky and other forms of life. Pleasure and hedonism form part of this experience and wine culture is the key to this liberation. Acquiring a wine culture sets you apart from the crowd and it is easier to see the functions it occupies in Japanese society where 'distinction' matters as far as consumption is concerned and where nature is reinvented through the act of wine drinking.

As Bouissou (2006: 249) has noted, manga appeared in a very specific cultural and historical context, characterised by the unique experience of the atomic cataclysm and the traumas inflicted on Japanese society by fast-track modernisation under the pressure of external forces. The crisis of capitalism hit the country as rapidly as globalisation and Japanese society had to come to terms with the past and what it still considers as traditional Japanese values. This is the context in which both wine culture and wine manga met and enjoyed economic success and it could be argued that the wine manga provided a mean of coming to terms with the past and reinventing the present. Wine provides the key to social mobility and the return to a harmonious and balanced way of life, and as Shizuku stated, 'Wine is really a strange drink. This is absolutely not a simple alcohol nor a luxury commodity' (p.39).

Cultural Brokers and Burgundian Wine Culture

Another site of deployment could be found in China with the dissemination of French culture packaged for Chinese consumers. One of my Burgundian social media informers drew my attention a few years ago to two young and successful French women, Coralie Flandre and Lucie Houis, who had launched a joint venture around the concept of wine civilisation in Beijing. I sought out their website, winecivilisation.com, and was intrigued by their stories and decided to contact them for an interview. According to them, wine civilisation, as a concept, lies in an innovative and cutting-edge approach to wine that is encapsulated in Ernest Hemingway's quote cited on their website: 'Wine is one of the most civilised things in the world'. They started their blog in 2012, and their Facebook page, as well as their more recent website, is dedicated to the development of their vision with an emphasis on 'Bon et Beau' (Good and Beautiful). They epitomise a young, relaxed, clean, fresh, feminine approach to the product and its cultural surroundings as well as an array of social experiences from *Dimanche à la Française* to thematic wine tastings or *soirées* created to facilitate the engagement of the neophyte with European wine culture and, more precisely, French culture. As Coralie explained to me, 'this is more about talking about emotions, energy and how we feel. It addresses young urban consumers, who are often minded and ready to discover wine in a French context'. Their website, which combines *art de vivre* with wine and pleasure, emphasising the visual dimension of French sociability, romanticism, sharing a meal together. Their niche market focuses mainly on young consumers, Chinese or expatriates, as part of the intercultural and social experience they wish to sell. Most of the events they organise aim to mix both groups in a balanced way. This is a post-modern reinterpretation of wine culture with a strong cosmopolitan background defined by a clean, fresh, minimalist and sharp *mise en scène*. Coralie sums it up well: 'This is about young Chinese who want to have a good time, who have travelled to France or have studied there or even have lived in France and they wish to experience it again in China'.

The concept forms part of a global trend that I have also noticed in Burgundy and which is inscribed around the UNESCO Gastronomic Meal of the French. As we have seen, the deployment of food heritage themes can take different forms. Launched by a team of Americans – mother and daughter – in Beaune, the Cook's Atelier (https://www.thecooksatelier. com/) is dedicated to 'the connection between the producer and the cook through hands-on-cooking classes, market tours, workshops, seasonal suppers and wine tastings'. This example suggests that the social experience of sharing a meal has become a cultural artefact in itself, which can be marketed and sold for a substantial amount of money. Crisp images of people, often from either multicultural and ethnic backgrounds, involved in wine drinking, sociability, cooking or dining together and sharing culinary know-how, are all part of a new phenomenon which challenges the world wine hierarchy and traditional European wines. The *climats de Bourgogne* campaign has also captured this trend effectively by playing the card of a more modern type of wine consumption, illustrated by some of the events they have sponsored such as *la marche des climats* (the March of *climats*, see Chapter 8).

Coralie and Lucie's wine project resonates with some of these shifts that they had already perceived in France but they were only able to articulate after their encounter with American and New World culture: 'We wanted to translate this American relaxed way to approaching wine culture and then to repackage it as French for the Chinese market'. They left behind the rigid Michelin gastronomic landscape and highly constraining cultural context to propose 'a relaxed, informal and simple convivial moment'. At the core of the cultural translation is the idea of sharing a meal, which as a social idiom is already in decline in France, but which by the process of heritagisation becomes a new commodity to be packaged and sold by external cultural actors. Each new translation picks up a dimension for a particular niche market in order to translate it in a specific context. In Beaune, the two American women take American and Chinese clients to the local market, cook a regional meal in front of them and have lunch, tasting local wines, while the two girls in Beijing recreate the French way of life, inviting Chinese, Americans and French to share a meal that they have cooked and put in the middle of the table while tasting cheap and easy to drink wines. In the first case this is about experiencing Burgundy as a site through the eyes of Americans, while in the second case this is about experiencing Frenchness in China.

Interestingly, Coralie's trajectory is quite telling of this process of cultural encounter and how her own experience shaped the ways in which she translated and blended different cultural experiences to fit within the context in which she operates. As she recalled during the interview: 'I was born in a wine region, but not from a wine family. My mother is a Muslim and my step dad has a sister who is married to a wine grower'. Educated in a French context that she described as gastronomic and culinary, she went on to study for a BTS (Brevet Technicien Supérieur) and started to work for a famous *caviste* in Perpignan, her home town, where she won her spurs. Then she worked for a *bar à vins* and decided to go to the *École supérieure d'agriculture* (Agricultural college) in Angers to get more training. She was able to join the international Wine Masters in 2012 before taking the well-recognised WSTE (Wine and Spirits Education Trust) exam. During her training she lived in Spain and Portugal and was able to learn more about South European viticulture. Following her travels, she joined the wine company Sud de France in Montpellier who sent her to Shanghai to represent Roussillon both to importers and to consumers. Her adventure with China thus started in Shanghai, a more cosmopolitan Chinese city with a strong expatriate community, and she moved later to Beijing which she described as a 'more traditional and challenging city'. During her first stay in Beijing, she also worked for a Chinese winery for a few months and started to think about setting up her own business. The opportunity came when she met up again with her former fellow student, Lucie Houis, when their paths crossed during Vinexpo 2014 in Hong Kong. Hong Kong played an important role in relaying and disseminating wine culture to mainland China.

The two French women decided to launch a blog devoted to wine and civilisation and their objective was to link French wine culture more closely with art, music, film and modern cultural trends, targetting young Chinese consumers. Recently they promoted a new range of French wines that they named 'Less is more', putting emphasis on a philosophy based upon biodynamic or organic wine and also the ecological purity of the product. Yet their initiative also resonates with Chinese wine drinking culture, which focuses less on quality and more on price, so combining both is perceived by the two entrepreneurs as a trump card. According to Coralie, the Chinese market is anxious to have more organic wines because of the urbanised and polluted nature of Chinese cities, where there is a growing demand for cleaner and healthier products. During her interview, Coralie emphasised how difficult and reflexive the process of transforming drinking culture is. She argues that 'in China, both the lack of confidence in the wine market associated with frauds and the cheap nature and prominent role of Baiju, also known as shaojiu [cheap Chinese alcoholic beverage made from grains], make it difficult to create a democratic wine culture'. Baiju is sometimes translated as white wine or rice wine, but it is in fact a strong distilled spirit, generally about 40 to 60 per cent alcohol by volume. It is perceived as a social scourge, costing the Chinese authorities

huge amounts of money and they are keen to encourage wine production because of the problems attached to Baiju consumption. Both young
French women see their role as crucial and more far reaching than just
teaching about wine: 'This is a national health problem in China and one
way to stop it is to teach French wine civilisation and culture'.

On the other hand, as Coralie argued, Chinese culture has also been
deeply marked by a traditional tea culture and its rituals and its vast
array of geographically specific quality teas resonates strongly with the
European concept of AOC, and it appears to have generated close collaboration and cultural encounters between both sets of consumers and
producers. This has helped them to talk about regional French wines. As
part of this broader process of encounter, Burgundy and the Association
for the Climats de Bourgogne recently invited Chinese tea producers to
visit emblematic plots such as Romanée-Conti to explore the concept of
terroir by meeting the producers, geologists and the BIVB (Burgundy
Wine Board). These initiatives have to be read against the development of a
wine drinking culture in China which was already related to Chinese wine
production. The Chinese wine market first opened to Bordeaux wines in
the 1990s which progressively became the victim of their own success, with
prices soaring to unsustainable heights before the bubble burst leaving the
market awash with unwanted wines.

In 2012, Burgundy took advantage of the situation and became the
new fashion in China due, in part, to the campaign for UNESCO heritage
status which put Burgundy on the map. The role of importers and cultural
brokers was central to this reshaping of the Chinese wine market. Coralie
notes their significance to the process of importing selected new wines and
creating trends. She noted that 'What we do is sell the French lifestyle, we
are not selling wines. We select wines with the importers and advise them
of some of the new discoveries we have made when in France and then we
get them to import the wines that we are tasting with the consumers'. This
is not about performing wine tasting and buying and selling, this is about
living the dream and creating a snapshot of an imagined French lifestyle
that can be experienced. Wine civilisation is about going to the market
and eating simple food around a few glasses of wine and paying for this
artificially created, fragmented and compressed cultural experience. The
majority of the lunches are organised by mixing expatriates with young
Chinese consumers and the language dominating the encounter is often
French or English. Most of the Chinese consumers are Europhiles and
they have already travelled in Europe. The social events that they schedule
follow the Chinese calendar and the Asian culinary tradition. 'The aim is
to facilitate the intercultural dimension of the encounter as the Chinese are
keen to meet French expatriates and to live the French way'.

Yet the cultural encounter is sometimes difficult to manage and the market that both women are targetting is still tiny and specialised, requiring a certain degree of cultural openness. In Beijing, perceived as less economically and culturally open than Shanghai, the translation and dissemination of French culture is seen by both of our informers as more challenging. The picture would not be complete without mentioning the expansion of viticulture in China, often with the advice or guidance of French wine growers or oenologists. Indeed, several exchanges have taken place since the 1990s between French viticultural experts and Franco-Chinese companies to develop cooperation around specific technical issues, especially in 2011 following Burgundy's attempt to acquire UNESCO recognition.

Translating Terroir

On 4 July 2015 during the session of the 39th World Heritage committee of UNESCO, the *climats de Bourgogne* were added to the World Heritage list as a cultural landscape. In the light of the recommendations made by Portugal and Vietnam, the *climats de Bourgogne* were unanimously listed as a cultural landscape rather than a cultural site. The key point of reference in their argument was article 47 of the Operational Guidelines for the Implementation of the World Heritage Convention, which defines cultural landscape as 'cultural properties and represent the "combined works of nature and of man", designated in Article 1 of the *Convention*. They are illustrative of the evolution of human society and settlement over time, under the influence of the physical constraints and/or opportunities presented by their natural environments and of successive social, economic, and cultural forces, both external and internal'.

On hearing this announcement, I was reminded that this had been the first question I had asked when invited to join the scientific committee for the preparation of the sociological dossier by the Association pour la Candidature des Climats de Bourgogne. A 'cultural site' is understood as 'works of man or the combined works of nature and man and includes archeological sites which are of outstanding universal value from the historical, aesthetic, ethnological or anthropological point of view' (World Heritage Convention, art. 1.3). The choice of 'cultural site' as the heritage category can be explained by the wish to establish a distinctive and singular application, compared to Champagne or other viticultural and heritage objects (see Chapter 8). But it is also about the politics of place and especially managing the relationship between the two competing towns of Dijon and Beaune which both claimed the title of 'the gastronomic capital of France'.

Yet the global deployment of terroir can be seen as a negotiated space in which the use of categories such as 'cultural site' and 'cultural landscape' open different windows on to the cultural translation of terroir, going beyond quality and place and being also largely the result of a global process of keeping and maintaining hierarchies. During the session, several members of the Committee referred to the confusion created by the argument put forward in favour of the use of cultural site as a heritage category. The representative of Lebanon, for instance, mentioned the necessity of being clear about what is listed as one category or the other, criticising the use of cultural site as a hotch-potch category. Through my ethnographic observations, I have been very conscious of a shift operated and led by different social actors in terms of presenting wine landscape as an aesthetic and visual experience devoid of any human interaction or social activity or putting emphasis on nature, landscape and order of the vineyards as well as the resilience of some of the sites due to the difficult conditions of production. The heritagisation of wine landscape operates in a similar fashion to works of art showcased in museums and it is also telling that very little is said about the social structure and the people inhabiting these places. The questions were all about protecting the role of the state and regulating as much as possible the site. Following the discussions during the session, I was also immediately struck again by this feeling that landscape dominated the debate on wine culture. It was as if the real interest was the preservation of the site, how it could remain authentic, safe from the deleterious effects of modernity, including the *vignerons*.

Rather than competing with New World Chardonnay and Pinot Noir, Burgundy seeks to reinforce its image as the place of origin of distinct elite products, with its Montrachet or Clos de Vougeot having a very different historic, geographic and cultural resonance associated with its *climats*. Interestingly, what was once associated with Burgundian wines – an unreliable quantity and quality of production, changing according to the annual climatic cycle – now becomes an advantage. Cultural landscapes and cultural sites are constructed; that is to say, they derive meaning, and often even their physical form, from the actions and imaginations of people in society. Here, in the case of the Asian market, the number of Chinese visitors coming to Burgundy is now comparable to the number of American visitors and what is at the core of their oenological experience is to return home with one of the precious wines that they have tasted or to take a 'selfie' in front of the Romanée-Conti.[10] Rather than building a case around the contested concept of terroir, Burgundy has carefully crafted an application which endorses *climats* as a more 'natural, authentic and historical' term based upon a coherent geo-system in the modern sense of the combination of archeology and geography. Through the concept of *climats* and its deployment in tourist and cultural media, Burgundy seeks to create and impose a universal way of seeing Burgundy wines, proposing a more democratic consumption of these commodities of distinction which are normally consumed by a tiny, extremely wealthy portion of the world's population. It also seeks to create a prescriptive category for thoughtful action (Paxson 2010: 445) by mobilising professionals around key values, such as authenticity, natural and more ecologically sustainable viticultural practices.

Interestingly, when reading the documentation attached to the session and especially the ICOMOS report, it came to my attention that ICOMOS had also initiated a thematic study of Asian Tea Landscapes. This coincided perfectly with the visits of Chinese tea producers as well as Chinese universities to Burgundy a few years before. Indeed, in 2011 the BIVB, in collaboration with the Association pour la Reconnaissance des Climats de Bourgogne, organised an exchange with tea producers from the province of Fujian, an area already recognised by UNESCO for its architectural site. According to the French geographer, Jean-Robert Pitte who played a role in supporting the Burgundian application to UNESCO and was instrumental in promoting the concept of the Gastronomic Meal of the French, tea tasting as well as wine tasting allows consumers to regain intimacy with the spirit of each place. During their visit, the Chinese tea producers were taken to Vosne-Romanée by the interpreter and filmed in front of the Romanée-Conti touching the soil with their hands. One of the producers asked several questions about the climate, the nature of the soil and its composition to see how different it was from China. The visit was orchestrated by a local wine instructor at the Burgundy Wine School, who was keen to see a meeting take place between the two kinds of producers who shared the same concept of terroir: 'tea is the drink of the three powers, the sky, soil and men, it is the same definition of terroir as here'. In China, tea culture is ancestral, but producers still lack legal protection and a definition; this is why the tea producers are keen to come to France and understand the AOC classification system. They were then taken to one of the reputed wineries, where they tasted the wine and were able to draw some parallels between both tasting cultures. As the interpreter stated: 'this is the same, we check the colours, we smell, we taste!'.

Conclusions

The Burgundian model of terroir has often been analysed through the prism of the local rather than approaching it from a transnational perspective through its deployment and cultural translation in other sites of production and consumption. It is true that the export of Burgundy to non-European markets is something of a recent trend, despite earlier largely unsuccessful attempts, and it is partly explained by the improvement of modes of conservation and transport now available to wine producers. Yet these developments also reflect the transformation in the global hierarchy of wine. Burgundy has always been characterised as the model of the original relationship between taste and place and the recent UNESCO listing will provide another sign of this historically constructed quest for authenticity. Through the Asian examples, drinking encounters take on different forms and lead to new imaginary constructions. The globalisation of the original experience of terroir, as it is historically mediated by groups of producers and elites, contributes to the dissemination of the Burgundy terroir or *climats* model. As we have seen, this is a model based upon diversity, complexity and the hierarchy of AOCs, which have in common the evocation of a single and heavily loaded name – Burgundy.

In our study we have evoked primarily the Côte d'Or as the site of our ethnographic encounter, but it is clear that other areas of Burgundy will benefit by proximity from this powerful story, which risks fossilising the core area under the UNESCO heritage site label, while opening new avenues for marketing and selling other less well-known *appellations*. In this dual process of internal differentiation, it is not clear if the consumer will benefit from a proper understanding of what is consumed and where it comes from, as Burgundy might mean a wide range of products and huge differentials in terms of price and quality.

The different Asian case-studies discussed in this chapter also demonstrate how wine culture is malleable, fluid, the object of interpretation, and, first and foremost, the basis of cultural, social and commensal forms of encounters. Whether in Japan, China, Hong Kong or South Korea, Burgundy and the terroir model circulates through a wide range of channels and is far from offering one monolithic interpretation of what the relationship between place and taste signifies. For Japan it is about upholding notions of tradition and the past, while confronting modernity and presenting Japan as a modern and open country. The Chinese market, which for a growing number of French epitomises the route to success, is far from being homogeneous and presents many challenges to newcomers, especially if they struggle to contend with the linguistic and geographic dimensions. The manga in South Korea exemplifies this challenge while playing both the democratic and elitist cards bringing together two different cultural forms and providing blended scenarios for individuals and groups from the East and the West. Production and consumption operate in different circles, but also share some common values. The process of translating back and forth reveals how these cultural forms reinforce one other while transforming the overall global story. One of the most fascinating dimensions is how wine culture is reinterpreted to suit both collective and individual processes of identity building in the process of being disseminated or negotiated in the social realm.

Burgundy offers an illuminating example of how both the local and the global influence each other through the weaving of a successful story in the world of wine. Burgundy's success, so often praised internationally by wine lovers, experts and producers, could be defined as an archetypal transnational investment terrain (Peace 2011: 251) and a successful world-wide cultural story. Its long-established reputation as a significant place, producing the best wines in the world, relies on the connections made between different imaginative discourses and experiences which promote place, producers and consumers in a quasi-religious encounter. These connections are by no means stable or carved in stone, but instead they continuously fluctuate in relation to the site of production and consumption and the nature of the social experience and drinking encounters that underpins them. The taste of place here takes on its full meaning, but it is passed on in different ways from the knowledge about the place to the taste of a particular wine and the story told in places far from its place of origin. Burgundy's model has, and remains, an emblematic and idiomatic expression of the close relationship between place and taste.

Notes

1. The diversity of the geological milieu, as well as the land structure, plays a major role in increasing the diversity of wines produced with Pinot Noir and Chardonnay along this small tapestry of vineyards.
2. BIVB newsletter, June 2013.
3. David Pilling, 'Asia's First Master of Wine', *Financial Times*, 5 March 2010. https://www.ft.com/content/968cb2dc-27e0-11df-9598-00144feabdc0. Consulted in November 2016.
4. See http://gestion-des-risques-interculturels.com/risques/un-manga-japonais-a. Consulted on 22 November 2017.
5. http://www.glenatmanga.com/histoire-du-manga.asp. Consulted on 14 June 2017.
6. https://www.soas.ac.uk/jrc/events/meiji-jingu/01oct2014-washoku-on-the-world-stage-japanese-traditional-cuisine-as-unesco-intangible-cultural-heri.html. Consulted 14 June 2017.
7. http://cdnsite.eu-japan.eu/sites/default/files/publications/docs/japanwinemar-ketreport-2014.pdf. Consulted on 20 November 2017.
8. Conférence de Presse BIVB, Hospices de Beaune, November 2012.

9. https://www.youtube.com/watch?v=ATaqwI6Zl3w. Consulted on 14 June 2017.
10. http://www.bourgogne-tourisme-pro.com/sites/default/files/bourgogne/001_PORTEUR-DE-PROJET/marches/Chine/Chine%20fiche%20march%C3%A9%202013.pdf. Consulted on 24 August 2015.

Chapter 7
CREATING TERROIR, BURGUNDY IN NEW ZEALAND

The cool, vibrant and modern city of Wellington in New Zealand, located at the southwestern tip of the North Island between Cook Strait and the Rimutaka Range, promotes itself with the slogan 'Thinking positively', and on 28 January 2013 it played host to the fifth New Zealand Pinot Noir festival. First held in 2001, this event attracts wine makers and enthusiasts from all over the world to Wellington and every four years it also moves to Queenstown (Central Otago). In 2013, I was invited to deliver a short presentation on Burgundy as part of a more extensive fieldtrip organised and funded by the COWA (Central Otago Wine Growers Association) and New Zealand wine producers in the context of the Burgundy-Central Otago exchange.[1] I took the opportunity of this invitation to further my on-going investigation into Burgundy as a global model. For the female middle-aged anthropologist that I am, swapping the traditional and folk-loric songs of the Cadets de Bourgogne for the powerful, mysterious and exotic Maori Powhiri was a unique *rite de passage* into the modern world of wine as presented by the New Zealand industry. From the outset, I was struck by the warm and generous hospitality of the locals. Equally note-worthy was their questioning attitude; from the first 'How do we define ourselves?' to the last 'Where do we go next?', there was a constant spirit of enquiry at the festival which was defined by a vitality and an openness to change that contrasts sharply with my experience of European viticulture.

My first encounter with the Burgundian model and its international deployment materialised during the keynote address given by the charis-matic and prolific American wine writer, Matt Kramer, author of a land-mark work *Making Sense of Burgundy* (1990), who is, as the Kiwis put it, 'a successful raconteur'. His controversial talk entitled 'Can Atheists Produce Great Pinot Noirs?' was published a few days later in the *Wine Spectator*[2] under the less polemical title 'In Pursuit of Ambiguity: Why Do Some Wine Lovers Insist on Exactitude?'. His lecture set the parameters of the debate that would unfold over the days that followed. According to Kramer, Pinot Noir producers are in pursuit of the Holy Grail as they want to seek to make 2 + 2 = 5 rather than 4. In his provocative, almost mystical talk, he argued for a return to nature and less control over wine production: 'We have become so reliant on rational control that we do not allow ourselves to take the necessary risks required for 2 + 2 = 5'. In line with his argument, he advocated mixing a variety of different clones, picked at optimum ripeness, making an analogy with a musical orchestra which has piccolos as well as double basses and bassoons. In his eyes, Burgundy incarnated this faith in 'the improvable-yet-possible'.

His powerful lecture, which was more esoteric and less well-structured than his polished article in the *Wine Spectator*, soon stirred up a controversy amongst the New Zealand Pinot Noir wine producers. Kramer's talk covered a wide range of issues from wine and religion to wine and science, whereas my own contribution was more focused concentrating specifically on the Burgundy story. I was the only academic invited to the 2013 Pinot Noir 2013 and one of the few women there. Lisa Perroti-Brown and Rebecca Gibb, both famous for their wine expertise, were also on the guest list. The gender dimension of wine writing and wine expertise is a characteristic of the global wine industry, with very few women visible in that area of wine culture, even if they are increasingly present in the global wine industry more generally.

I had, of course, come across a number of more nuanced retellings of the complex Burgundian global story, to which I return below, but I was vividly aware of the saliency and power of the simple narrative outlined in Kramer's lecture which was repeated throughout the event. His presentation of Burgundy as 'the mother house', encapsulated by his quotation 'It is where we all start, and in a strange way it is where we all end up',[3] would provide the benchmark for many discussions and presentations. Jasper Morris, a leading authority on Burgundy and the buyer for the famous London wine company, Berry Bros & Rudd, Emmanuel Bourguignon, son of terroir expert Claude Bourguignon, and Tim Atkin, author of the 2011 report on Burgundy and its wines,[4] all helped to reinforce the powerful message about Burgundy's 'great' wines,[5] the quality of the site and its historical legacy in terms of excellence. To some extent, even my own contribution, which was critical of the mythical Burgundian model, became part of the broader discussion on quality wines. Almost invariably cited as the classic model of viticulture, Burgundy's success derives from a unique combination of noble grape varieties, Pinot Noir for the red and Chardonnay for the white wines, and a complex array of microclimates and landscapes actively crafted by the heightened care and attention of the wine grower. The historical dimension is one of the main features associated with Old Europe, and Burgundy and its deployment among wine lovers and professionals is undoubtedly very persuasive. Its long-established reputation as the home to the best wines in the world relies on the connections made between different discourses and experiences, which promote place, producers and consumers in a quasi-religious encounter.

The Burgundian Story

The Burgundian story, as it was told, debated about and engaged with during the 2013 New Zealand Pinot Noir festival, was composed of three main ingredients which resonate globally and appeal to consumers and producers alike in particular ways. The religious motif of the monks, the cultural, historical and traditional experience associated with Burgundy and the wine grower/peasant icon contributes to a powerful evocation of the quintessential nature of European viticulture and the Old World. Focusing on the ways in which the story was deployed during the festival and the controversies generated by Kramer's speech, I want to analyse what is hidden away and how it is rooted in people's imaginary. Jamie Goode's wine blog discussed with precision and clarity the use of the religious motif:

> For Kramer, the key aspect of Burgundy's history as a wine region is that in the past the people who began making it were, as he puts it, 'drenched in spirituality'.
> The vineyards were cultivated by Cistercian and Benedictine monks and nuns. These religious orders were also responsible for winegrowing in the Northern Rhone, the Loire, Champagne and the Mosel. Kramer argues that this religious aspect is what is chiefly responsible for each of these regions having just a single grape variety for red and a single one for white: 'You can make a more reliable wine by blending but for the most part there was no blending where the monks were. They confined themselves because they wanted to hear the voice of God through the voice of the land'. This attempt to hear the voice of God through wine resulted in the subdividing of the land: the impulse to demarcate terroir in this way is deep. He likens the Côte d'Or to Stonehenge, in that it is the creation of a deep religious impulse, with the intricately subdivided vineyards of Burgundy being a homage to spirituality in a similar manner to those remarkable standing stones.[6]

This short excerpt is representative of a widespread and largely mythical understanding of wine knowledge perpetuated by scholars, experts, critics and writers in Burgundy and elsewhere. The 2000 years of history of Burgundian viticulture is often reduced to the period of a few centuries during which enlightened monks had a vision about quality wines which still, centuries after, comes to legitimise specific places or locations. Even the recent award of UNESCO World Heritage status underlines the role of monastic orders:

> the success of a model of production which will delineate new places for the production of wine that will be added to the already established tapestry of *lieux-dits, futurs climats viticoles* [my italics]. With the intensive labour, which is one of the monastic rules, religious duty and an unlimited efficient workforce, it is easier to understand the success of a model *at least* [again, my italics] during the first century of the Cistercian order.[7]

What is striking in this story is that the emblematic places which make Burgundy's reputation today, be they Clos de Vougeot or *grand crus* Corton, are constructed as blessed by God to the detriment of generations of wine growers who have applied their minds, hearts and bodies to the task of creating quality wines. If it is possible that the monastic orders played an important role in cultivating their vines, creating a hierarchy in relation to the perceived quality of the soils and making sure that their rule of hospitality was defined by commensality and sociability, they nevertheless only represented a brief period in the long occupation of the land and have almost nothing to do with Burgundy's current wine production. Roger Dion (1959: 181–88) cited the role of monastic orders in the establishment of a viticulture of quality, but his scholarly work also emphasises the political, social and educational role they played in showcasing their wines and other agricultural products. Wine production was central to the Christian religion and was also one of their main agricultural interests, yet the knowledge of the monks and the role science played at the time are often over-exaggerated.

Another feature of the Burgundian global story which came back at several points during the Pinot Noir festival is the constant invocation of iconic producers cited as the great wine growers of our time. For example, most of the speeches at the festival referred to 'Aubert de Villaine' (Domaine de la Romanée-Conti), to the extent that one of the members of the audience reported that his name had been tweeted more than two million times, 'as often as the monks'. Even those chairing the sessions joked that they needed a system of yellow and red cards to stop the use of terms such as 'my friend Aubert'. The wine industry is well known for name dropping and the character, real or imagined, of a well-respected wine grower exercises a deep fascination to the detriment of the team of people involved in the management of the domains on a daily basis. I have discussed elsewhere (Demossier 2010) how the image of the wine grower as a paragon of quality has progressively challenged that of the place or geographical origin as the predominant factor in the definition of quality. Interestingly, this essentialisation of the producer as working the land and producing high-quality wines every year dominates the global story, while in reality many now rely more often on a workforce to look after their vineyards. New generations of wine growers in Burgundy find themselves facing an industry which is deeply rooted in these constructions, which can hinder any sense of change and sometimes leaves them alienated by these hegemonic discourses. It also hides the broader social configuration and the power differentials of specific stories in which access to knowledge is crucial to the making of quality wines (Ulin 2002). In Burgundy, more than anywhere else, the pace of change can at times appear to be glacial.

Finally, the Burgundian model is incarnated and exemplified through its traditional culture and encounters with it can be magical. As one New Zealander remarked: 'Great place to visit, the history, the contrast with here!'[8] Burgundy is seen as an attractive tourist destination and the Côte d'Or is the most visited area.[9] For the majority Burgundy is synonymous with wine, when in fact the region has so much else to offer. The local architecture, the city of Dijon, the Hospices de Beaune and the site of Cluny are added to the gastronomic landscape of the region and make it a hot spot for wine lovers and many others. On the one hand, the story is about a real and authentic social experience of contact with the wine grower, usually the head of the lineage with his close and enduring tie to the land that is recurrent in narratives about Burgundy. But, on the other hand, it is also about experiencing the showcase-bounded culture, the visit to the cellar, the story of the producer, and the visual and gustative initiation to a particular location or plot. Every year French, North American, European and Asian tourists are taken by minibus to the small vineyard of Romanée-Conti in front of which a notice proclaims in French and English the location of the sacred plot and the respect expected when encountering it.

Learning the grammar of the site and the language of its products thus becomes integral to the experience of drinking and to the social forms and shared sociability underpinning it. Individuals engage in different ways with the place and product, but the Burgundian story remains immutably linked to wines, landscapes, time and human experience. The encounter with a specific place is experienced in gustatory, emotional or sensorial terms and has a social and cultural resonance that can be easily disseminated, translated and shared worldwide. As one of my British friends said: 'I remember when I visited the domaine X, what an incredible experience!' Many wine lovers compete to access these stories as social occasions and dream of having visited and tasted the object of their desires. In a similar way, wine producers across the world have been inspired by the Burgundian model.

Tell Your Own Story!

If the Burgundian model served as the background to the 2013 New Zealand Pinot Noir festival, the local wine industry was nevertheless trying to write its own story. It was only in 2001 that the New Zealand wine producers decided to launch a Pinot Noir event to put their wines on the global map. Four successful events later, New Zealand Pinot Noir continues to be internationally relevant and cutting edge, attracting world renowned wine commentators and producers. The sunny and warm weather of Wellington (unusual apparently for the time of the year), the relaxed atmosphere and the fantastic hospitality of the organisers were amongst the ingredients necessary to create an idyllic fieldwork setting for any anthropologist. My ethnographic experience was one of freedom, pleasure and humour and it was radically different from my years of doctoral research in Burgundy which were only rarely punctuated by such moments as I had to prove myself worthy. Most of the speakers were hilarious although it took me a while to understand the nuances behind the Kiwi (and in some cases Australian) sense of humour. The whole event was orchestrated around a series of key questions for the industry which were summed up by one of my informers who stated succinctly: 'How are we doing? We think we are pretty good, but are we? How do we stack up? Where do we fit in the international market?'

Regionality rather than terroir was the central theme of the wine gathering. The representatives of the New Zealand Pinot Noir industry present at the festival were a young and dynamic group of around 110 well-educated producers, including wine makers, wine managers and wine sellers and showcasing 300 wines from five different 'regions': Wairarapa/ Martinborough, Nelson, Malborough, North Canterbury/Waipara Valley and Central Otago. The 2013 event was managed around these five 'regions' as part of an attempt to make sense of the diversity of their products. A new team (2013 Pinot Noir Board of Directors) was put in charge of the event and a format based upon regionality was proposed, marking a change from previous festivals. Overall, the New Zealand wine industry has adopted a de facto and broad-scale approach to regional labels, using provincial names, such as Marlborough or Hawke's Bay, even though these themselves do not have a precise geographic or legal definition (Murray and Overton 2011: 424–25).

The programme, orchestrated around the slogan 'New Depths, New Characters, New Zealand', combined a series of talks with wine tastings and the discovery of three main regional areas: Central Otago (36 producers), Marlborough (37 producers) and the Pioneers (38 producers) – from Wairapara, Nelson, North Canterbury/Waipara Valley. For each of the main regions we were told a different story of the vineyards, while participating in a series of intense tastings to make sense of the diversity intrinsic to each of them. The regional theme was again showcased at lunch time with three dishes from 'Marlborough, home of the world-famous salmon; Central Otago, home of thyme, wild rabbit and apricots; and the Pioneers artisan food'. Wine tasting occupied most of the time during the first three days and it was organised in ways that were similar to comparable events I have attended in France and elsewhere. The only striking difference was the more collectivist and inclusive nature of the gathering. Each individual wine grower had his or her own stall with wines presented and sometimes a map of its 'blocks', that is to say its vineyards or plots within them. Each area presented first the region in terms of location, climate, geology, geography and history, focusing then on particular stories.

Central Otago opted for an informal, relaxed and lively presentation of the region with lots of photographs and *témoignages*; the two other areas were more formal and less confident in their outlook. The joint display of photographs, maps and bottles was notable for the greater emphasis placed upon the original story told by the Pioneers, which meant that it looked more like a museum exhibit than a wine fair. A caption was even included below each of the pictures associated with the beginnings of Pinot Noir production. Several names emerged from this story, including David Jackson, Danny Schuster, Richard Smart, Herman and Agnes Seifried, Ivan and Christine Donaldson, Stan Chifney, Neil McCallum and Clive Paton. They were either photographed planting their first vines or quotations from them were used to give context to the site of production. Place making was unfolding under my own eyes at a rapid pace, a theme that would to be picked up a few days later by Jasper Morris during his keynote speech: 'You are moving very fast, you seem to say we are mature, we are getting there'.

The concept of 'telling a story' was central to the 2013 New Zealand Pinot Noir event. The speakers were given instructions to tell their own story whether wine producer, film star, wine writer or anthropologist. Most of the tales I heard during the four days were always about uncertainties, self-deprecation, the lack of historical depth and the domination of science.

They contrasted vividly with years of ethnographic fieldwork conducted in Burgundy where, in the 1990s, questions were rarely asked. 'Why do I do that?' was not at the time part of the regional discourse. Unlike Burgundian viticulture, most of the wine producers in New Zealand are comparatively new to the profession; they were sometimes in the dairy industry, but often they had left the city behind them, investing their money in planting a vineyard and starting a new life. These stories reflect the youthful character of the national wine industry. Yet the role of European migrants in developing viticultural areas is also a major characteristic of New Zealand history. These families, two or three generations later, still play a major role in the national economy. One family I met and had lunch with owns a winery of repute near Auckland that I visited a few days after the event. It was originally established by the great grandfather who came from Croatia in 1944 to a small country settlement, ten miles away from Auckland, to build his winery. Three generations later, the family-run business is central to the regional economy and its story crystallises the various influences of its family members and of their global connections to the wine industry: 'In 1983 M travelled to gain valuable work experience in Bordeaux and Burgundy which has been so important in shaping the wine philosophy of KR'. Interestingly, Jasper Morris concluded his talk on the last day of the festival by advising New Zealand Pinot Noir wine producers 'to tell their story rather than being told', underlining the necessary step of becoming a benchmark at the international level.

Taste, Science and Nature

Yet behind this scene, a wide range of attitudes and opinions added another dimension to the understanding of the complexity of the Burgundian model and its interpretation, understanding and translation in different places. To make sense of the process of translating terroir, some background is necessary. New Zealand is a small and recent player in the global wine trade (Murray and Overton 2011: 423). It occupies fifth place internationally in terms of Pinot Noir production and it accounts for only about 0.5 per cent of total global wine production. The international wine industry has traditionally been characterised by the heavy involvement of capital and by contradictory processes of globalisation and localisation. In the global mapping of the New Zealand wine industry terroir has been used over the last four or five decades as a trump card, while a weak legislative framework was preserved for protecting and defining place names as GIs (Geographical Indications). In the early 1990s, the New Zealand Wine Institute was pressed to engage with global agreements through the

TRIPS (The Agreement on Trade-Related Aspects of Intellectual Property Rights) mechanism of intellectual property (Moran 2000). Legislation for Geographical Indications (Wine and Spirits Registration Act 2006) was eventually passed, but it was never fully implemented, relying instead on voluntary registration (Murray and Overton 2011: 423). The situation remained largely unaltered until the time of my trip to Wellington. Today the New Zealand wine industry counts no fewer than 703 wine companies compared to 421 in 2003. The area under production has doubled during that time to reach 33,400 ha, and 178 million litres were exported in 2012. While Sauvignon Blanc production dominates, representing 51.78 per cent of the overall wine production area in that year, Pinot Noir and Chardonnay account for 14.45 per cent and 11.35 per cent respectively.[10] In terms of volume of wines exported (millions of litres), these figures suggest the remarkable success of the wine industry which has more than doubled in volume during the last decade.

The development of Pinot Noir in New Zealand captures in microcosm the historical trajectory of the industry and the constant preoccupation with quality rather than quantity. In a seminal article discussing the history of the New Zealand wine industry, Warren Moran (2000) cites the work of the scientist, Romeo Bragato, in the nineteenth century who acknowledged the potential offered by the geography of New Zealand for the cultivation of vines. According to Moran (2000: 539), the varietal composition of each region was always strongly influenced by its history and its level of development. As far as Pinot Noir is concerned, its history can be traced back to the work of a handful of pioneers who have led the revival of the wine industry over the last few decades. The improvement of varietal selection and clones as well as the canopy technique and the viral status of the vines contributed to better quality wines. From the 1990s onwards, regional specialisation became more apparent especially in the main wine regions. At that time, the majority of the Pinot Noir was blended with Chardonnay to produce effervescent wines (Moran 2000: 539). It was only at the end of the 1990s that the quality of Pinot Noir wines was promoted through the development of Marlborough as the principal region of production. But it was Wairarapa which established the reputation of New Zealand in relation to Pinot Noir, which was followed quickly by others such as Nelson (Moran 2000: 540). This story was told during the pioneers' regional programme by some of the actors involved in this enterprise, most of them highly educated in the science of wine and well-travelled. From the black and white photographs forming part of the exhibition, it was easy to understand the adoption of the term 'pioneers' and to imagine the hard work attached to their experiments with viticulture.

When discussing the great success of New Zealand wines, three main areas of discussion came to the fore during the 2013 Pinot Noir festival. They concerned different types of publics – from wine experts and critics to wine growers and scientists – and reflected the ways in which ideas, norms and values circulate and are debated, cause conflict or are even strongly contested. They also offer useful vignettes to the ethnographer. To an anthropologist preoccupied with the flow of culture and the study of ideas, people and objects through a multi-sited approach, they give a sense of the cultural complexity at stake and of the layers of analysis attached to the study of a commodity such as wine at the global level. How to make sense of 'culture' in the anthropological sense of the term in the midst of this complexity? For the New Zealand wine industry and especially the world of wine critics, taste plays a crucial role when benchmarking Pinot Noir wines.

Geneviève Teil (2004; and with Barrey 2009: 428) has argued convincingly that viticulture is strongly structured around the gustative appreciation of wines, which contributes not only to the evaluation of their quality, but also to their level of pricing. Taste therefore plays a central role in the structuration of global wine culture and its attendant economy. The gustative appreciation or evaluation of wine is, according to Teil,[11] a question of reflexive engagement of people and objects of which the outcome is uncertain. Taking the example of Pinot Noir in New Zealand, I keep wondering how wines become economically valued and recognised and what makes the difference between a great and a bad wine. Experts have plenty to say about it, but, for the wider public, taste does not matter so much; pleasure is the key and this is defined by the social context in which tasting takes place. Yet for the wine expert or critic, to taste is his/her job, and when comparing and describing it he/she sometimes gets it wrong. How do these practices translate in economic terms? What are the parameters in fixing prices and getting your wines recognised? To answer these questions, what follows could be described as an attempt to define 'taste' through the insights provided by my ethnographic peregrinations.

In relation to Pinot Noir, one of the benchmarks is best illustrated in a quotation by the famous British female wine critic, Jancis Robinson, which sets the international standard regarding the taste of the grape regardless of terroir:

> Pinot, as I have said, can vary enormously but its essential characteristic is charm. It tends to be fruity, perfumed and haunting. It dances on the palate rather than overpowering it. Heavy tannins and deep colour are not essential elements in a fine Pinot Noir – not even in a young Pinot Noir. In fact some of my favourite burgundies are not grand, long-living monsters but lively,

sprightly essences of place, sometimes just a general village wine – not one labelled with the name of a *grand cru* or even a *premier cru* but one carrying simply the name of a village.[12]

To sum up her thoughts rather less eloquently, Pinot Noir is about fruits, tannins and depth; it also develops over time. Interestingly, Jasper Morris, one of the finest commentators on Burgundy, who lives in the region and is highly esteemed locally, made a point in his lecture to the 2013 New Zealand Pinot Noir festival. He argued that Pinot Noir taste has to be about 'fruits at the back rather than at initial attack' and that New Zealand wines are 'nearly mature, we are getting there', indicating the direction to follow for producers to reach the benchmark and even go further in terms of quality. This international benchmark for Pinot Noir is the result of a collective and international process of common evaluation and agreement, largely dominated in this part of the world by the Anglo-Saxons, about taste and quality.

In organising events such as the Pinot Noir festival, the local industry positions itself, puts its products both on display and under scrutiny, and engages with wine critics who will, in return, write about it and legitimise, or not, the wines tasted. RC, one of the wine commentators at the 2013 New Zealand Pinot Noir festival, presented his notes online, acknowledging the difficulties in codifying the regions through the wine tasting he has conducted:

> The over-riding impression I gained was the incredible diversity of style between the wines from this very different collection of wineries. This is to be expected, as the wines are from very separate regions, sites and terroirs, and made by very individual people with their own philosophies. Being a person who is organised and enjoys categorising and 'putting things into boxes', I tried to find commonality with the wines tasted according to their region. I felt the North Canterbury wines were marked by their serious extract and structure; the Nelson wines notable for their rich fruit expression, and the Wairarapa wines by their soft, substantial natures. Of course, within each regional group, there was a range of styles.[13]

Yet his notes synthesise the attempts made by the wine industry to propose a new reading of New Zealand Pinot Noirs which to compete with the best in the world have to satisfy the international taste standard, but also suggest a particular interpretation of the place, 'between a general framework for Pinot Noir, based on the general structure on the palate, and specific detail which comes from the sense of place: flavour profile, balance of fruit, acidity, tannin etc.'[14] The notes showcase fine wines, regional diversity, artisanship and complexity, putting New Zealand on the map next to Burgundy.

Interestingly, the discourse used by the wine producers was about regionality rather than terroir and this trope will be analysed later. The wine market constituted by social actors from different perspectives will then use these signs of quality to attribute economic value to products. Food and wine critics who were present at the festival play a major role in validating local systems of classification and promoting specific producers. Other factors also come into play, such as marketing, reputation, image, ecological positioning and rarity.

Another major and much more visible area of debate is the role of scientific knowledge in viticulture versus empirical experience. Anthropologist Robert Ulin (2002: 691) has argued that the relationship between artisanship and science is a point of conflict and tension in the self-definition of wine-growing culture in southwest France. As we can see in the case of New Zealand, it goes beyond the traditional cleavage between New and Old World wines. The multimedia storm created by Matt Kramer and his speech on atheists and great wines reveals the underpinning norms and values which define the world of wine at the global level. Several websites reported the speech, and inflammatory comments illustrating clearly the philosophical/religious divide as well as the relationship wine growers have with science were noteworthy. As one of the contributors put it: 'The idea that there is an arbitrary limit to the boundaries of what scientific method can contribute – based on the idea that there are current limits at any given time in history – is patently stupid and quite frankly typical of so much anti-scientific rhetoric', and later, 'You'll surely concede that chemistry is not the only science involved in wine. Additionally, the fact that science currently struggles to explain all the complexity of the drink and its associated process does not remotely mean that it never will'.[15] It is clear from the long list of reactions generated by Matt's talk that the topic of science was highly polarised among wine professionals. It was seen by a majority of New Zealand producers as one side of the equation; empirical knowledge and experience of previous vintages clearly also matter. Indeed, a number of my informers have pointed out and emphasised how empirical knowledge has played an important role in their mastering and crafting of quality, especially when dealing with viticultural matters. Small- and middle-sized independent New Zealand producers present themselves as artisans rather than wine growers and some of the wineries are showcased as wine boutiques.

The use of empirical knowledge is, for example, telling when discussing the choice of clones planted by the pioneers. According to one my informers, they define themselves as different from the other producers:

We have the benefit of living in London and understanding much wider tastes and wine habits that gives us a different perspective. We are really hands on in every aspect of our wine development even from this distance. Then we have a different context to the rest of the New Zealand industry. Our professional background is different, we are coming from the business professions where you undertake appropriate research before embarking on anything. When you fully understand what you want to do and what you need to achieve that then we execute it. Owning fully our vineyard with no investors or minor shareholders enables us to just get on with it.]

Key players in New Zealand viticulture, they base their philosophy around empirical investigation and identify good practices to follow:

We went to Beaune in Burgundy and made a study of all the clones that we thought would be suitable. We found a fabulous wine library there and we purchased every book in English that was relevant. We then read for months before making the final selection then we consulted with our viticulturist and our consultant for a second opinion. There was one book that was our main insight written by the Ministry of Agriculture Fisheries and food CTPS titled 'Catalogue of Selected wine Grape varieties and clones cultivated in France'. We have only two clones that are not Dijon, clone 5 California and Able which is New Zealand. We purchased our clones from a New Zealand nursery due to the quarantine and horticulture laws, that is the way that you have to do it.[16]

Several producers emphasised a less pragmatic approach on their websites and most of them would take local viticultural guidance. Our field trip to Central Otago confirms this strong polarisation within the group between an emphasis on using traditional know-how and a more technical and scientific approach.

In the quest for quality, the reference to Burgundy starts with the selection and plantation of vines. It even goes as far as the DRC myth, known also as the Gumboot or Abel Clone, which is widely shared and laughed about by producers. The story is recalled on the website of one of the most famous wine growers from Martinborough who I had the pleasure of meeting during my stay. The story is told as follows: in 1982, soon after purchasing the Ata Rangi home block, Clive, a well-known wine producer, called Auckland winemaker Malcolm Abel and volunteered to work on the production of a vintage. He knew that Malcolm was also chasing premium Pinot Noir, and the two soon became close friends. Malcolm died unexpectedly a year later and the Abel Vineyard itself was ultimately lost to urban sprawl. But Malcolm had already given Clive some promising pinot cuttings, the offspring of a single vine cutting allegedly taken by a traveller from Burgundy's finest estate, Domaine de la Romanée-Conti. The illegal cutting had been intercepted and confiscated at Auckland airport, where Malcolm, coincidentally, was working as a customs officer in the mid 1970s. He immediately understood its significance, and sent it straight to the state-owned viticulture research station of the day. Malcolm waited patiently for the first cuttings to become available, and duly planted them. To this day, the Abel Clone, or Gumboot Clone (legend has it the stolen cutting was hidden inside a Kiwi gumboot), remains at the heart of Ata Rangi Pinot Noir. Its website claims that:

> We love the texture, and length of palate it delivers. Its tannins are substantial, yet are incredibly silky and fine. From our site it brings dark cherry, and a brooding, savoury feel. The Pinot Noir grapevine is genetically very unstable, so there are literally hundreds of naturally occurring variants referred to as clones. Premium pinot needs the complexity that a range of these clones brings. We have over a dozen planted, with Clone 5/ Pomard [note the spelling] also considered very valuable, giving the wine a solid mid-palate structure and wonderfully vibrant, aromatic fruit. The much feted Dijon Clones, selected by the research unit at Dijon University in the late 1980s, are less textural but have more front palate weight, and beautifully perfumed high notes.

Several other examples could be cited about the circulation of Burgundy clones all over the world in legal and illegal ways. By the mid-1980s, interest in European clones was increasing, especially in Oregon (USA). The Oregon wine grower organisation and Ron Cameron at Oregon State University worked together and successfully established relationships with Raymond Bernard at the ONIVINS (Office Nationale Interprofessionnelle des Vins de Bourgogne) in Dijon and Alex Schaeffer at the research institute for viticultural and oenological experimentations (INRA – Institut National de la Recherche Agronomique) in Colmar.[17] Most of the vines imported into the USA were controlled by UC Davis (University of California, Davis) and several selections of Pinot Noir were imported from France and Switzerland, including Pommard (UCD 5) and Wädenswil (UCD 1A). Most of the trade became legally controlled and the Dijon clone started to propagate, following international agreements:

> The first Dijon clones of Pinot Noir (113, 114, 115) were brought legally into Oregon in 1984. The second set of shipments of Pinot Noir clones (667, 777), were sent in 1988 as a result of a subsequent trip by Adelsheim. Chardonnay clones 76, 95 and 96 were also part of these first shipments of clones. The French Dijon clones were first shared with FPMS in California in 1988-89. This program at Oregon State University was eventually discontinued upon the retirement of the permit holder less than ten years later. The laboratory technicians at Oregon State University had named the imported cuttings, Dijon clones, after the return

address on a shipping container of clones from Dijon, France. The name quickly became part of viticulture lexicon. Dijon clones imported into the United States are designated by numbers assigned by the French Ministry of Agriculture known as the Comité technique permanent de la sélection (Committee of Selection of Cultivated Plants, or CTPS) and include the most widely planted CTPS clones 113, 114, 115, 667, and 777 (and more recently 459 and 943). FPMS assigned the same 3-digit numbers to the Dijon clones.[18]

Yet smuggling clones was an integral part of the mythical story about Burgundy. Several of the producers I met in New Zealand talked about it with amusement. The French are highly protective of their vineyard names and by the mid-1990s, they threatened legal action against any Americans who were found to be using grapevine cuttings from their famous vine-yards, especially if they were vocal about it. Many rumours arose of vines being smuggled in suitcases from such famous vineyards as La Tâche and Romanée-Conti (so-called DRC clones) which were planted in California vineyards, but no one admitted to it for fear of violating French intellec-tual property law, not to mention US importation laws. The plantings are simply referred to as suitcase or heritage clones in the viticulture trade and wine publications today. New Zealand producers, on the other hand, cite the legally imported Dijon clones in some of their websites, but there has been no serious academic or scientific study of the clones or of their legal or illegal planting in New Zealand.

New Zealand's legal importation of Pinot Noir clones began in the early 1960s, when government viticulturist Frank Berrysmith put Clone AM10/5 through quarantine. Selected by the Wädenswil Research Station in Switzerland, 'Ten Bar Five' is responsible for most of the initial plantings of Pinot Noir in Otago, Martinborough and Canterbury. The 1970s wit-nessed a series of importations, largely from the University of California, Davis (UCD). The early UCD series, comprising Clones 5, 6, 13 and 22, provided winemakers with a new favourite – and UCD Clone 5 has gone on to become one of the mainstays of Pinot Noir wine making in many regions of the world. Clone 5 and Clone 6 and, to a lesser extent, Clone 13, were widely used in the next wave of Pinot Noir plantings in New Zealand, which occurred in the late 1980s. While there are still some plantings of Clone 6 (more so in Otago than other regions), Clone 5 proved a real winner, and it has become a favourite part of the mix in most vineyards today. Another 1970s accession, the Abel selection, comes complete with a colourful and uniquely New Zealand pedigree. The story is recalled with some variations compared to the initial one put on Clive's website, but it remains an enduring trope cited with amusement by most of the wine growers I met there.

Science and nature overlap in the discussion on quality as the key question is how to produce the perfect bottle. Most of the recent discussion around, for example, DRC in Burgundy builds on the mystical and esoteric aura of the domain which adds panache and a marketing lustre to the wine produced. It is also part of a worldwide shift from geologically based arguments to the recognition of the wine grower as the mediator in the expression of terroir (Demossier 2010). This shift has been part of a growing reinterpretation of terroir which places a strong emphasis upon nature and promotes an organic approach to viticulture. Geneviève Teil (2010) argues that the new link between taste and environment which has been emphasised by French organic producers has added complexity to marketing strategies. It has also given impetus to the use of environmentally-friendly vine-growing practices that have helped to encourage the production of wines that are strongly identified with terroir.

The recent development of environmental norms in viticulture has transformed the rules of the game and has also given a new dimension to terroir. In 2007, New Zealand launched an ambitious five-year sustainability policy aimed at placing all wines under independently audited environmental programmes by 2012. Recent estimates suggest that it was a success; 94 per cent of vineyards are now estimated to be sustainable and certified. During my field trip to Martinborough, with my friend and fellow anthropologist Peter Howland, we observed that the majority of the wineries displayed the label of certification on their gate. *Biodynamie* was another prominent philosophy advocated by some of the wine growers we met during our trip. The example offered by Mana (Marlborough Natural Winegrowers) exemplifies the wider trend in local viticulture: 'We believe the less we manipulate the soil, the grapes, the wines, the more the wines will express where they come from, highlighting the regional and sub-regional influences more completely in the wines'. When visiting different sites in Central Otago, Martinborough or in the North of Auckland, I was struck by the polished and carefully controlled vine training of some of the vineyards encountered, which clashed with more organically driven or biodynamic sites which were less numerous. It was clear to me that lots of human intervention had gone into the vine tending. This was in some cases acknowledged by my informers: 'I was trained at the University of Lincoln and I am still connected to them through some of their discussions through tweeters. I am a scientist, I managed forty vineyards'. Moran (2000: 544) has described the second or third generation of wine growers as highly educated, having been trained either in Australia (Roseworthy) or California (Davis) or Lincoln in New Zealand, and having completed a first degree in humanities or social sciences. Many have also travelled the world and often worked in French vineyards, usually in Bordeaux or Burgundy, during their training. Yet it is in Central Otago more than anywhere else that this deep fascination for Burgundy was most visible.

Central Otago and the Quest for the Holy Grail?

On the Saturday following the 2013 New Zealand Pinot Noir festival, while the wine critics and writers joined a Pinot Noir safari which was going to take them to Marlborough, I flew to Queenstown, Central Otago. If there was a place on the map which could be described as blessed by God, it is here. The wind-whipped landscapes, vast open spaces and treeless vistas give a sense of space and scale like no other region in New Zealand. The linear sweep of the skylines and the almost unbroken form of the land is a photographer's paradise. When you discover the region, with its overpowering sense of clean, decongested space, you are pleasantly surprised to discover that there are still sites like this in the world. RB, one of the most respected wine growers in Central Otago, sums it up nicely in the leaflet presenting his wines: 'In Central Otago, every day is a holiday. This landscape is so fantastic and the region is so strikingly beautiful. And it's a bonus to grow grapes so well here'. To locals, the space and scale provide a sense of place that is difficult to take for granted. The unequalled beauty is heightened by the presence of open plains and steep, cutting valleys. The high mountains with their snowy peaks, a beautiful blue sky and the majestic lakes all define a continental climate locked in deep valleys. The region sits just 100 km west of Milford Sound, the second wettest place on Earth with around 10 metres of rain annually. However, with the Southern Alps protecting the region, almost all the water is deposited in the mountains as either rain or snow. By the time you travel through Central Otago's vineyards to the east, you will have reached the outskirts of New Zealand's driest farm, with only around 250 mm of annual rainfall. Temperatures throughout the year are often around 31 to 32º in the summer, but the nights are cool.

The climatic contrast between Central Otago and the more humid, warmer wine regions of the North Island can be illustrated by the difference in the timing of the grape harvest. In the more northerly vineyards, picking generally takes place in late February or early March, while in Central Otago the harvest begins in mid- to late April – a difference of some six to seven weeks. The structure of the soil also differs considerably from the country's other wine-growing regions, with heavy deposits of rough-edged mica and other metamorphic schists in silt loams. This soil drains easily, and given that most vineyards are positioned on hillside slopes, artificial irrigation is usually essential, as we witnessed. All these characteristics make the region a privileged site of Pinot Noir production, with all the challenges it presents.

According to Jancis Robinson, cited by Jasper Morris, many believe it is where the Pinot Grail is to be found: 'New Zealand is setting its cap at Pinot Noir and certain examples from Martinborough/Wairarapa just north-east of Wellington in the south of the North Island and Central Otago towards the south of the South Island suggest that they may well have a real claim to be the next great Pinot region'.[19]

On my arrival at Queenstown airport I was welcomed by the COWA president and taken on a tour of the region and a visit to some of the vineyards he manages. Like several other wine growers who have combined different careers, he qualified and worked as a chartered accountant for a decade before retraining in viticulture at Lincoln University, and he has been growing grapes ever since. He is also the wine grower for Mt Extreme wines, amongst others. His company employs around ninety people and covers 300 ha of production. He advises on plantation and visits each site on a regular basis. Our tour began with a visit to Queenstown and the Gibbston valley, taking me to various sites of wine production and ending up at Rippon.

The history of the place is one associated with a young wine producing area and external investments as well as periods of crisis. I was quite surprised by the number of abandoned vineyards, especially along the main road we followed with new blocks of vines appearing on the slopes and hills. There was a clear sense that experimentation was ongoing and that people learned from it very quickly. In this part of the world, vines are ready to produce in their second year, while in traditional European viticulture it is not until the fourth year that they are considered as legally ready. The lack of a strong legal framework facilitates the development of the New Zealand wine industry and explains its fast pace. For my informer, the Burgundian model, even if it is recognised for quality, is not necessarily the one to follow as 'there are too many regulations'. Instead, it is treated more as something to learn from, a tableau for the selection of information which can then be applied to Central Otago. On the viticultural front, Central Otago is, according to him, where it needs to be in terms of quality, but the next step is related to the implementation, or not, of the IGP (Indication Géographique de Provenance, or Protected Geographical Indication) and the regional dimension of its applicability.

Taking me to the vineyards located near Mt Difficulty, he wanted to illustrate that terroir could be 'constructed' anywhere: 'Look we have three different plots close to each other, located on different parts of the hill or the flat bit, they share various characteristics in common, but are also very different in nature'. They correspond to three different ways of making wines and three different price and marketing brackets: a single block or vineyard on the hilly site; the estate which is formed of several blocks; and what we call the urban, which is basically the site along the road. The vineyards belonging to Mt Difficulty Wines are on several different sites on the south side of the Kawarau River at Bannockburn. They were planted early in the 1990s and their names refer to people and events from New Zealand's historic gold rush which is part of the Otago story: Long Gully, Manson's Farm, Target Gully, Pipeclay Terrace and Templars Hill. Each has a specific terroir, largely influenced by climate, and offers a variety of soil types, from open gravels to heavier clays. They are all low in fertility, and include light sands, clays, loams and gravels. Germanic man-made soils, which came about as a result of hydraulic mining and sluicing in the gold mining era of the late 1800s, can also be found on some blocks. The so-called Bannockburn soil is one of the few soils in the world classified as man-made. One feature common to all local vineyard soils is the high pH levels: sweet soils are tailor-made for the production of quality wines. Since 2001, Mt Difficulty Wines have become renowned for the Single Vineyard wines it produces from the best sites on its Bannockburn Estate properties. With variations in soils, microclimates and grape clones, the sites each have markedly different features. The philosophy of Single Vineyard wines is to display the characteristics that are particular to their terroir, thus each wine tells the unique story of its own place. Again, as elsewhere in the world, creating differences and legitimising them with an individual narrative contributes to the global wine industry and its core value.

During the 2013 New Zealand Pinot Noir festival several of my informers drew my attention to Central Otago as the place where the Burgundian model 'was the most emulated'. My invitation to New Zealand was indeed part of the cultural exchanges set up by one of my old New Zealand friends, Nick, met during my fieldwork in Burgundy nearly twenty years ago. Among the students working on one of the domains I studied, he and I met when he came to discover 'how *grands crus* were made'. Nick was the second youngest of six of a family of Otago Pinot Noir producers and he stayed for one year to learn his trade. Following his experience, Nick, then Sophie who owned the domain where he was placed, and years later their children, went to visit Nick and to share the Burgundian wine model. Nick's wife, Jo also worked for six months at the Domaine de Monthelie, owned by Aubert de Villaine and managed by his nephew. In 2010, Nick, now the president of the Central Otago Winegrowers Association (COWA), invited me to come and discuss the terroir strategy with local producers, an invitation I could not accept at the time. Asked why terroir was of interest to New Zealand wine producers, Nick responded that 'in defining Central Otago's own viticultural path forward, it has been, and will continue to be, essential to look towards the classic model of Burgundy and its *climats* for inspiration and guidance'.

This feeling was confirmed by other local wine growers when I discussed it with them. As RB, a well-respected producer in Central Otago, explained when commenting on the Burgundian model: 'a very complex mosaic, we in Central Otago only can learn from it, as we are still shaping our pieces not knowing yet what the mosaic will look like'.[20] In a letter addressed to the Association pour la Reconnaissance des Climats de Bourgogne on 6 November 2010, Nick argued:

> With a truly noble variety content to grow here, along with expressive schist-based soils and a complex array of microclimates and landscapes, the region naturally looks now to seek clarity in the potential of each site and how this might be manifested in the glass. It is clear that inspiration and direction may be gained in this endeavour by considering the classical model of Burgundy and the heritage of les climats.

Through Nick's attachment to Burgundy and his admiration for the *grands crus* model, several strategies were promoted in Otago to imitate its success. Nick's letter underlined the growing interest in the relationship between a site and its concrete gustative and sensorial expression in the glass through the taste of the place. At the core of Otago wine producers' concerns is the role of the wine grower, seen as one of custodianship 'in an ongoing pursuit of quality', as emphasised by Nick. Yet what this cultural exchange between Otago and the Côte d'Or wine producers tells us is how some of the dominating conceptions of wine and regulation of the market – traditionally defined by their relationship to nature (the Old World equals nature as a driving determining force, and in the New World, nature is seen as an enemy that must be controlled and dominated by science) – can overlap in some local circumstances and lose their initial meaning in the process of transnational circulation.

Invited and funded by the COWA to come and discuss the Burgundian model from the perspective of an anthropologist, I was joining a list of eminent invited personalities who had expertise on Burgundy, including Matt Kramer, Jasper Morris, Jancis Robinson, Sylvain Pitiot and others. For example, a session was organised in 2011 on the natural geography of Burgundy and on what defines a place most accurately. My talk, which took place after the 2013 New Zealand Pinot Noir event, was about terroir in Burgundy and its critical analysis. A large audience of wine producers attended and I must confess that it was one of the most enjoyable intellectual debates I have had in years, even compared to academic settings. Nick and his fellow wine growers had a specific set of questions in mind which they wanted me to explore. I had given them a sense of what I intended to cover when I gave them a copy of an article I had published in the *Journal of Royal Anthropological Institute*, entitled 'Beyond Terroir'. My briefing was clear: I needed to talk about Burgundy and the terroir model.

The COWA president defined the background as follows: 'We are right in the throes of defining sub-regionality at present within the Central Otago region and have called a meeting for this coming week to try to understand more fully what defines the sub-regions (starting with the apparently simply concept of geographical borders, which seems appropriate given our very short wine growing history)'. Interestingly, a few weeks before my trip Nick sent me a list of points he wanted me to cover more precisely:

> you talk about how you see the regional elites dominating the Burgundy's sense of place and identity over a long period of time (les *climats* being the most current example). Yet the process has benefited the majority of wine produc- ers, and the UNESCO campaign is another example of the shift of *terroir* to consolidate the economic positioning of the elites at a time of drastic European reforms and global changes. The majority of the wine-growers will only realise the impact of such initiatives in the longer term, and without really having embraced or contested what is underpinning the shift in the *terroir* ideology.
>
> What I don't get from you is, although it may well not be in the scope of your research … is this a correct (ie natural) sequence? Should the regional champions maintain their firm grip on the ship's wheel? Or does a social anthropologist chose not to judge?
>
> And, more importantly for the 'Regionality Session' 'It is after all about place-making in an interconnected world where globalisation remains trans- lated and interpreted in local terms. This production of locality, however, does not benefit all members of the community in the same way'.
>
> Can it? Should it?

This interesting exchange set the tone for the intellectual discussions which were to follow and provided me with an example of how knowledge is selected and then passed on or learned from or engaged with critically. My presentation lasted forty-five minutes and questions came from different parts of the audience, covering a wide range of topics from knowledge, regional governance to more cultural aspects. The discussion also focused on the UNESCO bid for heritage status and why Burgundy had decided to launch it.

One of the main aims of COWA was to invite the Association for les Climats de Bourgogne to Otago and Nick was hoping to get the president of the Association pour la Reconnaissance des Climats de Bourgogne to be directly involved. For this purpose I was asked to play the role of mediator between the two projects and to go back to the Association on my return to give them the background behind this initiative and what was expected from them. My purpose was to get a better understanding of what circu- lated between the two geographic areas and how knowledge was transmit- ted, selected and used in a global context. The opportunity offered by Nick was timely as the UNESCO bid had just been postponed until 2014 and its international dimension needed to be consolidated. In this context, the trip was planned for June 2013 and it was organised just before the 37th session of the UNESCO Committee in Phnom Penh in which the Association intended to participate. The exchange, if successful in attracting the famous co-owner of DRC, was likely to put Central Otago on the global map of Pinot Noir and this did not escape his attention: 'Yes I can see that there is some interest in what we are doing ... Nick has always tried to emulate what we do here in Burgundy'. It became clear after my meeting that the exchange was seen by both sides as an opportunity. It was not spelled out properly, but the silence surrounding the exchange was revealing. It was only because it would benefit both communities that it was going to take place and even then, Burgundy would define its own terms.

Yet the visit to Nick's estate in Central Otago illustrated in microcosm the global nature of the wine industry, and especially the extent to which a more ecologically friendly attitude towards wine production has become part of the modern global wine economy and culture. On the day of my arrival I was joined by two of Nick's importers from Hong Kong and taken on to a tour of his wine estate that had been founded in the 1970s. His parents moved back to the family farm in Wanaka in 1974. Acting largely on a hunch born when observing the schist slopes of the Douro Valley many years earlier, they planted a few short rows of experimental vines on a small steep bank above their house. Despite the mostly negative opinions of the viticultural experts of the time, the climate data that Nick's father, Rolfe, was collecting was encouraging enough for them to plant their first commercial vineyard block in 1982. The growing confidence they had in the site's potential to produce fine wines was soon to be rewarded. Today, the total area under cultivation is fifteen hectares with the majority of plantings in Pinot Noir and Riesling.

The family is very much hands on in every aspect of the estate management. The winery exports all over the world to a select number of prestigious outlets such as Grands Crus Paris, Artisans Cellar in Singapore and Altaya Wines Limited in Hong Kong. The latest promotional leaflet presenting Rippon is noted as follows:

> The impressive list below is the culmination of several years of good work. It takes not only sales volume but also long-term commitment and integrity to gain the trust of our suppliers. Each year, we visit every single one of them to exchange ideas on sales and marketing and to taste and select the new vintage's wines. This partnership naturally becomes friendship and each buying trip is as much for business as it is to enhance our relationship, illustrating the niche market in which Rippon wines are sold today.

As a committed biodynamic wine grower, Nick incarnates the new generation of young producers eager to learn and engage with the global wine industry without compromising their own principles or family values. Biodynamics is central to his philosophy which aims to reveal the true essence of the place. According to Nick, 'Granted custodianship over this very special piece of land, the family's principal goal is to create *vins de terroir*, wines that are an accurate reflection of their surroundings'. The family story is embedded in the website and this is an integral part of experiencing the place as their guests have the immense privilege of staying over at Lois' house at the top of the hill, with a breathtaking view over the lake. Three generations are involved in the management of the vineyard and the newly built Rippon Hall, devoted to the organisation of musical and cultural events throughout the year, adds another dimension to the site. Most of the wineries that I visited have chosen to develop other activities to attract tourists and locals, and Peter Howland's work on New Zealand wine consumption in Martinborough shows a similar pattern (Howland 2008).

What is fascinating about Rippon and its vineyard is the location itself, at 330 metres altitude, on the shores of Lake Wanaka. Maybe it was time for me to believe in 'a terroir blessed by God'. Again here, the whole experience of the site, the cleanness and crispness of the air and the majestic Wanaka Lake with its small island, make it one of the most beautiful places on earth. The holistic wine philosophy of Nick is summed up by the presentation on the family website:

> It is the micro-life in our soils which, in their ability to metabolise minerals into a form that vines can assimilate, are the link between plants and the soil. This simple biology is the essential framework in producing a wine which is true to its roots and site. With this understanding comes an absolute respect for the land and life therein and it is for this reason that Rippon is run biodynamically.

Yet this ecological commitment is not only a rhetorical marketing tool or a way of ticking the box organically and environmentally, it is about Nick and his family and every corner of the site breathes their philosophy. All the property's organic waste matter is recycled to make around 40 tonnes of fungal dominant compost every year and lots of care is invested in developing specific areas of the site. For example, Nick's sister has started apiculture so that bees will pollenate the vines while cows are kept on the property as a way of using natural fertilisers.

The artisanal and crafted dimension of the Rippon vineyard is apparent throughout the visit and even when one is taken to the cellar for the traditional wine tasting, it is clear that wine making is impregnated with the same philosophy. The Rippon experience contrasted vividly with the visit earlier in the day at Mt Difficulty where a more technological approach dominated. Everything in Bannockburn was neat, tidy and highly organised from the commercial looking cellar door to the long row of aluminium vats, the high-spec technological viticultural material within. Yet Rippon was closer to my Burgundian experiences of wine. The site of production is articulated around a similar discourse on terroir and the sense of place was the defining theme throughout the visit to the vineyards. The climatic conditions, as well as the position of the vineyards close to the shores of the lake and the waterfall creeks, make it a unique site. According to one of the New Zealand wine writers, 'N has a deep, almost spiritual, connection to the vineyard and that's reflected in his wines. They have a level of detail etched into them that few can match. If Pinot Noir tells the story of site more than most varieties, then the narrative that comes through Mills' wine is suitably dramatic and compelling'.[21]

Conclusions

Translating terroir between Burgundy and New Zealand, from the original model of European viticulture and the emerging Pinot Noir producing regions of New Zealand, offers an interesting example of the global process of culture and its flow. It is clear that the two regions are radically different. In the objectives mentioned in the draft report on Central Otago and Burgundy,[22] it is stated that Burgundy has been producing wines for many centuries and has long been celebrated as having some of the finest vineyards in the world. Burgundy is reputed to possess an immense depth of empirical knowledge, meaningful tradition and rich cultural heritage. Central Otago, on the other hand, has only been producing wine consistently since the late 1980s. The region's youth and pioneering outlook has allowed it to approach its craft with freshness and energy, relatively free from legal or historical constraints and it has fostered an ability to learn extremely quickly. The New Zealand experience seems to have had little in common with that of Burgundy, which could be defined as almost hermetically sealed in its own materiality and temporality, while Central Otago could be seen as open, soaking up external influences.

Yet what both areas have in common is the global wine industry defined by capitalism as well as consumers cultivating 'differential distinction'. In this global context although they started from different historical positions they are both engaged in the same pursuit of excellence. In this competition the position they have respectively reached determines to some extent their attitude towards each other. For the majority of its wine producers,

Burgundy has nothing to learn from Otago, while Otago has everything to gain from a cultural exchange. This is therefore an unequal relationship in the context of the global cultural economy. Globalisation therefore appears as both a homogeneous and a heterogeneous process in which the notion of scale plays a major role. Nick has chosen to borrow ideas, cultural practices and techniques from his experience working with the Burgundian *grands crus*, while at the same time translating them in a critical fashion in the context of his own place. Biodynamics makes sense to him as a way of following the family tradition rooted in an environmental and ecological ideology while playing down the capitalistic enterprise associated with the Hall and its development as a touristic site.

As Crang (Cook and Crang 1996) has argued, globalisation takes place through conceived, perceived and lived spaces and the cultural flow is filtered and interpreted according to the local culture in which it takes shape. Moreover, local culture and its production are constantly in flux through the interventions of local actors who are embedded in the wine industry and have a longstanding interface with the global as a result of the process of direct or nearly direct commercialisation. The global has become part of the equation as wine growers have begun to travel widely and have become more educated. At the local level, however, the context in which globalisation is played out, contested, interpreted or resisted through social practices, political initiatives or cultural developments is filtered by the nation. In Burgundy the AOC system imposes constraints on viticulture and its capacity to innovate, borrow, or change while in Otago the lack of a legal framework means that innovation is an intrinsic part of the global pursuit of excellence. The existence of specific networks of producers-buyers-wine critics-consumers attached to the production and commercialisation of wines worldwide has created the conditions for encouraging differentiation and 'distinction'. Marketing, but more importantly 'taste' as a social experience is central to the process of identifying specific networks. As the Australian founder and partner of the Prince Wine Store in Melbourne, Philip Rich, said to me: 'the consumers of Burgundy wines are very knowledgeable, they know what they want to drink. Burgundy sells very well. They are discerning buyers'. The Burgundy model has through globalisation established itself as a benchmark for the discerning buyer who has a certain level of social, economic and cultural capital. This is considered as the model to aspire to in terms of wine production, but also in terms of taste and consumption. Otago's place in this hierarchy is still being defined and, as we have seen, its pathway is complex, multi-formed and partly inspired by the Burgundian model. It has yet to finish writing its story.

Notes

1. This exchange between the two regions began in 2006 and was initiated by two wine growers and close friends from each respective region.
2. http://www.winespectator.com/webfeature/show/id/47981. Consulted on 5 March 2013.
3. For a full version of the talk, see http://www.wineanorak.com/wineblog/new-zealand/making-sense-of-matt-kramer-pinot-noir-2013-keynote. Consulted on 5 March 2013.
4. For more information, see http://www.timatkin.com/. Consulted on 14 June 2017.
5. The concept of 'bad wines' is never or rarely associated with the Burgundian story; it is all about greatness and quality. If there are bad wines, they are never singled out.
6. http://www.wineanorak.com/wineblog/?s=Kramer+Burgundy. Consulted on 8 August 2017.
7. See CD Les climats du vignoble de Bourgogne, Dossier, January 2012.
8. JD, personal communication, January 2013.
9. http://www.insee.fr/fr/themes/theme.asp?theme=13&sous_theme=5&nivgeo=22&type=1. Consulted on 5 March 2013.
10. For a statistical overview, see the following report: https://www.nzwine.com/media/2135/nzw_annual_report_2012_web1.pdf. Consulted on 21 November 2017.
11. Teil et al. (2011).
12. http://www.jancisrobinson.com/articles/jrs03402.html. Consulted on 8 August 2017.
13. http://www.raymondchanwinereviews.co.nz/blog/pinot-noir-2013-day-two-the-pioneers. Consulted on 14 June 2017.
14. Jasper Morris, personal communication.
15. http://www.vinography.com/archives/2013/01/matt_kramer_can_athiests_make.html. Consulted on 14 June 2017.
16. J.B from Central Otago.
17. http://www.ucanr.org/sites/intvit/files/24389.pdf. Consulted on 14 June 2017.
18. http://www.princeofpinot.com/article/1268/. Consulted on 14 June 2017.
19. http://www.jancisrobinson.com/articles/jrs03402.html. Consulted on 14 June 2017.
20. R.B, personal communication, 4 March 2013.
21. See http://www.rippon.co.nz/wine/reviews/. Consulted on 14 June 2017.
22. Central Otago and Burgundy: A Growing Fraternity. Draft Report 2012. Communicated by Nick.

Chapter 8
FROM TERROIR TO THE
CLIMATS DE BOURGOGNE

During my fieldwork trip to New Zealand in 2013, the question of why Burgundy should seek to obtain UNESCO World Heritage status was repeatedly brought to my attention by the actors of the local wine industry. Yet the response was far from simple. Appointed in 2008–2009 as the 'anthropological/sociological expert' on one of the scientific committees established by the Association pour la Reconnaissance des Climats de Bourgogne, I witnessed part of the process of putting together a 'convincing and solid' application to UNESCO. As a result, I was associated with some of the key stages of the process. In this context, I was able to conduct a reflexive ethnography and to use my experience as a springboard for a new investigation of terroir. Throughout my continuous and regular periods of fieldwork, new ethnographic vignettes continually called into question my analysis of the tensions between the single boundedness of the site and its wider circulation at the global level. The UNESCO dossier, which I had first started to work on in 2008, provided me with a useful timeline to revisit some of my previous ideas and to conduct a different kind of anthropological investigation in the context of a more globally defined industry.

In 2012, the French national committee[1] for UNESCO decided to favour two other dossiers, The Grotte Chauvet and the Volcans d'Auvergne,[2] ahead of those proposed by Burgundy and Champagne, respectively the *climats de Bourgogne* (cultural site) and the *paysages de Champagne* (Champagnes Landscape). Like my New Zealand informers, I was surprised by the subsequent sudden re-emergence of Burgundy's candidature. Interestingly, it was in 1990 that Burgundy had first sought World Heritage status, and a project had been launched only to succumb[3] to local right-wing opposition under Mitterrand's presidency.[4] After more than twenty years of fieldwork in Burgundy, I know how hard it is to persuade individuals and communities to engage with cultural or heritage issues. I worked throughout the 1990s with the local heritage taskforce, the DRAC (Regional Directorate for Cultural Affairs), on various local projects involving the wine growing profession. On several occasions, we raised concerns about the sustainability of land ownership and generational transmission, the management of local festivals and identity politics, knowledge and viticultural norms as well as historical changes and social configuration, in particular the tensions between *négociants*, wine growers and *propriétaires* which hindered any coherent professional vision of the local wine industry. Yet our call for debate remained largely unanswered. Interestingly, some of these issues resurfaced in the context of the UNESCO application.

My status as a French female anthropologist[5] in exile in a British university explained, in part, why I was invited to join the committee, something which was justified to me as: 'You are far away, but we need a sociologist'[6] (in the words of the project coordinator who was less sensitive to the distinction for an anthropologist ...) for the dossier. I accepted the task of writing a report on the *climats* from an anthropological perspective because I wanted to use this experience as a way of pursuing my long-term ethnographic investigation into terroir and its historical transformations through a single bounded site. It provided me with a unique perspective into a set of questions that I have grappled with over the years. Why is terroir such a powerful discourse about place? How is modernity affecting the place, the people and the products? Finally, what can the UNESCO application tell us about terroir?

This chapter seeks to unravel the complexities at stake in the context of the UNESCO application and to better understand how the politics of heritage might affect the Burgundian wine industry. The UNESCO application reveals some of the deeper issues discussed in the previous chapters, offering a window onto the cultural realm of a local society and the constant work of individuals or groups to try and guarantee the permanence of the fit, and facilitating the isomorphism of space, place and culture (Gupta and Ferguson 2002). Through the concept of terroir and its globalisation, the Côte d'Or *grands crus* offer a classic example of a geographically and historically stable site and a fluctuating, but strongly culturally defined, group of producers working in a particular ecological milieu. This evocative and powerful construction of place as a natural site protected from any external changes has progressively been consolidated in response to the increasing internationalisation of the wine supply and the growing competition in the market. If quality was not explicitly spelled out at the core of this social edifice of Burgundian wines, it is because the main story was one of a historically stable terroir defined as an imaginary discourse about the enduring relationship between a specific place, one acquired with difficulty and through hard labour, and a specific wine grower and his family. The terroir story fossilises social relations, work, and land ownership (Ulin and Black 2013: 84). Yet this terroir story is today reframed in heritage terms, the *climats de Bourgogne*, adding further lustre to an already economically highly valued site.

The *Climats de Bourgogne* Dossier

The management of the UNESCO project was entrusted to the GRAHAL (Groupe de Recherche Art Histoire Architecture et Littérature, Bureau d'étude pour la connaissance, la gestion et la valorisation du patrimoine, The Office for Knowledge, Management and Development of Heritage) located in Paris. The GRAHAL successfully led previous UNESCO dossiers such as Saint-Emilion and the Great Saltworks of Ar-et-Senan. It was represented at the national level by a young officer and at the local level by a young female project coordinator, who works alongside the President of the Association pour la Reconnaissance des Climats de Bourgogne, the well-known and respected co-owner of the Romanée-Conti (known as DRC). It is undeniable that without the continuous engagement and efforts of the president and the efficient team management of the project, the application would not have seen the light of the day. Not only has it generated several local initiatives in relation to tourism and rural protection, but it has also opened up environmental debates and stimulated collaboration involving the local university, the political milieu and the wine profession. More than 52,000 volunteers joined the campaign, helping to organise different events and supporting the association. The project has certainly transformed the local landscape. Through the candidature for the *climats de Bourgogne*, a constellation of social and professional actors have started to collaborate on issues spanning environmental and ecological concerns to urban planning and rural heritage protection as well as tourism. The application has already given an impetus to several initiatives and developments aiming at mapping Burgundy in the twenty-first century. Heritage, whilst ostensibly about the past, is always about the future, and the *climats* application offered a new way of redefining terroirs in the modern context while at the same time ensuring the continuity of the narrative about the cultural site, its past and present, and of consolidating a new territorial appropriation by the local elites.

Most of my encounters with Burgundy over the years have been characterised by an economy of words and what the Burgundians would define as a kind of silent, implicit understanding of specific issues. The application was generally presented in heritage and touristic terms with the aim of protecting terroir, while the consequences of such categorisation have not been fully debated at the local level.[7] That ambiguity is evident in an interview given by the president of the Association to Berthomeau[8] during the campaign. In the interview, in which he underlines the standardisation of tastes as well as the modern conditions characterised by increasing urbanisation and globalisation as driving the application to UNESCO, he argued that:

> We do it at a moment in history when the world and European regulations try to create global viticulture according to the same mould, where the AOC have lost some of their aura and where it was felt that the INAO serves more as a relay of European decisions than a defence of our French specificities where, in a rapidly changing world, it is essential to mark the values that distinguish you from others, when planning the venue needs to be controlled (sometimes almost too late!) and where it is vital that Burgundy shows that it is at the forefront in protecting its heritage, where sustainable development has been a key in terms of development strategy and conquest of the market.[9]

Yet the UNESCO application also needs to be understood in relation to the major debates affecting the world of wine: the wine reforms and the discussion on the TRIPS agreement (Trade Related Aspects of Intellectual Property Rights), the decline of distinctive and traditional values attached to local viticulture, the growing contestation and criticism of the Denomination of Origin, the increasing threat posed by urbanisation, and the sustainability of viticulture in the face of new challenges.

Nothing is, however, said about the competitive and changing context in which Burgundy tries to maintain its symbolic and economic status, nor about the recent wine frauds which have impacted upon its global reputation. Banks and Overton (2010: 58) have argued that a new approach is needed to reconceptualise the multiple worlds of wine as cross-cutting, contingent and contextual. Both differentiation and localisation characterise the contemporary worlds of wine and venerable dichotomies such as Old and New World no longer capture the complexity of an industry in which competition has increased. One part of the global consciousness generally includes environmental ethics and criticisms of worldwide market economies. The *climats* dossier, paradoxically, discreetly integrates environmental ethics while avoiding accusations of greediness and quest for profits by playing the *climats* card as devoid of any economic dimension. Yet heritage recognition has huge economic implications.

The extract from the interview cited above sheds some light on the background behind the declaration of exceptional universal value which was constantly underlined by the coordinators during our research meetings.[10] The *climats de Bourgogne* were proposed on the heritage list as a 'cultural site' and not as a landscape. They were understood as 'works of man or the combined works of nature and man and areas including archeological sites which are of outstanding universal value from the historical, aesthetic, ethnological or anthropological point of view' (article 1, paragraph 3 of the World Heritage Convention). The choice of 'cultural site' as the heritage category can be explained by the wish to establish a distinctive and singular application, compared to that of Champagne or other viticultural and heritage objects. The dossier argued that 'the exceptionality is based on the material character of these plots which refer back to a culture of taste diversity' (Rapport, volume 2: 64).

Previously UNESCO had given heritage status to nine cultural landscapes where viticulture plays a role, and three where there is a mixture of cultural and natural elements, but where viticulture is however present.[11] The Piémond Italien (2006) and the vineyards of Primošten, Bucavac Veliki, in Croatia were the only sites to benefit from World Heritage status under the category 'cultural site', while the majority of the other artefacts related to viticulture were presented under 'cultural landscapes'. I myself made the mistake at the beginning of the project of confusing landscape and site and was quickly reminded of the relevant category. Yves Luginbühl, an eminent geographer appointed to the *climats* dossier whose expertise includes the Côte d'Or landscape, argued that the exceptional universal value defined *climats* not as 'landscapes', but as 'cultural sites', 'attesting that they are not considered as landscapes, but as a localised set of plots, that is to say material goods that are identifiable in the space and clearly delineated'[12] (emphasising the private nature of the goods). Moreover, they could be identified through the taste of their wines. Yet the outcome of the UNESCO's deliberations has proven that a confusion between site and landscape was more than just a rhetorical issue, and Burgundy was finally classified as a landscape.

At the core of the application is the uniqueness and exceptionality of the site which arguably determines some of the logic behind the application, especially in terms of the heritage categories listed. Luginbühl's research report cited above served as the foundation for the rationale of the choice of categories. As the dossier combined cultural and natural elements as well as historical buildings and towns, including also the legacy of the legal denomination of origin which is territorially defined, the concept of site has imposed itself.[13] Luginbühl's work and his years of experience as an expert on UNESCO viticultural heritage sites have helped to craft a narrative about *climats de Bourgogne*. His intellectual contribution as a human geographer was central in building the case, alongside that of Jean-Pierre Garcia, geologist and archaeologist at the University of Dijon.[14] Criteria III and V were proposed to support the application, emphasising 'the unique or at least exceptional testimony to a cultural tradition or to a civilization which is living, or which has disappeared' (criteria III), and being 'an outstanding example of a traditional human settlement, land-use, or sea-use which is representative of a culture (or cultures), or human interaction with the environment especially when it has become vulnerable under the impact of irreversible change' (criteria V). On the basis of what the dossier defined as a 'coherent' geo-system, transmitted for generations, and the accumulation of technical-scientific knowledge attached to local viticulture, the *climats* are seen as a unique cultural phenomenon. For the local communities, the *climats* refer to both time and place as markers of excellence, quality and diversity characterising local wine production, and the work of man to unleash the natural potential of the site.[15]

What is striking about the *climats* dossier is the absence of the human dimension. Since the 1990s, a paradigm shift has occurred from the geological argument to the recognition of the wine grower as the mediator in the expression of terroir (Demossier 2011 and 2015) and, more recently, to a more symbiotic and ecologically determined relationship between man and nature. *Climats* encapsulate these shifts remarkably. According to the association, 'the *climats* are representative not only of a multi-secular culture, but also of human interaction with its environment'.[16] But how are they defined?

According to the dossier, the *climats* are defined as the Burgundian translation of the word terroir, taking on a different sense than that usually associated with meteorological conditions. Particular to Burgundy, it designates a parcel of land dedicated to a precisely delimited vineyard, known by that name for hundreds of years, and therefore a precise plot, soil, subsoil, exposure and microclimate, forming together within a vineyard characteristics that constitute a personality, unique to one terroir and one cru. These *climats* have created an exceptional mosaic of vineyards with a hierarchy of crus and an international reputation. The association website emphasises through an interactive map this diverse patchwork of plots. The fact that no fewer than 1,247 *climats* were debated at the meeting of our committee[17] and then chosen for the application reveals the difficulties in mapping the area with precision. It is worth noting that the French national committee overseeing UNESCO bids initially rejected the project on the grounds of 'mapping'.[18]

The issue of delineation is indeed central in heritage terms as it underlines processes of inclusion/exclusion in the heritage process and market. It is why several maps were integrated into the dossier to contribute to the cartography of place. The application itself was constructed around a precise delineation or perimeter which includes two zones: the central zone (13,475 ha) at the heart of the application, and a buffer zone (49,755 ha). In order to guarantee the future protection of the site, a territorial charter was ratified on 8 April 2011 by thirty-six mayors, the main local professional bodies, the INAO (Institut National des Appellations d'Origine), the chamber of commerce as well as the representatives of the regional and general councils. That charter lists the individual *climats* with the date of their cadastral recording and their size. The recent publication of the work of Marie-Hélène Landrieu-Lussigny[19] and Sylvain Pitiot (Pitiot and Landrieu-Lussigny 2012) has contributed to the recognition of the *climats* as a collective good, but has also established and fixed the perimeter of the heritage site under consideration.

By combining rural landscape with the towns of Beaune, Nuits-Saint-Georges and Dijon, already recognised for their emblematic and monumental architecture, the candidature aimed to fulfil several objectives. Broadly speaking, it sought to serve national and local political interests incarnated by the local *maires* and their respective projects around gastronomic culture and heritage. Dijon and Beaune in particular have long competed against each other for the title of 'gastronomic capital'. More precisely, the main objective is the protection of material and cultural heritage followed by the raising of public awareness of its exceptional value, enhancing and managing a unique area and finally, and handing down that legacy to future generations. As Lowenthal (1996: xv) noted about the heritage fever of our modern societies, 'in domesticating the past, we enlist heritage for present causes. It clarifies pasts so as to infuse them with present purposes'. If the *climats de Bourgogne* could be read as a new type of regional project at a time of crisis, it is only part of the story. The *climats de Bourgogne* certainly represent another stage in reasserting Burgundy's place in the global world of wine where quality and excellence have been radically recast and contested through the growing attack on the denomination of origin. By claiming heritage status, it seeks to ensure that distinctiveness in cultural and economic terms is preserved. Heritage is mobilised to shift emphasis onto the geographic site as a natural area to be protected and to mobilise local actors behind the UNESCO banner with the aim of transforming local practices and local/global perceptions of the place. Authenticity was presented as the main objective behind the application.

Enhancing Identity and Producing Distinctiveness

In a leaflet circulated to all the volunteers and supporters of the *climats de Bourgogne*, Bernard Pivot, the Honorary President of the supporting committee, former journalist and presenter of the intellectual and cultural programme 'Bouillon de Culture' (Cultural Melting-pot), himself a wine grower in nearby Beaujolais, asserted that 'terroirs and territories need to fade'. His appeal was an eloquent invocation of the *'esprit du lieu'* (Berliner 2012: 773), but also the wish to move away from the past. The *climats de Bourgogne* offer a perfect example of a complex politics of scale which aims to refashion terroir as a local and global place and make it a recognisable and enduring site by creating a differentiated local and global sense of place. UNESCO World Heritage status is a phenomenon that is constructed in a transnational field of interests, perspectives and locales.

As is pointed out by Hannerz (1992 and 1996), cultural processes are often shaped by the centre/periphery relationship. As wine is a global commodity, the relationship between centre and periphery is transformed. The success of the *climats de Bourgogne* application was finally officially announced during the annual Hospices de Beaune wine auction in 2015, which is an economic and emblematic site where local and global interests meet. It then progressively developed as a regional political project and was characterised by the main protagonists as a 'smooth and easy process of collective mobilisation at the local level' up until its encounter with the sphere of international heritage politics.

Both the French Ministry of Culture and the Ministry of the Environment were highly supportive of the *climats* project which struck a chord with the shift towards food heritage and the recent Paillotin environmental report.[20] In 2011 the local wine magazine *Bourgogne aujourd'hui* published a special issue investigating organic wines, entitled 'When Burgundy goes green', attesting to the rise of the debate on environmental issues. Despite a few minor political hurdles, the whole project succeeded in creating a bridge between politicians and wine professionals in a tense political climate marked by electoral change at the national level.[21] The competition between Dijon and its socialist mayor, Jean-François Rebsamen, and Beaune with its conservative RPR/UMP mayor and parliamentary deputy, Alain Suguenot, was centred around the race for the title of gastronomic capital. They both, however, supported the *climats de Bourgogne* application. Yet even if the national dimension was not obvious, there was nevertheless a strong French flavour to the local project, illustrated by the food heritage dimension which has, over the years, become central to French identity and its global recasting.

The World Heritage status given to the *climats de Bourgogne* is part of a process which aims to transform local places into objects of international interest, bringing local, national and international politics into the arena. Heritage valorisation represents not only a fashionable trend, but also political determination and the impact of social and economic interests (Bessière 1998: 32). The uniqueness of the site constructed by local actors moves the focus away from the product – wine – which has become more contested in the context of the public health issues associated with excessive alcohol consumption and prompted by the national governments and the World Health Organisation (WHO). In response, the wine lobby places greater emphasis on the material, 'natural', 'authentic', ecological and concrete element of production, the *climats*. It seeks to create a stronger identification between peoples and places.[22] Using a new category of landscape perception, the *climats*, and through the constant work and 'repeated acts' which establish relationships between the site and its visitors, it aims to transform the collective, cultural and regional identity. The intimate features of locality are used to rework understandings of the global or the world beyond (Tilley 2006: 25). In this context, the *climats* are intended to offer a new reading of the place, suggesting a text characterised by uniqueness/diversity or singularity/plurality which will be read differently and have a plurality of meanings for both groups.

As Bessière (1998: 28) has argued, historical context, origins and roots are the most important ingredients for a successful heritage market. The *climats* dossier endorses and essentialises these three conditions. The project challenged the economic reading associated with the now dated AOC system, which is increasingly disputed by consumers and producers (Teil et al 2011 and Teil and Barrey 2009). It argued very strongly for a clearer identification of the place and the product at a time when food security debates and issues of authenticity are to the fore. Rather than the consumer simply drinking the product, the *climat* locates its provenance and source with a clear mental image of geographical place and individual plots. The uniqueness of one *climat* is constructed against the extreme diversity of 1,246 others and to the further complexity of more than 100 AOCs, all located in a single site. The visual dimension is telling and instrumental to the construction of this new reading. The organisation of photographic exhibitions, as well as a series of public conferences on the *climats* and of publications accompanying the application, all participated in the construction of the site as a project to engage with at the local level. The Marche des Climats, which was attended by more than 3,000 people, was timed to coincide with the ratification of the territorial charter and provides another example of the strategies put in place to enhance the visibility of place. The initiative developed by the Burgundy tourist offices of a new kind of guide called a 'greeter'[23] is another way of facilitating cultural encounters. According to the bold claim of the website: 'A greeter is a local volunteer who takes you on a free and informal tour of his or her neighbourhood. Greeters share with you their personal anecdotes and interests, their everyday lives, and their love for Burgundy, so that you can be "a Burgundian for a day" too!' Other recent initiatives include targetting local schools and children and helping them to understand the local landscape and wines, and the renaming of the local wine festival as Saint-Vincent Tournante des Climats;[24] this is all part of a new reframing of the local wine culture.

It could be argued that through these new activities a more democratic and collective sharing of place will emerge in a space that was traditionally dichotomised and segregated in terms of its social functions and uses and even in terms of perceptions. Most of the Dijonnais interviewed by the local newspaper, *Le Bien Public*, in 2012 did not know what *climats* meant.[25] The *climats*, if they were understood at all, were usually conceptualised by the locals as a particular category of landscape distanced from everyday social practices and only experienced in their productive sense by the wine growers. Pierre Poupon sums it up very neatly: 'For the Côte d'Or wine grower, *lieu-dit* (locality) is what he calls a *climat*, that is to say the physical portrait of a plot of land, located in a specific place, having a particular shape, with a specific soil accompanied by cultural constraints and powerful forces having an impact on the quality of the final product' (Landrieu-Lussigny 1983: 10).

At the local level, it can already be said that the application has transformed the sense of place by putting *climats* at the core of this refashioning of the landscape. Moreover, increased tourism is likely to enable the visitor to better understand the complexity of the local milieu and thus to have access to a drink that normally they are unable to afford and consume. *Climats* are a remarkable example of a new invented discourse of place which has become accepted and effective and has proved its ability to mobilise large number of volunteers to join in, and campaign for UNESCO recognition. As a result, the *climats* are rapidly being integrated into the regional heritage alongside monuments such as the Hospices de Beaune, the Clos-de-Vougeot or the Palais des Ducs, but they will also be at the core of the new construction of the territorial identity of the region. Thierry Bonnot (2002) has argued that Burgundy is generally presented as a place where living is fine, landscapes are magnificent, gastronomical traditions reach back several centuries, and sumptuous monuments constantly bring to mind a glorious past. By introducing wine and rural landscape into the equation, it adds another dimension to the heritagisation of the region.

In the case of the *climats de Bourgogne*, several themes are embedded to contribute to the construction of distinctiveness and singularity of the site in local, national and global terms, illustrating a politics of scale as well as a subtle use of heritage for economic and commercial purposes. Above all, there is a clear political context which is marked by the decline of France as a world actor and its attempt since the 1980s and 1990s to singularise and protect its so-called traditional culture. In 2010, the Gastronomic Meal of the French was inscribed on the representative UNESCO list following a long series of initiatives dating back to the 1980s under the culinary heritage inventory, which was first launched at the regional level by the CNAC (Centre National des Arts Culinaires, or National Centre for Culinary Arts). If the Gastronomic Meal of the French and its invented imaginary seems highly questionable academically speaking, it is nevertheless an example of heritage being used to demonstrate the political dimension of anthropological concepts (Tornatore 2012: 342). This is not, however, the case with Burgundy, where there was a conscious decision not to mention cultural practices, idioms or traditions.

Jean-Louis Tornatore, a social anthropologist and former ethnological advisor on industrial *patrimoine*, has argued that the politics of heritage could be a way of reconsidering the relationship between territory and sovereignty. What benefits Burgundy clearly benefits France as the articulation of nation and region are important tropes in French identity. Yet following Tornatore's argument (2012: 347), the Burgundian take on the UNESCO Convention is to bend it to one's own tradition in bending oneself to it in turn. Heritage plays a major role in creating new territorialities in a constant game of territorialisation, deterritorialisation and reterritorialisation (Tornatore 2012: 344). Through the *climats* dossier, Burgundian regional identity becomes part of a 'heritage distinction' process in which the site is constructed as a 'key model of viticultural production and terroir' and 'an example of a human community, which has chosen the reference to place and time as markers of quality'. By including Dijon and Beaune, the application builds on the respective attempts of both cities to be recognised as 'gastronomic capitals', and, by the same token, it integrates an older heritage category, urban monumental heritage which is already recognised: 'This urban and territorial project articulates the historical monuments of Dijon, urban Burgundy and the world of wine'.[26] As a result, the site presents some unique characteristics compared to other UNESCO viticultural sites, but it also claims a uniqueness founded on the old emblematic towns of Beaune and Dijon, both famous for their architectural monuments, and produces an added value in the heritage market. The core of the dossier emphasises this uniqueness, distinctiveness and representativeness.

At the core of the dossier, the term *climats* was chosen by the local actors to avoid any references to terroirs which 'appear in other vineyards'. *Climats* was proposed as a modern interpretation of the old word terroir which has recently come under critical scrutiny (Teil 2010). Throughout the various discussions taking place in the context of the research committee, *climats*, despite being an almost totally invented category, was never really questioned. Most of the intellectual encounters I had were with Yves Luginbühl and the president of the Association, while the majority of the sessions were, I felt, dominated by general intellectual apathy. Both the geographer and the geologist attempted to trace the etymology of the term *climats*, using historical dictionaries or other historical sources. They cited several historical records, including the work of nineteenth-century folklorists and local historians. Yet they never fully problematised the concept of *climats* in its current form and the committee did not leave any space for such contestation which would have appeared out of place. Thus, for all the carefully crafted publicity, *climats* in Burgundy remains a twenty-first century invention.

The weakness of the *climats* argument, as presented in one of the documents circulated to the public,[27] is not difficult to spot, not least because it jumps from the seventh century to the seventeenth century without any apparent connection or archival justification. It is claimed that the central concept of *climats* originated in the sixteenth century, and yet we are told that the Chambertin, the Romanée, the Montrachet and the Clos de Bèze were identified as early as the seventh century. It seems unlikely that the early medieval monks had the same conception as those writing a thousand years later and equally improbable that the sixteenth-century authors thought of these parcels/vineyards in the same way as the twenty-first century advocates of the universal and exceptional *climats de Bourgogne*. One eminent professor of Burgundian legal history noted during one of the sessions of the committee that *climats* was first and foremost an erudite term used by local *sociétés savantes* (scientific societies) which gradually became more common. Yet in the vineyards and communities of the Côte d'Or the term was unknown before 2006, and I cannot recall hearing it used once during the many years of fieldwork that I conducted there from the late 1990s until that date. During my years of fieldwork, my informers always referred to the name of their parcels rather than using the term *climats*. When writing my report for the committee, I underlined the legal and private ownership issues attached to the parcel through the filiation and genealogical transmission, arguing for the importance of taking into account 'work' as a meaningful anthropological experience of the wine grower. The notion of *climats* was not part of the vocabulary and the terms *parcelles* or *cru* were more common. The notion of *climats* was not part of the vocabulary and the terms *parcelles* or *cru* were more common as they both integrated another dimension attached to the knowledge and experience of the place, referring to climatic and technical characteristics of land ownership (Chapter 4). Yet this dimension has been largely silenced and any mention of the changes in terms of social configuration have been left to one side.

The application was constructed around the *climats* as the centrepiece and as an enduring and permanent category of the local landscape mainly emphasised through its geographical, archaeological, geological and historical deployments which, it is claimed, form a unique and coherent whole or 'geo-system'. What is endorsed in the dossier is the relationship between man, history and nature. The term 'geo-system' relies on the articulation of three elements which have progressively been developed and are presented as complementary and inseparable: a productive element which includes the *climats* zones with the villages; an element of political and regulative power followed by a scientific and technical pole incarnated by Dijon, capital of Burgundy; and, finally, a commercial and *négociants* orientated element in Beaune. This provided the political and social configuration of the dossier, while the historical narrative refers to the slow but continuous construction of the site as one characterised by the constant quest for quality. It is encapsulated by the trope of the monk performed during the Marche des Climats to tell the *climats* story.[28] The *climats* are presented as historical and geographic markers of excellence and the social history that accompanies their emergence has been largely silenced or erased.

The narrative adopted by local actors is one privileging the soil and the material heritage, including the historical monuments and the urban political power of the dominant towns, Beaune and Dijon. What emerges clearly from the dossier is the lack of a social dimension which is hardly mentioned. The narrative emphasises the long-lasting engagement with place-making, the investment of 'man' to construct 'a unique, multi-scalar and anthropic site'.[29] Even during the discussions, when I mentioned the social configuration and the key issue of land ownership, I was reminded by the president that 'We need to use only one word, wine grower; there are no small or big wine growers, but only the accomplishment of a collective work transcending any sociological tensions'.

In a similar vein, when I asked the research officer in charge of the project to organise a focus group to discuss my hypothesis, insisting on having all the various social groups represented, only the president of the association and the prestigious established wine merchant, the Family D, attended, together with some local personalities, politicians and representatives of the wine industry. Wine growers were absent from any of the discussions during the different stages of the process I witnessed.

Yet the history and ethnography of Burgundy demonstrate the fact that social and cultural conflicts are endemic, and throughout the process I was reminded of the less than collective nature of the enterprise. During the meeting organised for the presentation of the socio-economic and anthropological reports, the president of the association, responding to some of the points I had raised during our discussions, defined terroir by referring to the work of wine growers, which, he claimed, was inspired by a philosophy and a vision which he termed the 'génie bourguignon' (Burgundian spirit). That term was already widespread in the Burgundian folkloric literature of the 1930s. This romantic and nostalgic vision of terroir, which is still commonly evoked in public discourse not only in Burgundy, but also in French vineyards more generally, neglects the socio-political realities of knowledge and of its transmission in the wine sector.

What comes out strikingly from the dossier is that in Burgundy, perhaps more than any other wine region in the world, place has been revealed and defined with constant reference to geography and geology. This relationship to place and wine has materialised through a landscape, a system of interdependent parcels, which illustrates a model of viticultural art that has resisted historical changes, ruptures and crisis. The dossier gives a prominent place to geology, history and geography. Burgundian culture in the late twentieth century was defined by a concept of terroir based on the AOC system and underpinned by a belief in the determining power of geology, which was itself confirmed by the price of land.[30] This construction worked to the advantage of local elites and tended to be rather conservative as the soil was at the core of this ideology. As wine has been transformed into a global commodity, it has impacted local social stratification in terms of economic and social differentiation, making it more diverse and heterogeneous in social terms (see Chapter 6).

As a result, the wine growers have become more receptive to the idea of taste, engaging more actively in the making of better quality wine and contesting more openly the role of geology in the definition of quality. This has led to a challenge to the classic definition of terroir based upon land, tradition and soil, with a new emphasis on the wine grower, who emerged as the key to unleashing the potential of the vineyards. With the proliferation of international wine guides and a genuinely global market, successful wine growers have established themselves as major actors in their own right. This has called into question distinctiveness among social categories and the UNESCO application could be seen as a way of reasserting Burgundy's position and by adding the lustre of heritage. Place can be a decisive marketing tool in the wine industry, and distinctiveness at the local or even micro- level is a strategy that allows for the exploitation of the power of monopoly rent. (Overton 2010: 759). The example given by DRC exemplifies the heritage distinction strategy. The example of the DRC exemplifies the heritage distinction strategy, and yet the paradox remains between being a public good and an almost inaccessible commodity.[31] By focusing on the place rather than the product, this friction can be reconciled.

Integrating Culture into Nature

As argued before, the image of monks and the soil in Burgundy have long served as a powerful symbol of the region and its reputation for excellence. In contrast to viticulture in the New World, history here is used to claim a rootedness and uniqueness. A further ingredient in this elaborate construction is the relationship between man and nature. It is presented through the trope of the monk as possessing a mythical or spiritual association with nature and the environment. Yet this theme, perhaps unconsciously, reveals a line of tension in local viticulture as it separates the wine growers, as workers of the land, from the others, *propriétaires* and *négociants*. As discussed previously, wine growers generally defined themselves as the 'workers of the land', and even if this category has become fashionable in public discourse, wine growers differentiate amongst themselves, identifying those who work the land from the rest. The experience of many years of intensive fieldwork makes it clear that the majority of wine growers are in agreement with this definition, which hints at deeper political, religious or ideological divides. The *climats* application, on the other hand, is dominated by the educated *propriétaires* and *négociants*, with wine growers almost totally absent, and it is clear that even if it has successfully engaged the public, the wine growers have not been so clearly visible in the cultural scene except for in the Marche des Climats.

Our perceptions of cultural landscapes derive their meanings from the actions and imaginations of people in society.[32] In fact, in Burgundy like elsewhere, the landscape has been so comprehensively altered by human activities over long periods of time that the distinction between cultural and natural is largely meaningless. Yet nature has been placed at the centre of the claims for heritage status made on behalf of *climats*. However, a number of European sites involve wine-producing districts, as this form of land use in more-developed nations has proven most resistant to change, at least to change that produces a visible effect on the landscape (Aplin 2005: 104–113). As one of the young volunteers in the *climats* campaign interviewed on YouTube expressed it: 'we need to realise how lucky we are, we have history. We have to learn from our previous mistakes, especially the intense mechanisation of the 1960s-1970s'. The *climats* dossier used heritage as a powerful drive for sustainability and as a way of controlling and stopping past practices that are seen as harmful for the environment. Interestingly, this side of the debate has been largely confined to the professional milieu and has not been debated at the regional level or in the public domain. The only public reaction was that of a respected wine grower from Monthelie,[33] former steward of the Hospices de Beaune, who criticised the lateness of the UNESCO project. In a YouTube video, he denounced the fact that intense mechanisation had devastated the area, local stone walls called *murgers* had been destroyed and vineyards had expanded to increase production.

Since the 1960s, the Burgundian vineyards have undergone important internal transformations as well as external ones which were imposed by commercial pressures (Cerveau 2000). The productivist mentality that dominated wine production in the post-war period added to the development of clonal selection, and the increasing resort to oenology, the use of pesticides and potassium hydroxide have all radically transformed the landscape and the product. As a result, the period was marked by a strong opposition between the modernists who were in favour of all these technical changes and a minority of traditionalists who favoured the protection of genetic plant material and the particularisms of terroirs. In the late 1990s, the balance between these groups shifted (Cerveau 2000) to the advantage of the younger and more modern wine growers who privilege the production of quality wines using ecologically sound practices while the traditionalists are now those who still favour productive methods hiding behind the AOC system. It was during the same period that the wine sector decided to organise a series of conferences on the issue of soils and their management. Fieldwork conducted at the time confirmed that there was an emerging discourse in the wine profession emphasising the need to use fewer pesticides and other chemicals and to return to more natural and ecologically friendly techniques.

Today, the *climats de Bourgogne* candidature tells another story. By using heritage as a tool to develop sustainability and protect what is left after years of intense mechanisation, a group of highly regarded producers are seeking to shake up local viticultural practices. Headed by the emblematic Aubert de Villaine, the bid has promoted a new era, but the route traced remains paved by obstacles. Interestingly, all of the brochures used to publicise the UNESCO campaign were coloured in ecologically friendly green with abundant pictures of vines, the soil and the site. No wine growers are present in these pictures. Yet the ecological turn is far from being universally popular. The contribution of one charismatic advocate of ecological methods to the scientific committee during the application process was met with criticism and accusations of non-scientific rigour by some members of the panel. In addition, the BIVB (Burgundy Wine Board) is traditionally composed of a wide range of producers from the south to the north of Burgundy, including *négociants* and wine growers who have divergent interests and face different challenges. Coherence and a collective willingness to address some of the current issues, such as the threat of disease, are not helped by the sub-regional identity divisions, and the *climats* dossier was not seen by all as a tool for an inclusive regional development.

Yet the *climats de Bourgogne* campaign has been accompanied by other types of local initiatives encouraging sustainability and more ecologically friendly practices. A project of sustainable development, Paysage de Corton,[34] initiated by Denis Fetzman, the manager of the Latour domain, who also presided at BIVB technical commission, situated in Aloxe-Corton, was launched in 2010 to 'protect the authenticity' of the landscape by proposing an approach that includes the integrity, the vitality and the diversity of the soils, the quality of the ecosystems and the biodiversity in the environment, the evolution of environmentally friendly practices, the development of an aesthetic, cultural and historic heritage, and the management of a scientific literary resource. The project includes bee keeping and other more ecologically friendly practices involving the local domains.[35] Another example is provided by the newly created association for the safeguarding of the diversity of grapes in Burgundy, which is composed of around fifty domains and seeks to preserve the varieties of Pinots Noirs traditionally cultivated in the area. These initiatives form part of the broader ecological and heritage shift of the place which seeks to construct the site as 'natural'.

Sustainable wine growing can be a means of ensuring the long-term future of vineyards in a context of increased economic competition (Boulanger-Fassier 2008). The majority of French wine growers have begun to turn towards this form of viticulture, prompted by consumer demand as well as new environmental pressures both from within France and from the European Union. Sandrine Barrey and Geneviève Teil (2011) have argued that in this new ecologically driven context, the question of authenticity has come to the fore. As part of the heritagisation of terroir, which has become an important strategy to protect and preserve specific areas of agricultural production, authenticity has emerged as a central feature attached to the definition of quality wine at a time of criticism of the AOC system.

Mike Bennie, an influential Australian wine 'writer' and 'talker', chose to give his keynote lecture during the 2013 New Zealand Pinot Noir festival on the concept of authenticity and its definition in the wine industry. The commentators interviewed by Bennie summarise with acuity the essence of the concept and multiple interpretations from the different perspectives of wine growers, wine managers or sommeliers:

Terroir and integrity… truth… it is real, reflecting where they come from… really purity… honesty, character… where it is from, comes from the right place… the real place, it is consistent… from nature… humans can be true from themselves, the land… the earth, it is what it is… his individual wine maker, his style, we know that there are people who do it for money, but it is not right… someone who tries to be like someone else is not authentic… are amongst the comments cited.

As Michael Glover of the Bannockburn vineyard put it: 'All around the world, there are baddies and goodies, there are promoters, charlatans and there are monks, people who believe that they are doing the right thing, so the Clos de Vougeot I want to have it in my cellar, what I want is the Echezeaux, someone who does not care about score, this is authenticity'.

In the age of global heritage, re-inventing Burgundy means re-locating its value within the confines of the traditional boundaries defining the product, that is to say what is left of the historical legacy, its historicised landscape. By focusing attention upon *climats*/terroir as a long-lasting category of identification – 'they have always been here' – and by playing the natural card, heritage becomes a tool for hiding change and fossilising what Burgundy ought to be in the eyes of the main local actors. The anthropologist Muriel Faure has demonstrated how agricultural products such as the Beaufort cheese in the Northern Alps have been 'refined' as cultural products by promoting them in a specific fashion and linking more closely the cultural characteristics of the products to their markets (Faure 1999). It is undeniable that Burgundy too seeks to safeguard its position in a global competition at the top of the hierarchy. The only way to preserve its leadership is to use history and place-making as the guarantees of its success and by gaining heritage status to preserve this positioning while using it as a tool for disguising major viticultural changes.

Isomorphism and Social Differentiation: Artisanship and Work

The authenticity of *climats* lies in their multi-scalar deployment as stable and enduring historically rooted places. For a product, the reference to a specific taste – in both its singularity and plurality – enables the relationship between taste and place to be established as the truth and as a unique and identifiable object of trust in the market economy. The heritage validation, if successful, will enhance and consolidate the identification between product and place of what is already defined as the 'lien au lieu' (link to a location). This strategy, which is similar to that developed in the luxury goods industry, has emerged at a time when frauds are commonplace.

As products become increasingly easily reproducible, so authenticity, if proven, gains a new value (Schofield et al. 2008: 2). It is why, in the current global wine context, where all the traditional divisions in terms of viticultural practices and wine definitions seem to be blurred by differentiation and homogeneisation, authenticity becomes a crucial area in which unique narratives matter. For Burgundy, it means re-enacting some of the global references linking place to taste by fossilising and historicising the site of production which is presented as a stable, trustworthy and reliable place. Interestingly, that image is itself a modern invention and for centuries Burgundy was unable to ensure reliable quantities or a high quality of production. Time is absorbed and embedded in the *climats*. As the protection of place of origin has gradually been accepted as an element of 'intellectual property', it has become one of the few aspects of local protection that has been allowed in the more liberalised world trade environment (Josling 2006): this is a trump card for Burgundy.

As discussed in this chapter, not only do the *climats de Bourgogne* seek to preserve spaces, places, monuments and objects, but they also aim to 'make do' by 'creating new aesthetic forms, historical narratives, politics of transmission and more generally new social configurations (Berliner 2012: 771). Yet this part of the candidature remained implicit in the dossier, only becoming clear after closer examination of its content. The project aimed, therefore, not only to protect, but also to foster and to create and nurture a new relationship with the heritage object, the *climat*, which in turn will generate its own social practices as part of the process of safeguarding its uniqueness in heritage and economic terms. What is showcased is a return to a pre-modern conception of nature, a kind of emblematic and nostalgic mythical land, untouched and blessed by God (or the monks). As Massey (cited by Tilley 2006: 19) indicates, nature, represented as solid and unchanging) indicates, human reflections on nature, represented as fixed and unchanging, may encapsulate a sense of national identity or conjure up romantic notions of a true human identity in relation to place. The *climats* are presented as 'authentic' and immutable sites, preserved from any historical changes. They are, according to the dossier, part of a common collective regional heritage despite being the subject of a long history of private ownership. The dossier was silent on the private nature of the goods or the recent history of the push for viticultural expansion.

On 4 July 2012, a wine grower explained in a YouTube video[36] how to shape the terroir in accordance with the INAO regulations concerning the protection against erosion. Traditional stones were usually employed to build small walls as a way of stopping water flowing. The work was carried out in his Pommard 1er Cru 'Clos des Arvelets':

I did pull the old vines planted in the direction of the road, removed it and kept this beautiful earth, dug the mound and filled the bowl that prevented the mechanised work and restored the land, rebound the separation wall and replanted a young vine in the direction of the slope. In April 2010, we planted the vine, it will be productive in four years.

His positioning, even if not shared by the majority of the wine growers, forms part of a wider attempt to manage the land while preserving traditional features such as stone walls. What the *climats* dossier aims to achieve is to create a set of new norms which will inspire and encourage a more respectful relationship to the site. By focusing on nature and *climats* rather than culture, Burgundy wishes to create a difference by combining tradition, history and heritage with more environmentally friendly practices in an area where it could make a real difference. What is proposed is to manage nature as a heritage good, which implies containing the market rationality (Barrère, Barthélemy, Nieddu and Vivien 2004: 121). As part of that process, the *climats* are presented as the product of a long history and constant striving for quality. Banks and Overton (2010: 59) have already pointed out that 'centuries of trial and error have perfected viticultural and winemaking techniques that are suited to particular places'. Yet as any anthropologist confronted by the growing fragmentation of the cultural groups he/she studies knows, making sense of this diversity of worldviews is problematic. The idea of linear progress remains highly questionable as the production of excellence is often a question of cultural and economic capital as well as differentiated experience and knowledge.

During the UNESCO application process, the only reference to human intervention or to that of the cultural realm was located in the narrative about the past, and especially the role of monastic orders, or featured tangentially as part of a broader discussion of regionalism (Laferté 2006). This type of iconography was nothing new as it was part of an innovative reading of French regionalism that Laferté characterises as a 'commercial regionalist folklore', initiated during the inter-war period by republican elites who devised a marketing strategy for their wines based upon the traditional images of wine grower, terroir and authenticity. To counteract this commercial regionalist folklore, the dossier has carefully avoided any mention of the sociological or anthropological dimension of the site, despite having commissioned me to write this side of the report. It is striking that only a few pages of the two volumes of the *climats* dossier discuss people, and this is only in the section on folklore (volume 1), or traditional know-how, from the 1950s as recorded by the local wine museum.[37]

A sense of permanence characterises Burgundy and it is even showcased through local wine tourism and the cultural *mise en scène* where the emphasis is placed upon authenticity, history and tradition. Very few changes are visible to the naked eye of the anthropologist returning for an annual field trip, and it could be argued that globalisation has not visibly affected the local wine industry. The façade of an unchanging place, 'a terroir blessed by God', remains superficially convincing, and the issue of how individuals mediate globalisation seems almost incongruous in this context. Against the background of globalisation, which is for the majority of wine growers a synonym for acute competition, business failure and anxiety, local political actors and elites have developed strategies to use global forces to redefine in their own terms part of the local environment (Crenn and Téchoueyres 2004). Using rhetoric which emphasises terroir not only as a natural and ecological concept, but also as a historicised and heritagised construction of place, the elites have created a suggestive and powerful image that can be passed on, narrated or consumed by a discerning group of consumers.

This powerful construction is partly inspired by what is happening in other vineyards, such as in New Zealand or California. By the same token, the wine growers reinvest this already emblematised place with another set of values and meanings which encompass past and present practices, local and global representations echoing other contemporary preoccupations. It is after all about place-making in an interconnected world where globalisation is translated and interpreted in local terms. The erosion of the 'natural' connection between place and culture has undeniably taken centre stage in most analyses, leading us to think of a globalised world as a culture without space. Rather than being mutually exclusive, the local and the global feed upon and reinforce each other, and the production of locality relies on imagination mediated by local agency, but articulated differently by individuals depending on their social positioning at local and global levels.

Conclusion

Using the case-study provided by Burgundy's campaign for UNESCO World Heritage status for the *climats de Bourgogne*, this chapter helps to understand how Burgundian wine and its political and economic elites emphasise history, nature and heritage concerns by claiming the right to global recognition. Burgundian wine elites have sought to use heritage as a new means of serving the definition of specific micro identities to counter-globalisation. Yet the recent project of applying for UNESCO recognition of the *climats* of Burgundy for World Heritage status offers an insight into the continuing strength of a traditional model of terroir deployed by intellectual and cultural elites. The project was put together by the region

231

of Burgundy, the department of Côte d'Or, the towns of Beaune and Dijon, the BIVB (Bureau Interprofessionel des Vins de Bourgogne) and the Confrérie des Chevaliers du Tastevin. The co-manager of the Domaine de la Romanée-Conti was the president of the association established to campaign for UNESCO recognition and most of the meetings have taken place under his leadership. Having been invited as an expert to participate in the definition of the *climats de Bourgogne*, I was able to unpack the construction of a historical narrative around the notion of '*climats*', a twenty-first century invention but one that is embodied in imagined notions of an enduring and thus authenticated social configuration. An exploration of its deployment and the complex politics of scale accompanying it through the various debates and scientific committees attended makes it clear that the application was as much about 'making do' as preserving. Emphasising the historical and geographic continuity of the place encapsulated through the use of 'geo-system', Burgundy seeks to produce singularity by combining the place as a historically defined list of 1,247 sites in which man and nature have interacted with the diversity of tastes underlying it. Moreover, it has provoked fierce debate about terroir constructed as a world heritage commodity, raising questions about long-term ecological and environmental issues. Terroir thus provides a window onto the mechanisms by which societies are able to use globalisation and modernity to suit their own purposes.

Notes

1. The formal nominations submitted by the state parties to the Convention are processed by UNESCO and assessed by the expert bodies before the World Heritage Centre reaches its final decision.
2. The Chauvet-Pont-d'Arc Cave in the Ardèche department of southern France is a cave that contains some of the earliest known cave paintings, as well as other evidence of Upper Paleolithic life, while the volcans d'Auvergne are a natural site, part of the regional natural reserve of Auvergne Volcanoes which covers a large part of Cantal and continues northward on to Puy-de-Dôme.
3. The first attempt took place during the time of the Rio summit when the environment and development were the two keywords of the era.
4. http://missglouglou.blog.lemonde.fr/2012/07/16/*climats*-de-bourgogne-a-lUNESCO-tout-ce-que-vous-avez-toujours-voulu-savoir/. Consulted on 9 May 2013.
5. The Burgundian wine milieu remains largely dominated by a male culture especially as far as the academic world is concerned.

6. A sociologist from Paris, Gilles Laferté, student of Florence Weber, refused for ethical reasons to contribute to the project despite having played a major role at the local level by publishing a book in 2006, *La Bourgogne et ses vins: image d'origine contrôlée*, which partly inspired the local Burgundian elites to put together the UNESCO application. The main strength of his work was to show how various key social figures, landowners for the wine industry, the tourist industry, the political sphere and the university, have all contributed – through the establishments of networks constituted by alliances between wine producers, political elites, the food industry and the University of Dijon – to the creation and management of a still dominant rural and folk image of Burgundian wines. For more details, see http://www.h-france.net/vol9reviews/vol9no18demossier.pdf, consulted on 9 May 2013.

7. Personal communication with wine growers and presidents of AOC *syndicats*.

8. Jacques Berthomeau is a wine consultant who was appointed by the Ministry of Agriculture in 2001 to write a report on French wines and globalisation which aimed at 'establishing the goals and means to be deployed in terms of people, regulations and finance for a winning strategy for French wines as we approach the year 2010', but who met with strong opposition. His blog can be read at http://www.berthomeau.com/ and the interview I extracted at http://www.berthomeau.com/article-3-questions-a-aubert-de-villaine-l-inscription-des-*climats*-du-vignoble-de-bourgogne-au-patrimoine-mondial-de-l-UNESCO-66114900.html, consulted on 9 May 2013.

9. http://www.berthomeau.com/article-3-questions-a-aubert-de-villaine-l-inscription-des-climats-du-vignoble-de-bourgogne-au-patrimoine-mondial-de-l-UNESCO-66114900.html. Consulted on 14 June 2017.

10. I attended three research meetings overall ether as part of a short committee or as a member of the scientific committee. I also contributed to a conference and attended a number of key events as part of my ethnographic enquiry.

11. Internal research report entitled 'Analyse comparative des *climats* de Bourgogne', Yves Luginbühl, 2009, 47pp., which was circulated to a small number of members of the scientific committee, including myself.

12. Ibid.

13. For a broader discussion about the heritage process and the categories involved, see Demossier (2015).

14. Professor Garcia edited the volume *Les climats du vignoble de Bourgogne comme patrimoine mondial de l'humanité* (2011) which presents the conference proceedings of the scientific committee.

15. www.climats-bourgogne.com/en/. Consulted on 23 November 2017.

16. Technical dossier published and circulated in 2012. The dossier coloured in variations of green presents the site and the argument behind the application.

17. The figure was not confirmed by the INAO representative who acknowledged the confusion between different terminologies, be it *lieux-dits*, *crus*, *Aocs* or '*climats*'.

18. Underlined by the project coordinator.

19. Landrieu-Lussigny's initial work, which was a master's thesis conducted in 1963, was published in 1983 under the title *Les lieux-dits dans le vignoble bourguignon*. It constitutes the first academic contribution to the dossier, even if she was not directly appointed on the scientific committee. The preface to her book was written by a famous local *négociant* who was also a terroir writer, Pierre Poupon, who mentions '*climat*' as a term frequently used by wine growers (Landrieu-Lussigny 1983: 10). His son-in-law, Sylvain Pitiot, manager of the Clos de Tart and topographer engineer by training, followed in their footsteps by publishing a series of maps in collaboration with Pierre Poupon and then the Burgundy wine board. In the context of the candidature, both Landrieu-Lussigny and Pitiot, together with Jean-Charles Servant and Bernard Pivot, have published *Climats et lieux-dits des grands vignobles de Bourgogne: Atlas et Histoire des Noms de Lieux* (2012). This book provides the definite mapping of the *climats*.
20. Rapport Paillotin, February 2000. L'agriculture raisonnée, Ministère de l'Agriculture, 57p.
21. Nicolas Sarkozy supported the Burgundian application since his wife, the model and singer Carla Bruni, had been asked to chair the annual Hospices de Beaune auction, while François Hollande had a marked preference for the Champagne dossier.
22. For an analysis of people and places, see Cresswell (2004) and Massey (2006).
23. The greeters can be contacted at: http://www.bourgogne-greeters.fr/index.php?lang=en. Consulted on 9 May 2013.
24. This festival was held for the first time in 2012 simultaneously in Beaune, Dijon and Nuits-Saint-Gorges.
25. http://missglouglou.blog.lemonde.fr/2012/07/16/climats-de-bourgogne-a-lunesco-tout-ce-que-vous-avez-toujours-voulu-savoir/. Consulted on 23 November 2017.
26. *Le Bien Public*, 8 November 2011.
27. Dossier technique. Projet, Critères, Cartographie et Calendrier.
28. See http://www.youtube.com/watch?v=VnFErwQlQtE. Consulted on 9 May 2013.
29. Dossier de candidature pour l'inscription des *climats de Bourgogne* sur la liste du patrimoine mondial de l'UNESCO. CD circulated to the scientific committee, February 2013, 2 volumes.
30. The value of plots varies from just 30,000 euros per hectare to as much as 2,760,000 euros per hectare for the best locations (Agreste Bourgogne 2010: 4).
31. Kirschenblatt-Gimblett (2006), citing Klamer and Zuidhof.
32. See, for example, Schofield et al. (2008: 155).
33. www.youtube.com/watch?v=3SLLjdBRLQQ. Consulted on 8 May 2013.
34. See http://paysagedecorton.fr/
35. See, for example, the Poisot domain: http://www.domaine-poisot.fr/blog/a-la-vigne/les-abeilles-du-charlemagne.html. Consulted on 9 May 2013.

36. http://www.youtube.com/watch?v=V7M21ji8GPc. Consulted on 9 May 2013.
37. See volume 1, p. 343–45.

CONCLUSION

On 30 March 2016, one of the longest established wine merchants in Burgundy[1] was involved in a major fraud concerning the blending of wines from different AOCs. This was nothing new as regular crises have punctuated the history of local viticulture. However, his arrest shook the profession as it came immediately after the announcement of UNESCO recognition for World Heritage status and the seemingly successful recrafting of the Burgundian terroir story. This crisis was reported in the local press as well as in the national newspapers, but perhaps surprisingly it failed to reach international audiences. As we have seen, issues of authenticity and provenance have become part of the place-making project and of the wider global story used to sell the image, and bottles, of Burgundy wines. In this context, any accusation of fraud jeopardises that position, leaving it vulnerable to the charge of deception, robbing Burgundy and its producers of what should a major trump card in a competitive global market.

Over the years, frauds have been reported both in terms of mass production and the blending of different AOCs as well as the sale of fake wines affecting the *grands crus*. In the 1930s, Burgundy wines were often blended with those from Algeria or other parts of France, but they were intended, first and foremost, for local consumption, urban centres and neighbouring cities and only a small number of premium wines were destined for international or quality markets. One of the great achievements of the period prior to the 1930s was the regulation and organization of the wine market by the wine profession and landowners, to the detriment of the *négociants*, who had previously dominated the region. In the course of the twentieth century, Burgundy wine acquired a global status due to better conditions of transport and conservation and a fall in its costs. Yet for all the efforts at the local level to ensure that wines remain defined according to '*usages, bons, locaux, loyaux et constants*',[2] frauds surrounding the denomination of origin have always existed and were likely to reappear, especially when new

236

social actors entered the local market with the aim of making money in the context of neoliberal economies.

Wine frauds have always been part of the global wine economy, but the nature and scale of the frauds have changed following the increasing value of certain wines or *grands crus* and the rising number of wealthy wine lovers across the world. Distinction and the quest for social status are both drivers behind the sale of these rare commodities. Prices for *grands crus* oscillate between 20 euros to 12,000 euros or more for a bottle within the same limited geographic area named Burgundy. To put this in perspective, one bottle of DRC (Domaine de la Romanée-Conti) recently sold for 850 euros, while older vintages could reach up to 12,000 euros per bottle and these expensive wines are the object of intense international speculation. Yet they coexist with ordinary bottles of Burgundy costing no more than 10 euros. Frauds can therefore take different forms, from the blending of different AOC wines on an industrial scale to the extremely precise reproduction and copy of *grands crus* sold at exorbitant prices. In this context, the Burgundy story becomes more powerful than most others. This wide range of fraudulent strategies reflects the divisions which polarise the viticultural community, between producers and wine merchants, wine investors and financial sharks, passionate and *routiniers* (in the sense of traditionalists) as well as ecologically minded versus *terroirists*.

The puzzling hierarchisation and differentiation attached to this tiny geographic area of excellence is one that often escapes the average consumer, unless he/she has started to be initiated, and progressively drawn, into the Burgundy story. That narrative has proven remarkably adaptable, capable of consolidating a cultural edifice to promote both ordinary and rare wines. Wine is revealed to be capable of story-telling in a more effective way than almost any other commodity. What my nearly thirty years of fieldwork have demonstrated is how the crafting of *grands crus* is a serious matter which requires a constant monitoring of the processes of production at every stage, and a consistent and durable narrative to be deployed against global forces and their impact on the local community. Globalisation offers a new challenge, as it is no longer a question of selling your wines, but also of positioning them in a global market where competition is fierce and certainties are few. The periodic process of crafting together different stories, as well as ensuring that there is a common goal to be pursued by the local actors, remains a challenge, especially in a group where differences provide the fundamental means of ensuring your economic future and competition makes cooperation less likely. What is fascinating in this canvas is the role played by some of the local producers and elites in preserving this story against the pressure of newcomers and opportunists. This is where both anchoring yourself into the local terroir narrative, while imbricating into the global world of wine, is essential for survival. This dual strategy is reflected by both terroir as the foundation for excellence and the reverse engineering terroir ideologies which enable Burgundy to remain in charge of its own destiny.

The deeply rooted social construction of wine at the local level and its reflexive imbrication have been powerful and ubiquitous rhetorical devices employed by producers when asked about their personal professional lives. The story of terroir is presented here as a particular case of extreme localisation, whereby three, four, five or even more successive generations of the same family have established a working relationship with a particular milieu and a specific 'noble' plant – Chardonnay or Pinot Noir – in an ecological milieu which has been presented as unchanged, despite being the subject of intense agrarian transformations and commercial expansion. These families have anchored themselves to a specific place and village and, consequently, they have accumulated a wealth of experience, albeit not one that was necessarily a synonym of 'quality'. As one female informer explained to me: 'It is not easy to move the goal posts here when belonging is counted in centuries'.

The terroir story has provided the intellectual foundations of a viticultural ideal based upon quality, permanence and care of the site. This ideology, largely rooted in local familial cultures, was linked to the perception of working the land as the primary factor in the making of what was defined as quality wines in the context of an economy largely in the hands of the *négociants* and a few elites. From the 1970s onwards, with the increasing development of direct commercialisation and the exportation of wines abroad, this ideology of care started to go beyond the level of the local discourse to become a socially recognised collective undertaking. It was very clear from the initial fieldwork I conducted in the 1990s that an 'education of attention'[3] was starting to emerge amongst the most educated or entrepreneurial young wine growers. Yet it would be naïve to assume that each wine grower engages in the same way with this education, while also learning to manage the weather cycle and building an experience driven knowledge within the same geographic area. Wine in Burgundy can only be defined by a complex interface of a multiplicity of factors – natural, social, cultural and political – which influence the final quality of the product. This is about wine's complicated relationship to place. Care here takes a different and more complex form and remains largely socially differentiated.

A recent example of this imbrication of the Burgundy story into the global wine hierarchy is illustrated by a YouTube clip circulating in the context of Chardonnay Day,[4] an event organised by the wine board. On that occasion, one of the most reputed producers in Meursault responded to the question 'Do we produce Chardonnay in Burgundy?', as follows:

In Burgundy we do not produce Chardonnay, we produce different Meursault, different Puligny, different Chablis, wines from Mâcon and this is what we have learned to do, this is what our ancestors have shown us as well, we have a viticulture of terroir and thus we are always in the search of the best expression of the place that we try to give to our clients. Chardonnay is a tool, simply a tool to express the place.

This statement reflects both the recent work around crafting the Burgundy story into a world wine hierarchy based upon grapes, but also an attempt to educate the consumer about the various ways in which places could be enacted through wine consumption and the subtle reading of differences. Yet it is also an indication of a reflexive engagement with the product and the site of its production.

The Burgundy story has therefore been constructed on terroir and its reputation as the birthplace of that concept, while a constant effort to craft this authenticity has been led at key historical points of juncture by different groups of actors and in a diverse range of ways. There are, however, fundamental social differences in both the construction and the consumption of the place. Indeed, the very act of naming geographical entities implies a power over them, and more particularly over the way in which places, their inhabitants and their social function are represented (Harvey 1990: 419). The act of representation is inscribed in the making and remaking of the place and the *climats* story adds another layer to an already rich and colourful veneer. This is moreover about shifting the environmental agenda and positioning Burgundy in the new wine heritage landscape. By becoming a World Heritage site and promoting a new reading of terroir, Burgundians are seeking to maintain their hegemonic position in the global hierarchy of wine where place, taste and social experience still matter.

Burgundy thus offers a unique illustration of how a resonant and historically rooted story of terroir provides a structure for the contemporary deployment of new narratives about place. The application for UNESCO World Heritage status, led by the local elites, has reactivated under different guises the story of quality, soil, history and nature while closely guaranteeing that communities, wine growers, *négociants* and the local population engage with or, even more rarely, contest it. It is clear that the promotion of the *climats* story has been a great success. Yet in order to become more globally recognised, it will need to be embraced more widely, repeated, translated and experienced as well as being constituted as a new category of perception locally, nationally and internationally. In the pursuit of such a strategy, the iconic image of the vineyards provides an enduring symbol about place and its making through a diversity of plots supported by the emblematic and powerful Burgundian spirit of hospitality.

This kind of mythical construction, which is often underlined by a series of hegemonic discourses about locality, necessarily impacts upon a wide range of actors who contribute to the making of quality wine and to the sustainability of place in a rapidly changing economic context. It also has a huge economic impact and a growing potential for further speculation. Wine entrepreneurs in Burgundy do not seek necessarily to diversify and create multiple meanings of authenticity to accommodate, modify and at times, resist the effects of globalisation on local culture and economic life.[5] They paradoxically wish to engage, take control and master global forces by consolidating, reinforcing and perpetuating the story of their origins and authenticity, thus differentiating themselves from other producers at the local level. The heritagisation of the site as well as the ecological shift are far from collective and homogeneous processes because all too often it is forgotten that this will benefit some, but potentially harm others. This also opens the door to increasing divisions and growing contestation. Yet it consolidates the hegemonic position of Burgundy's wine in the global market.

The traditional collective values which were at the core of the Burgundian self-identity, such as hospitality, generosity and humbleness, have been progressively eroded by the impact of economic success and growing affluence that has led to the transformation of the place. Wine today is produced in multiple different locations and with a wide range of value attached to it, and Burgundy, with its 100 different AOCs and its 1,247 *climats*, offers a perfect example of the complex values, mechanisms and processes at stake when discussing wine and globalisation. Yet due to the limited volume of its production, Burgundy remains in a dominant position as 'there is nothing left to sell', highlighting the paradox of being a UNESCO site – the heritage of humanity – and yet also an object of elite consumption inaccessible to all but the most wealthy. By focusing on the place, producers and its commercial elites can present Burgundy as if it were accessible to all, part of the world's patrimony, rather conveniently forgetting that only a tiny minority will ever purchase a bottle of Romanée-Conti. By investigating the development of the Burgundy story in the long term, we can obtain a fascinating insight into some of the fractures of modern society and the constant battle between different strategies. But the story of Burgundy is also a crafted and enduring construction of place against the grain of globalisation, where every piece is assembled into a seamless puzzle through historical junctures and elitist enterprise. It is the story of that complex imbrication that I have followed, not only through the window offered by the locality, but through its powerful deployments in the face of globalisation.

The terroir story in Burgundy is presented as traditionally rooted and historically unchanged when, in fact, it achieves its powerful resonance from a close and reflexive, in the sense of carefully crafted, imbrication with global wine culture and its hierarchy of values. Yet for all its persuasiveness, it faces today uncertain times as climate and environmental change and the evolving global wine hierarchy call into question the dominant position of the *grands crus*. It is not surprising that a range of new initiatives involving charities have become more visible in the local landscape, complementing the traditional Vente des Vins des Hospices de Beaune. Agency is crucial to an understanding of why elites and wine growers are able to drive change and is partially explained by their economic and social positioning. The Climats du Coeur website[6] illustrates the new interest of wine growers and elites in philanthropic activities. The website states: 'In the same spirit of solidarity, eight Burgundian producers have founded a charitable association "Les Climats du Cœur" ... Since 26th June 2009, we've launched an offer of 1,000 cases of 4 magnums of 1er Crus from the vintage 2009 for the price of 1,200 €, ex-cellars Beaune and including VAT'. The money raised on this occasion goes to local charities: the Restos du Coeur, a charity that helps the destitute with food in winter, and other charities linked to the Abbaye de Citeaux, the Couvent de Béatitudes and the Abbaye de St-Vivant, to remind the public of the history that ties the wines of Burgundy to the convents. 'Without the monks, Burgundy would not be what it is today', states the website.

Yet if some of these initiatives are driven by a small group of elites, it remains clear that Burgundy is also largely made up of a large number of small wine estates, for some of whom the terroir story has not always been beneficial. I have often been reminded by wine growers of economic uncertainties or family crises or deaths which have marked local communities. For most of the producers, family business has become the defining feature of post-industrial capitalism, but it has also meant that the ways in which they operate have altered drastically. These changes have not affected the social fabric in the same uniform way, as the value of wine has always depended upon a wide range of factors and not everybody has been a winner in the Burgundy story. The economic and social position of each wine grower is often based upon the monopoly rent, which is defined by the portfolio of vineyards they inherited, but also on the position of their wines or *climats* within both the locality and the global hierarchy of wines.

New challenges will necessarily necessitate a *prise de conscience* as well as more collective responses and it could be said that they have been timidly articulated in this part of the world. The so-called decline of community values and the rise of individualism, accompanied by the stardom associated with the wine grower, are all features of our wine modernity. It is nevertheless essential to discuss more broadly how the future of the region will be shaped by the decline of these values. Like many other commodities, wine production requires some rethinking to become more ecologically minded, respectful of nature and embedded in a vision that will play an important role for future generations. This can only happen if the terroir story becomes one of greater care and more ecological engagement. While all the conditions for future success are undoubtedly present, it becomes an issue of making sure that the terroir story is one of inclusion and self-reflexive collective engagement, reflecting what the Burgundy experience is about for the visitor.

As a world-renowned wine region, Burgundy, like the roof of Beaune's emblematic Hôtel-Dieu, has over the last two centuries acquired a coating of imbricated scales which have established the foundations for the terroir story. This is a tale of the original and sometimes mythical links between place, culture and taste which has found a new resonance with the invention of *climats* and the acquisition of World Heritage status. New tiles have been added to protect the Burgundy story in the global hierarchy of wine by reiterating the original myth of terroir and by adding both the heritage and environmental varnish to the local politics of place. In the pursuit of this strategy, the iconic image of both the roof and the vineyards provide enduring and mythical clichés about place and its making through a diversity of tiles and plots supported by the emblematic and powerful Burgundian spirit. It is now maybe time for the local community to engage with the *climats de Bourgogne* by reasserting local viticultural practices in the new ecologically defined context of the twenty-first century.

Notes

1. See http://www.bienpublic.com/edition-cote-de-beaune/2016/04/01/fraudes-sur-les-vins-perqui-sition-et-garde-a-vue-chez-bejot. Consulted on 14 June 2017.
2. This means in accordance with local, fair and consistent practices or referring to fair and traditional practices. In the context of Burgundy, Jean-Francois Bazin, in his *Le dictionnaire universel du vin de Bourgogne* (2010: 695), defines the expression as part of the founding myth of the AOC as well as the legal framework by which wines have been traditionally produced in Burgundy since at least the nineteenth century.
3. See, for example, Ingold (2000) and Gieser (2008).
4. https://www.youtube.com/watch?v=77qZ9O99CDg. Consulted on 23 November 2017.
5. For a useful analysis of the social sources of authenticity, see Wherry (2006).
6. http://www.climats-du-coeur.com/. Consulted on 21 September 2016.

GLOSSARY OF KEY TERMS

❧❧❧

BIVB: The Bureau Interprofessionnel des Vins de Bourgogne (Burgundy Wine Board) which oversees the production and promotion of Burgundy wines. It now includes both wine producers and *négociants* as part of its board of directors.

Cabottes: Small stone shelters.

Clonal selection: In clonal selection, an ideal plant within a vineyard or nursery that has exhibited the most desirable traits is selected with all cuttings taken from that single plant. In Burgundy it started to develop in the 1970s through the work of Raymond Bernard of the University of Dijon. For an introduction to the history of clones for Pinots Noirs, see http://www.princeofpinot.com/article/945/.

Clos: A walled plot. It often refers to a monopoly in terms of wine production or to one distinctive AOC which can be divided amongst several producers.

Crus: Defined here as a specific AOC wine classification which refers to several vineyards assembled to constitute a specific vintage.

Cuvée: A French wine term derived from *cuve*, meaning vat or tank. In Burgundy, it has a specific meaning as it is often the tank in which grapes from the same plot or different plots are blended together to produce wine from the same AOC.

Esca: A disease of mature grapevines. The fungi Phaeoacremonium aleophilum, Phaeomoniella chlamydospora and Fomitiporia mediterranea are associated with the disease.

Fermage: A rent paid annually or given in bottles to the landowner in exchange for the care of the land.

Flying wine maker: A term used to describe wine professionals who travel around the globe to supervise viticulture and wine making. A handful of young Burgundy wine growers have started to go global with their expertise.

INAO: The Institut national de l'origine et de la qualité (previously Institut National des Appellations d'Origine) is the French organisation charged with regulating French agricultural products with the status of Protected

Designations of Origin (PDOs). Controlled by the French government, it forms part of the Ministry of Agriculture and it regulates the use of names and the definitions of geographic areas entitled to produce a specific wine.

Landowners: This term has a specific connotation in the Burgundian landscape. It is often associated with wealthy families who own the most prestigious parts of the vineyards, but also who approach viticulture from a more financial and market-driven perspective. Owning the land distinguishes them from the producers who cultivate it. They were also traditionally part of the Catholic rural bourgeoisie, but made their fortunes by working in legal or business environments.

Massale selection: Historically massale selection was the empirical way by which wine growers selected plants to facilitate the propagation of grapevines. This was quite widespread in Burgundy until the 1980s and was often organised through family ties. In massale (or 'mass') selection, cuttings are taken from several vines of the same variety that have collectively demonstrated desirable traits.

Master of Wine: Abbreviated to MW, this is a qualification (not an academic degree) issued by the Institute of Masters of Wine in the United Kingdom. The MW qualification is generally regarded in the wine industry as one of the highest standards of professional knowledge. It was founded in 1955 and has since acquired a world reputation.

Métayage: Sharecropping, which is the norm in Burgundy.

Négociants: In Burgundy, these are the wine merchants who buy grapes from different wine growers and blend them to create AOC wine. They are represented by a handful of old Burgundian families, but also include newcomers who seek to make their fortune or are passionate about wine.

OIV: The International Organisation of Vine and Wine. For more information, consult http://www.oiv.int/en/the-international-organisation-of-vine-and-wine.

Phylloxera: In the late nineteenth century the phylloxera epidemic destroyed most of the vineyards in Europe, most notably in France. Hybridisation – the breeding of *Vitis vinifera* with resistant species – became a popular avenue of research to try and stop the phylloxera louse.

SAFER: The Société d'Aménagement Foncier et d'Etablissement Rural, the French rural agency which manages and regulates rural space.

Syndicat de l'appellation: The *syndicat de l'appellation* or AOC committees are voluntary associations which have taken the lead in governing the production of quality wine since the 1930s (Colman 2008: 39). For a more detailed account of their history in Burgundy, see the work of Olivier Jacquet (2009). The *syndicats* manage the AOC legal definition known as *cahier des charges* and are composed of both wine growers and *négociants* who are producers of that AOC.

Wine growers and ***vignerons***: These terms are used interchangeably throughout the text. Their definition corresponds to the embodiment of work they physically carry out unlike other wine intermediaries or actors.

BIBLIOGRAPHY

Agreste Bourgogne. 2010. *Viticulture en Bourgogne: progression des surfaces et de l'emploi Salarié.* Numéro 125 – décembre 011.http://agreste.agriculture.gouv.fr/IMG/pdf_R2611A14.pdf (accessed 11 November 2017).

Aplin, Paul. 2005. 'Remote Sensing: Ecology', *Progress in Physical Geography* 29: 104–13.

Appadurai, Arjun. 1995. 'The Production of Locality', in Richard Fardon (ed.), *Counterworks: Managing the Diversity of Knowledge.* London: Routledge, pp. 205–25.

Banks, Glenn A. 2013. 'Between Old Worlds and the New? Transcending Place and Space in the Contemporary Geography of Wine: Introduction', *EchoGéo* 23(1), http://echogeo.revues.org/13380 (accessed on 15 June 2017).

Banks, Glenn A. and John Overton. 2010. 'Old World, New World, Third World: Reconceptualising the Worlds of Wine', *Journal of Wine Research* 21(1): 57–75.

Barham, Elizabeth. 2003. 'Translating Terroir: The Global Challenge of French AOC Labelling', *Journal of Rural Studies* 19: 127–38.

Barrey, Susan and Geneviève Teil. 2011. 'Faire la preuve de "l'authenticité" du patrimoine alimentaire: Le cas des vins de terroir', *Anthropology of Food*, http://aof.revues.org/6783 (accessed 9 January 2014).

Barrère, Christian, Denis Barthélemy, Martino Nieddu and Frank-Dominique Vivien. 2004. *Réinventer le patrimoine: De la culture à l'économie, une nouvelle pensée du patrimoine.* Paris: L'Harmattan.

Bazin, Jean-François. 2010. *Le dictionnaire universel du vin de Bourgogne.* N.p.: Editions Belvédère.

Bender, Barbara (ed). 1993. *Landscape: Politics and Perspectives.* Oxford: Berg.

Bendix, Barbara. 1997. *In Search of Authenticity: The Formation of Folklore Studies.* Madison, WI: University of Wisconsin Press.

246

Bérard, Laurence, and Philippe Marchenay. 2006. 'Local Products and Geographical Indications: Taking Account of Local Knowledge and Biodiversity'. *International Social Science Journal*, 58: 109–116.

Berliner, David. 2012. 'Multiple Nostalgias: The Fabric of Heritage in Luang Prabang (Lao PDR)', *Journal of the Royal Anthropological Institute* 18: 769–86.

Berthomeau, Jacques. 2001. *Cap 2010: Le défi des vins français*. May 2002. Online Report, obs.viti.herault.fr/viti/download_file.jsp?id_doc=1603 (accessed on 15 June 2017).

Bessière, J. and L. Tibère, L. 2011. 'Editorial: Patrimoines Alimentaires'. *Anthropology of Food*, https://aof.revues.org/6758 (accessed on 15 June 2017).

Bessière, Jacynthe. 1998. 'Local Development and Heritage: Traditional Food and Cuisine as Tourist Attractions in Rural Areas', *Sociologia Ruralis* 38(1): 21–34.

Bestor, Theodore C. 2003. 'Markets and Places: Tokyo and the Global Tuna Trade', in S. Low and D. Lawrence-Zunigais (eds), *The Anthropology of Space and Place: Locating Culture*. Malden, MA: Blackwell Publishing, pp. 301–20.

Black, Rachel and Robert Ulin. 2013. *Wine and Culture: Vineyard to Glass*. New York and London: Bloomsbury.

Bonnot, Thierry. 2002. 'Des tuiles, des toits et des couleurs: de Beaune à Disneyland Paris, une tradition bourguignonne', *Terrain* 38 March: 153–62.

Bouissou, Jean-Marie. 2006. 'Pourquoi aimons-nous le manga? Une approche économique du nouveau soft power japonais', *Cités* 3(27): 71–84. www.cairn.info/revue-cites-2006-3-page-71.htm (accessed 4 October 2016).

Boulanger-Fassier, Sylvaine. 2008. 'La viticulture durable: une démarche en faveur de la pérennisation des territoires viticoles français?', *Géocarrefour* 83(3), https://geocarrefour.revues.org/6870?lang=en (accessed on 4 October 2016).

Bourdieu, Pierre. 1977. 'Une classe objet', *Actes de la recherche en sciences sociales* 17(18), November: 1–5.

Bowen, Sarah. 2010. 'Embedding Local Places in Global Spaces: Geographical Indications as a Territorial Development Strategy', *Rural Sociology* 75(2), June: 209–43.

Brereton, Derek P. 2004. 'Preface for a Critical Realist Ethnology. Part I: The Schism and a Realist Restorative', *Journal of Critical Realism* 3(1), May: 77–102.

Bruner, Edward. 1993. 'Epilogue: Creativity Persona and the Problem of Authenticity', in Smadar Lavie, Kirin Narayan and Renato Rosaldo (eds), *Creativity/Anthropology*. Ithaca, NY: Cornell University Press, pp. 321–34.

Cambourne, Brock, C. Michael Hall, G. Johnson, Nicky Macionis, Richard Mitchell and Liz Sharples. 2000. 'The Maturing Wine Tourism Product: An International Overview', in C.M. Hall, L. Sharples, B. Cambourne and N. Macionis (eds), *Wine Tourism Around the World*. Oxford: Butterworth-Heinemann, pp. 24–66.

Candea, Mattei. 2007. 'Arbitrary Locations: In Defence of the Bounded Field-site', *Journal of the Royal Anthropological Institute* 13: 167–84.

Cerveau, Marie-Pierre. 2000. 'Les égarements de la région viticole Bourguignonne ou les tribulations d'un bateau ivre', *Annales de Géographie* 109(614): 444–58.

Chatelain-Courtois, Martine. 1984. *Les mots du vin et de l'ivresse*. Paris: Belin, Le français retrouvé.

Chaudat, Philippe. 2012. 'Vin et monde viticole', in Jean-Pierre Poulain (ed.), *Dictionnaire des cultures alimentaires*. Paris: PUF.

Choo Lee, Jeannie. 2009. *The Asian Palate*. N.p.: Asset Publishing & Research Limited.

Cleere, Henry. 2004. 'World Heritage Vineyard Landscapes', *World Heritage Review* (35): 4–19.

Clifford, James and George E. Marcus (eds). 1986. *Writing Culture: The Poetics and Politics of Ethnography*. Berkeley, CA: University of California Press.

Colman, Tyler. 2008. *Wine Politics: How Governments, Environmentalists, Mobsters and Critics Influence the Wines We Drink*. Berkeley, CA: University of California Press.

Cook, Ian and Philip Crang. 1996. 'The World on a Plate: Culinary Culture, Displacement and Geographical Knowledges', *Journal of Material Culture* 1(2) July: 131–53.

Coover, Roderick. 1999. *A Harvest in Burgundy*, https://unknownterritories. org/A_HARVEST_IN_BURGUNDY/index.html (accessed on 14 June 2017).

Crenn, Chantal. 2013. 'Des invisibles trop visibles? Les ouvriers agricoles "marocains" dans les vignobles du Bordelais', *Hommes et migrations: Migrations et mondes ruraux*: 99–108.

Crenn, Chantal and Isabelle Téchoueyres. 2004. 'Enracinement, production de la différence et nécessités du marché: l'exemple du président du syndicat Ste Foy-Bordeaux', *Anthropology of Food*, 3 December. http://aof.revues.org/240 (accessed 4 October 2016).

Cresswell, Tim. 2004. *Place: A Short Introduction*. Oxford: Wiley-Blackwell.

Csordas, Thomas (ed.). 1994. *Embodiment and Experience: The Existential Ground of Culture and Self*. Cambridge: Cambridge University Press.

Cwiertka, Katarzyna Joanna. 2006. *Modern Japanese Cuisine: Food, Power and National Identity*. London: Reaktion Books.

Daynes, Sarah. 2013. 'The Social Life of Terroir among Bordeaux Winemakers', in Rachel Black and Robert Ulin (eds), *Wine and Culture: Vineyard to Glass*. New York: Bloomsbury, pp. 15–32.

Deffontaines, Jean-Pierre. 2005. 'Le terroir, une notion polysémique', in Laurence Bérard et al. (eds), *Biodiversité et savoirs naturalistes locaux en France*. Paris: Editions du CIRAD, pp. 38–43.

Delaplace, Marie and Elsa Gatelier. 2014. 'Patrimonialisation individuelle et collective et développement de l'oenotourisme en Bourgogne', *Territoire en mouvement Revue de géographie et aménagement* 21, http://tem.revues. org/2283 (accessed on 14 June 2017).

Delissey, Jean and Louis Perriaux. 1962. 'Les courtiers gourmets de la ville de Beaune: Contribution à l'histoire du commerce du "vin de Beaune" du 16ème au 18ème siècle', *Annales de Bourgogne* 34: 46–57.

Deloire, Alain, Philippe Prévost and Mary Kelly. 2008. 'Unravelling the Terroir Mystique – An Agro-socio-economic Perspective', *CAB Reviews: Perspectives in Agriculture, Veterinary Science, Nutrition and Natural Resources* 3(32): 1–9.

Demossier, Marion. 1992. 'La fête, miroir d'une communauté: la Saint Vincent tournante de Puligny-Montrachet', *Les Saints protecteurs de la vigne en Bourgogne*, Archives de la ville de Beaune, Musée du vin, 123–40.

_____. 1999. *Hommes et vins: une anthropologie du vignoble bourguignon*. Dijon: Éditions universitaires de Dijon.

_____. 2000. 'Food for Thought, Culinary Heritage in France', in S. Blowen, M. Demossier, J. Picard (eds.) *Recollections of France: Memories, Identities and Heritage in Contemporary France*. New York: Berghahn, pp. 141–153.

_____. 2010. *Wine Drinking Culture in France: A National Myth or a Modern Passion?* Cardiff: University of Wales Press.

_____. 2011. 'Beyond *Terroir*: Territorial Construction, Hegemonic Discourses, and French Wine Culture', *Journal of the Royal Anthropological Institute* 17: 685–705.

_____. 2013. 'Following *Grands Crus*: Global Markets, Transnational Histories and Wine?', in Rachel Black and Robert C. Ulin (eds), *Wine and Culture: From the Vineyard to the Glass*. New York: Bloomsbury, pp. 183–200.

_____. 2015. 'The Politics of Heritage in the Land of Food and Wine', in William Logan, Máiread Nic Craith and Ullrich Kockel (eds), *A Companion to Heritage Studies*. Oxford: Wiley-Blackwell, Companions to Anthropology Series.

_____. forthcoming. 'Reflexive Imbrications: Burgundy and the Globalisation of Terroir', in David Inglis and Anna-Mari Almila (eds), *The Globalization of Wine: The Trans-Nationalization and Localization of Production, Leisure and Pleasure*. London: Bloomsbury.

Dion, Roger. 1959. *Histoire de la vigne et du vin en France, des origines au XIXe siècle*. Paris.

Ditter, Jean-Guillaume. 2005. 'Reforming the French Wine Industry: Could Clusters Work?', *Cahiers du Ceren* 13: 39–54.

Dobronauteanu, Maria-Carla. 2014. 'The Wine Market in Japan: An Assessment of Challenges and Opportunities for Central and Eastern European Producers'. EU-Japan Centre for Industrial Cooperation, http://www.eu-japan.eu/sites/eu japan.eu/files/JapanWineMarketReport-2014.pdf (accessed 14 June 2017).

Douglas, M. 1987. *Constructive Drinking: Perspectives on Drink from Anthropology*, Cambridge University Press, Editions de la maison des Sciences de l'Homme.

Douglas, Mary. 1966. *Purity and Danger*. London: Routledge.
Dubost, Françoise and Bernadette Lizet. 1995. 'Pour une ethnologie du paysage', in Françoise Dubost and Bernadette Lizet (eds), *Paysages au pluriel: Pour une approche ethnologique des paysages*. Paris: Editions de la Maison des sciences de l'homme, Collection ethnologie de la France, cahier 9, pp. 225–40.
Dutton, Denis. 2003. 'Authenticity in Art', in Jerrold Levinson (ed.), *The Oxford Handbook of Aesthetics*. New York: Oxford University Press, pp. 258–74.
Dutton, Jacqueline. forthcoming. 'Taking Disciplinary Measures to Narrating French Wine Culture', Conference paper presented at the Worlds in a Wine Glass Conference, 9–10 May 2016, King's College London, Menzies Centre for Australian Studies.
Eriksen, Thomas. 2014 (second edition). *Globalization: The Key Concepts*. London: Bloomsbury.
Escobar, Arturo. 2001. 'Culture Sits in Place: Reflections on Globalism and Subaltern Strategies of Localization', *Political Geography* 20: 139–74.
Faure, Muriel. 1999. 'Un produit agricole "affiné" en objet culturel: Le fromage beaufort dans les Alpes du Nord', *Terrain* 33: 81–92.
Featherstone, Mike. 1991. *Consumer Culture and Postmodernism*. London: Sage.
Fernandez, Jean-Luc. 2004. *La critique vinicole en France: Pouvoir de prescription et construction de la confiance*. Paris: L'Harmattan, Logiques *sociales*.
Fewsmith, Joseph. 2007. 'The Political Implications of China's Growing Middle-class', *China Leadership Monitor* (Hoover Institute) 21: 1–8.
Field, Les. 2009. 'Four Kinds of Authenticity? Regarding Nicaraguan Pottery in Scandinavian Museums, 2006-08', *American Ethnologist* 36(3): 507–20.
Filipucci, Paola. 2004. 'A French Place Without a Cheese: Problems with Heritage and Identity in Northeastern France', *Focaal* 44 (Winter): 72–86.
Fillitz, Thomas and A.-Jamie Saris. 2012. 'Introduction: Authenticity Aujourd'hui', in Thomas Fillitz and A.-Jamie Saris (eds), *Debating Authenticity: Concepts of Modernity in Anthropological Perspective*. New York: Berghahn, pp. 1–26.
Fourcade, Marion. 2012. 'The Vile and the Noble', *The Sociological Quarterly* 53: 524–45.
Fournier, Dominique and Salvatore D'Onofrio (eds). 1991. *Le ferment divin*. Paris: Editions de la Maison des sciences de l'homme.
Frazier, Brandy N., Susan Gelman, Alice Wilson and Bruce Hood. 2009. 'Picasso Paintings, Moon Rocks, and Hand-written Beatles Lyrics: Adults' Evaluations of Authentic Objects', *Journal of Cognition and Culture* 9: 1–14.
Garcia, Jean-Pierre (ed.). 2011. *Les 'climats' du vignoble de Bourgogne comme patrimoine mondial de l'humanité*. Dijon: Editions Universitaires de Dijon.
Garrier, Gilbert. 1995. *Histoire sociale et culturelle du vin*. Paris: Bordas.
Geertz, Clifford. 1973. *Toward an Interpretive Theory of Culture*. New York: Basic Books.

Gieser, Thorsten. 2008. 'Embodiment, Emotion and Empathy: A Phenomenological Approach to Apprenticeship Learning', *Anthropological Theory* 8(3): 299–318.

Gille, Zsuzsa and Seán Ó Riain. 2002. 'Global Ethnography', *Annual Review of Sociology* 28: 271–95.

Giroir, Guillaume. 2015. 'L'entreprise Changyu, acteur majeur de la construction du système viti-vinicole émergent en Chine', *Cultur* 8(3), http://www.uesc.br/revistas/culturaeturismo/ano8-edicaoespecial/12-giroir.pdf (accessed 14 June 2017).

Grazian, David. 2003. *The Search for Authenticity in Urban Blues Clubs*. Chicago, IL: University of Chicago Press.

Gupta, Akhil and James Ferguson. 2002. 'Spatializing States: Toward an Ethnography of Neoliberal Governmentality', *American Ethnologist* 29(4), November: 981–1002.

Guy, Kolleen. 2003. *When Champagne Became French: Wine and the Making of a National Identity*. Baltimore, MD and London: The Johns Hopkins University Press.

Gwynne, Robert N. 2008. 'UK Retail Concentration, Chilean Wine Producers and Value Chains', *The Geographical Journal* 174: 97–108.

Hall, C. Michael, Liz Sharples, Richard Mitchell, Nicky Macionis and Brook Cambourne (eds). 2003. *Food Tourism Around the World: Development, Management and Markets*. Oxford: Butterworth Heinemann.

Handler, Richard. 1986. 'Authenticity', *Anthropology Today* 2(1): 2–4.

Hannerz, Ulf. 1992. *Cultural Complexity: Studies in the Social Organization of Meaning*. New York: Columbia.

———. 1996. *Transnational Connections: Culture, People, Places*. London: Routledge.

Haraway, Donna. 1988. 'Situated Knowledges: The Science Question in Feminism and the Privilege of Partial Perspective', *Feminist Studies* 14(3): 575–99.

Harvey, David. 1990. 'Between Time and Space: Reflections on the Geographical Imagination', *Annals of the Association of American Geographers* 80(3): 418–34.

Heller, Chaia. 2006. 'Post-industrial "Quality Agricultural Discourse": Techniques of Governance and Resistance in the French Debate over GM Crops', *Social Anthropology* 14: 319–34.

Herzfeld, Michael. 2004. *The Body Impolitic: Artisans and Artifice in the Global Hierarchy of Value*. Chicago, IL: University of Chicago Press.

Hirsch, Eric and Michael O'Hanlon (eds). 1995. *The Anthropology of Landscape: Perspectives on Place and Space*. Oxford: Clarendon Press.

Holt, Mack. 1993. 'Wine, Community, and Reformation in Sixteenth-Century Burgundy', *Past and Present* 138(1): 58–93.

Horn, Pierre-L. 1991. 'Comics', in Pierre-L. Horn (ed.), *Handbook of French Popular Culture*. New York: Greenwood Press, pp. 15–38.

Howes, David (ed.). 1991. *The Varieties of Sensory Experience*. Toronto: University of Toronto Press.

Howland, Peter. 2008. 'Martinborough's Wine Tourists and the Metro-rural Idyll', *Journal of New Zealand Studies* 6-7 (October 2007-October 2008): 77–100.

Humbert, Marc and Yoschimichi Sato (eds.). 2012. *Social Exclusion: Perspectives from France and Japan*. Sato: Tohoku University.

Inda, J. and R. Rosaldo. 2002. *The Anthropology of Globalization: A Reader*. Malden, MA: Blackwell.

Ingold, Tim. 2000. *The Perception of the Environment: Essays on Livelihood, Dwelling and Skill*. London: Routledge.

———. 2012. 'Toward an Ecology of Materials', *Annual Review of Anthropology* 41: 427–42.

Jacquet, Olivier. 2009. *Un siècle de construction du vignoble bourguignon: Les organisations vitivinicoles de 1884 aux AOC*. Dijon: EUD, Coll. Sociétés.

Jacquet, Olivier and Gilles Laferté. 2013. 'La route des vins et l'émergence d'un tourisme viticole en Bourgogne dans l'entre-deux-guerres', *Cahiers de géographie du Québec* 57(162): 425–44.

Joly, Nathalie. 2004. 'Ecrire l'événement: Le travail agricole mis en mémoire', *Sociologie du travail* 46: 511–27.

Johnson, H. 1989. *The Story of Wine*. London: Mitchell Beazley.

Jones, Jason. 2015. 'Delightfully Sauced: Wine Manga and the Japanese Sommelier's Rise to the Top of the French Wine World', *Japanese Studies Review* XIX: 55–84.

Josling, Tim. 2006. 'The War on *Terroir*: Geographical Indications as a Transatlantic Trade Conflict', *Journal of Agricultural Economics* 57: 337–63.

Jullien, André. 1824. *Topographie of All Known Vineyards*. London.

Jung, Yuson. 2014. 'Tasting and Judging the Unknown Terroir of the Bulgarian Wine: The Political Economy of Sensory Experience', *Food and Foodways* 22(1–2): 24–47.

Jung, Yuson and Nicolas Sternsdorff Cisterna. 2014. 'Introduction to Crafting Senses: Circulating the Knowledge and Experience of Taste', Special Issue of Food and Foodways, *Food and Foodways* 22(1–2): 1–4.

Karpik, Lucien. 2010. *Valuing the Unique: The Economics of Singularities*. Princeton, NJ: Princeton University Press.

Kirshenblatt-Gimblett, Barbara. 2004. 'Intangible Heritage as Metacultural Production', *Museum International* 56: 52–65.

———. 2006. 'World Heritage and Cultural Economics', in Ivan Karp, Corinne A. Kratz, Lynn Szwaja, Tomás Ybarra-Frausto, with Gustavo Buntinx, Barbara Kirshenblatt-Gimblett and Ciraj Rassool (eds), *Museum Frictions: Public Cultures/Global Transformations*. Durham, NC and London: Duke University Press, pp. 161–202.

Kjellgren, Björn. 2004. 'Drunken Modernity: Wine in China', *Anthropology of Food*, 3 December. http://aof.revues.org/249 (accessed 4 October 2016).

Kockel, Ullrich. 2007. 'Reflexive Traditions and Heritage Production', in Ullrich Kockel and Máiréad Nic Craith (eds), *Cultural Heritages as Reflexive Traditions*. Basingstoke and New York: Palgrave, Macmillan, pp. 19–33.

Kramer, Matt. 1990. *Making Sense of Burgundy*. William Morrow & Co.

Krzywoszynska, Anna. 2015. 'What Farmers Know: Experiential Knowledge and Care in Vine Growing', *Sociologia Ruralis* 56(2), April: 289–310.

Labbé, Thomas. 2011. 'La Revendication d'un terroir viticole: La Côte-de-Beaune à la fin du XVIIIe siècle', *Histoire & Sociétés Rurales* 1*(35)*: 99–126.

Lachiver, Marcel. 1988. *Vins, vignes et vignerons: Histoire du vignoble français*. Paris: Fayard.

Laferté Gilles. 2003. 'La mise en folklore des vins de Bourgogne: la "Paulée" de Meursault', *Ethnologie française* 3(33): 435–42.

———. 2006. *La Bourgogne et ses vins: Image d'origine contrôlée*. Paris: Belin, Socio-Histoire.

———. 2011. 'The Folklorization of French Farming: Marketing Luxury Wine in the Interwar Years', *French Historical Studies* 34(4): 679–712.

Lagendijk, Arnoud. 2004. 'Global "Lifeworlds" Versus Local "Systemworlds": How Flying Winemakers Produce Global Wines in Interconnected Locales', *Tidjschrift voor Economische en Sociale Geografie* 95(5): 511–26.

Landrieu-Lussigny, Marie-Hélène. 1983. *Les lieux-dits dans le Vignoble Bourguignon*. Marseille: Editions Jeanne Laffitte.

Lash, Scott and John Urry. 1987. *The End of Organised Capitalism*. Cambridge: Polity Press.

Lavalle, Jean. 1855. *Histoire et statistique de la vigne et des grands vins de la Côte d'Or, with the help of Joseph Garnier, Delarue and a large number of owners and wine producers*. Paris: Dusacq; Dijon: Picart; Gray: Joeger.

Lem, Winnie. 1999. *Cultivating Dissent: Work, Identity and Praxis in Rural Languedoc*. Albany, NY: Suny Press.

———. 2013. 'Regimes of Regulation, Gender and Divisions of Labor in Languedoc Viticulture', in Robert Ulin and Rachel Black (eds), *Wine and Culture: Vineyard to Glass*. London and New York: Bloomsbury Academic, pp. 221–40.

Lowenthal, David. 1996. *Possessed by the Past: The Heritage Crusade and the Spoils of History*. New York: The Free Press.

———. 2005. 'Natural and Cultural Heritage', *International Journal of Heritage Studies* 11(1): 81–92.

Lucand, Christophe. 2010. *Les négociants en vins de Bourgogne: De la fin du XIXe siècle à nos jours*. Bordeaux: Éditions Féret.

———. 2015. 'Le commerce des vins de Bourgogne à la conquête des concessions françaises en Chine au début du XXe siècle', *French Cultural Studies* 26(2): 152–62.

Luginbühl, Y. 2014. 'Préface', in S. Angles (ed.), *Atlas des paysages de la vigne et de l'olivier en France méditerranéenne*. Versailles: Quæ.

Maby, Jacques. 2002. 'Paysages et imaginaire: l'exploitation de nouvelles valeurs ajoutées dans les terroirs viticoles', *Annales de Géographie* 624: 198–211.

Malinowski, Brownislaw.1922. *Les Argonautes du Pacifique occidental.* French translation, 1963. Paris: Éditions Gallimard.

Massey, Doreen. 1992. 'A Place Called Home?', New Formations 17: 3–15.

_____. 2006. 'Landscape as a Provocation: Reflections on Moving Mountains', *Journal of Material Culture* 11 (July 2006): 33–48.

Micoud, André. 2004. 'Des patrimoines aux territoires durables: Ethnologie et écologie dans les campagnes françaises', *Ethnologie française* 1(34): 13–22.

Miller, Daniel. 1988. 'Appropriating the State on the Council Estate', *Man* 23(2): 353–72.

_____. 1997. 'Coca-cola: A Black Sweet Drink from Trinidad', in Daniel Miller (ed.), *Material Cultures.* London: UCL Press, pp. 169–87.

_____. 1998. *A Theory of Shopping.* Cambridge: Polity Press.

_____. 2008. 'The Uses of Value', *Geoforum* 39(3): 1122–32. 10.1016/j. geoforum.2006.03.009 (accessed 14 January 2016).

Mitchell, Richard, Stephen Charters and Julia N. Albrecht. 2012. 'Cultural Systems and the Wine Tourism Product', *Annals of Tourism Research* 39(1): 311–35.

Moeran, Brian. 2005. 'Drinking Country: Flows of Exchange in a *Japanese* Valley', in Thomas M. Wilson (ed.), *Drinking Cultures.* Oxford: Berg, pp. 25–43.

Mollevi Bortolo, Gemma. 2012. 'Le paysage de la vigne et du vin', *Territoires du vin* 4: Varia sur les Territoires du vin, 8 March 2012. http://revuesshs.u-bourgogne.fr/territoiresduvin/document.php?id=1521 ISSN 1760-5296 (accessed 4 October 2016).

Molz, J. Germann. 2004. 'Tasting an Imagined Thailand: Authenticity and Culinary Tourism in Thai Restaurants', in L.M. Long (ed.), *Culinary Tourism.* Lexington, KY: University Press of Kentucky, pp. 53–75.

Moran, Warren. 1993. 'The Wine Appellation as Territory in France and California', *Annals of the Association of American Geographers* 83: 694–717.

_____. 2000. 'Culture et nature dans la géographie de l'industrie vinicole néo-zélandaise', *Annales de Géographie* 614–615: 525–50.

_____. 2001. 'Terroir – the Human Factor', *Australian and New Zealand Wine Industry Journal* 16(2): 32–51.

Morris, Jasper. 2010. *Inside Burgundy.* London: Berry Bros & Rudd.

Murray, Jasper and John Overton. 2011. 'Defining Regions: The Making of Places in the New Zealand Wine Industry', *Australian Geographer 42(4):* 419–33.

Murray, Warwick E. and John Overton. 2014. *Geographies of Globalization.* 2nd edition, Routledge Contemporary Human Geography Series. London: Routledge/Taylor and Francis.

Musolf, Peter. 2008. Review, Tadashi Agi (writer) and Shu Okimoto (illustrator), 'Kami no Shizuku: Les Gouttes de Dieu'. *Journal of Wine Economics* 3(2), Fall:

217–22. http://www.wine-economics.org/aawe/wp-content/uploads/2012/10/JWE2008-V3-No2-Reviews.pdf (accessed 4 October 2016).

Normand-Marconnet, Nadine and Jason Jones. 2016. 'From West to East to West: A Case Study on Japanese Wine Manga Translated in French', *TranscUlturAl* 8(2): 154–73.

Nossiter, Jonathan. 2004. *Mondovino*. Production Goatworks films and films de la croisade.

Ong, Aihwa and Stephen J. Collier. 2005. *Global Assemblages: Technology, Politics and Ethics as Anthropological Problems*. London: Blackwell Publishing.

Overton, John. 2010. 'The Consumption of Space: Land, Capital and Place in the New Zealand Wine Industry', *Geoforum* 41(5): 752–62.

Overton, John D., Warwick E. Murray and Glenn Banks. 2012. 'The Race to the Bottom of the Glass? Wine, Geography and Globalization', *Globalizations* 9(2): 169–86.

Parker, Thomas. 2015. *Tasting French Terroir: The History of an Idea*. Berkeley, CA: University of California Press.

Paxson, Heather. 2010. 'Locating Value in Artisan Cheese: Reverse-Engineering Terroir for New World Landscapes', *American Anthropologist* 112(3): 442–55.

———. 2012. *The Life of Cheese Crafting Food and Value in America*. Berkeley, CA: University of California Press.

Peace, Adrian. 2011. '*Barossa* Dreaming: Imagining Place and Constituting Cuisine in Contemporary Australia', *Anthropological Forum* 21(1): 23–42.

Petric, Boris. 2014. 'Transformer le désert chinois en vignes', *Le Monde diplomatique* 13: 14, http://www.monde-diplomatique.fr/2014/07/PETRIC/50619 (accessed 14 June 2017).

Phillips, Lyne. 2006. 'Food and Globalization', *Annual Review of Anthropology* 35: 37–57.

Pitiot, Sylvain and Marie-Hélène Landrieu-Lussigny. 2012. *The Climats and Lieux-dits of the Great Vineyards of Burgundy: An Atlas and History of Place Names*. Editions De Monza.

Pitte, Jean-Robert. 2005. *Bordeaux et Bourgogne: Les passions rivales*. Paris: Hachette littératures.

———. 2008. *Bordeaux/Bourgogne: A Vintage Rivalry*, translation. Berkeley, CA: California University Press.

Pomel, Bernard. 2006. *Réussir l'avenir de la viticulture de France*. http://static.canalblog.com/storagev1/beaujolaisdemain.canalblog.com/docs/rapport_pomel_mars2006.pdf (accessed 8 November 2016).

Pottier, J. 1996. 'Food', in A. Barnard, and J. Spencer (eds), *Encyclopedia of Social and Cultural Anthropology*. London: Routledge, pp. 238–241.

Pratt, Jeff. 2007. 'Food Values: the Local and the Authentic', *Critique of Anthropology* 27(3), September: 285–300.

Pye, David. 1968. *The Nature and Art of Workmanship*. London: StudioVista.

Redding, Cyrus. *1833. A History and Description of Modern Wines*. London: Whittaker, Treacher and Arnot.

Rigaux, Jacky. 2010. *Le réveil des terroirs – Défense et illustration des 'climats' de Bourgogne*. Éditions de Bourgogne.

Ritchie, Ian. 1991. 'Fusion of the Faculties: A Study of the Language of the Senses in Hausaland', in D. Howes (ed.), *The Varieties of Sensory Experience: A Sourcebook in the Anthropology of the Senses*. Toronto: University of Toronto Press, pp. 192–203.

Rofel, Lisa. 1992. 'Rethinking Modernity: Space and Factory Discipline in China', *Cultural Anthropology* 7(1): 93–114.

Rogers, Susan Carol. 1987. 'Good to Think: The "Peasant" in Contemporary France', *Anthropological Quarterly* 60: 56–63.

Roudié, Philippe. 2002. 'El paisaje y los parajes del Patrimonio Mundial de la Humanidad de la UNESCO', in *Paisaje y ordenación del territorio*. Seville: Consejería de Obras Publicas y Transporte, Fundación Duques de Soria, pp. 183–92.

Rovani, Pierre-Antoine. 2001. 'The 1999 Red Burgundies part 2', *Wine Advocate* 136: 10–24.

Royer, Claude. 1980. *Les vignerons: Usages et mentalités des pays de vignobles*. Paris: Editions Belin.

Schodt, Frederik L. 1983. *Manga! Manga! The World of Japanese Comics*. Kodansha International.

Schofield, John, Graham Fairclough, Rodney Harrison and John H. Jameson Jnr (eds). 2008. *The Heritage Reader*. London: Routledge.

Shapin, Steven. 2012. 'The Tastes of Wine: Towards a Cultural History', in *Wineworld: New Essay on Wine, Taste, Philosophy and Aesthetics*, n.s., 51 (3/2012), anno LII: 49–94, https://scholar.harvard.edu/files/shapin/files/shapin-tastes-of-wine.pdf?m=1441312630 (accessed 14 June 2017).

Skinner, William. 2015. 'Fermenting Place: Wine Production and Terroir in McLaren Vale, South Australia', PhD thesis. University of Adelaide, degree conferred December 2015.

Smith, Laurajane and Natsuko Akawaga (eds). 2009. *Intangible Heritage*. London: Routledge.

Stanziani, Alessandro. 2005. *Histoire de la qualité alimentaire (XIX-XXième siècle)*. Paris: Liber.

Sutton, David. 2010. 'Food and the Senses', *Annual Review of Anthropology* 39: 209–23.

Taylor, John. P. 2001. 'Authenticity and Sincerity in Tourism', *Annals of Tourism Research* 28(1): 7–26.

Teil, Geneviève. 2001. 'La production du jugement esthétique sur les vins par la critique vinicole', *Revue de Sociologie du Travail* 43: 67–89.

———. 2004. *De la coupe aux lèvres – pratiques de la perception et mise en marché de vins de qualité*. Toulouse: Octarès.

———. 2010. 'The French Wine "Appellations d'Origine Contrôlée" and the Virtues of Suspicion', *Journal of World Intellectual Property* 13(2): 253–74.

————. 2012. 'No Such Thing as Terroir', *Science, Technology & Human Values* 37 (September): 478–50.

Teil, Geneviève and Susan Barrey. 2009. 'La viticulture biologique: de la recherche d'un monde nouveau au renouvellement du goût de terroir', *Innovations Agronomiques* 4: 427–40.

Teil, Geneviève, Sandrine Barrey, Pierre Floux and Antoine Hennion. 2011. *Le Vin et l'environnement*. Paris: *Presses des Mines*.

Terrio, Susan. 1996. 'Crafting *Grand Cru* Chocolates in Contemporary France', *American Anthropologist* 98(1), March: 78–96.

————. 2000. *Crafting the Culture and History of French Chocolate*. Berkeley, CA: University of California Press.

Tilley, Christopher. 2006. 'Introduction: Identity, Place, Landscape and Heritage', *Journal of Material Culture* 11(1–2), July: **7–32.**

Tornatore, Jean-Louis. 2012. 'Anthropology's Payback: The Gastronomic Meal of the French. The Ethnographic Elements of a Heritage Distinction', in Regina Bendix, Aditya Eggert and Arnika Peselmann (eds), *Heritage Regimes and the State*. Göttingen: Universitätsverlag Göttingen, pp. 341–65.

Trébuchet-Breitwiller, Anne-Sophie. 2011. 'Le travail du précieux: Une anthropologie économique des produits de luxe à travers les exemples du parfum et du vin', PhD thesis. Paris: École Nationale Supérieure des Mines de Paris.

Trubek, Amy. 2008. *The Taste of Place: A Cultural Journey into Terroir*. Berkeley, CA: University of California Press.

Trubek, Amy and Sarah Bowen. 2008. 'Creating the Taste of Place in the United States: Can We Learn from the French?', *Geojournal* 73: 23–30.

Tsing, Anna. L. 2005. *Friction: An Ethnography of Global Connection*. Princeton, NJ: Princeton University Press.

Uchiyamada, Yasushi. 2004. 'A Review of Ingold's "The perception of the environment"', *Journal of the Royal Anthropological Institute* 10(3): 723–24.

Ulin, Robert C. 1996. *Vintages and Traditions: An Ethnohistory of Southwest French Wine Cooperatives. Washington, DC: Smithsonian Institution Press.*

————. 2002. 'Work as Cultural Production: Labour and Self–identity Among Southwest French Wine-growers', *Journal of the Royal Anthropological Institute* 8: 691–712.

Ulin, Robert C. and Rachel Black. 2013. *Wine and Culture: Vineyard to Glass*. London and New York: Bloomsbury Academic.

Urry, John. 2001. 'Globalising the *Tourist* Gaze', published by the Department of Sociology, Lancaster, at http://www.lancaster.ac.uk/fass/resources/sociology-online-papers/papers/urry-globalising-the-tourist-gaze.pdf (accessed 14 January 2016).

Vaudour, Emmanuelle. 2002. 'The Quality of Grapes and Wine in Relation to Geography: Notions of Terroir at Various Scales', *Journal of Wine Research* 13(2): 117–41.

Veblen, Thorstein. 1899. *The Theory of the Leisure Class*. New York: Macmillan.

Wang, Ning. 1999. 'Rethinking Authenticity in Tourism Experience', *Annals of Tourism Research* 26(2): 349–70.

Warnier, Jean-Pierre. 2013. *La Mondialisation de la Culture*. Paris: Editions la Découverte.

Weber, Max, Peter R. Behr and Gordon C. Wells. 2002. *The Protestant Ethic and the 'Spirit' of Capitalism* and other Writings. London: Penguin.

Weiss, Brad. 2011. 'Making Pigs Local: Discerning the Sensory Character of Place', *Cultural Anthropology* 26(3): 438–61.

Wherry, Frederick F. 2006. 'The Social Sources of Authenticity in Global Handicraft Markets: Evidence from Northern Thailand', *Journal of Consumer Culture* 6: 5–32.

Wilson, Thomas M. 2005. *Drinking Cultures: Alcohol and Identity*. Oxford: Berg.

Wilson, James. E. 1998. *Terroir: The Role of Geology, Climate and Culture in the Making of French Wines*. Berkeley, CA: University of California Press.

Zanettin, Frederico. 2008. *Comics in Translation*. Manchester: St Jerome Pub.

INDEX

New Directions in Anthropology

General Editor: **Jacqueline Waldren**, *Institute of Social and Cultural Anthropology, University of Oxford*

Twentieth-century migration, modernization, technology, tourism, and global communication have had dynamic effects on group identities, social values and conceptions of space, place, and politics. This series features new and innovative ethnographic studies concerned with these processes of change.